"...towards better relations between all people."

from the

★

Irwin Uran
Gift Fund

Learning about the Holocaust

A Student's Guide

RONALD M. SMELSER

Editor in Chief

volume 4 **S-Z**

Macmillan Reference USA

an imprint of the Gale Group

New York • Detroit • San Francisco • London • Boston • Woodbridge, CT

Learning About the Holocaust

Macmillan Reference USA   Gale Group
1633 Broadway   27500 Drake Road
New York, NY 10019   Farmington Hills, MI 48331

Library of Congress Catalog Card Number: 00–062517

Printed in the United States of America

Printing Number
1 2 3 4 5 6 7 8 9 10

Library of Congress Cataloging-in-Publication Data
Learning About the Holocaust: a student's guide / Ronald M. Smelser, editor in chief.
    p. cm.
    Includeds bibliographical references (p.) and index.
    ISBN: 0-02-865536-2 (set) – ISBN 0-02-865537-0 (v. 1) –
ISBN 0-02-865538-9 (v. 2) – ISBN 0-02-865539-7 (v. 3) –
ISBN 0-02-865540-0 (v. 4)
    1. Holocaust, Jewish (1939–1945)–Study and teaching (Secondary)
I. Smelser, Ronald M., 1942-

D804.33 .L4 2000
940.53'18—dc21   00-062517

Contents

VOLUME 1

A

B

Contents

VOLUME 2

Contents

VOLUME 3

M

N

O

P

R

Contents

VOLUME 4

S

Glossary 159
Primary Source Documents 171
   Nazi Party Documents 171
   Official Laws, Orders, and Regulations of the Third Reich 179
   Secret Nazi Documents 186
   Nazi Correspondence 190
   Jewish Resistance 193
   Life in the Ghettos 197
   Testimony 199
Resources for Further Study 201
Photo Credits 207
Text Credits 211
Index 215

Timeline:
The Holocaust in the Context of World Events

1918 November 9: The Weimar Republic is established in Germany.

November 11: The war that would come to be called World War I ends after four years. Germany is defeated.

1919 June 28: The Treaty of Versailles is signed. It establishes the League of Nations and punishes Germany for its aggression in World War I.

September 16: Adolf Hitler joins the German Workers' Party, precursor of the National Socialist German Workers (Nazi) Party.

1920 January 16: The League of Nations convenes for the first time.

August 8: National Socialist German Workers' Party (known as the Nazi party) is founded.

1921 Adolf Hitler takes control of the National Socialist party.

1922 October 27: Benito Mussolini is appointed the premier of Italy.

1923 November 11: Adolf Hitler is arrested for his attempt to overthrow the German government in Bavaria in the Beer Hall Putsch.

1924 April 1: Adolf Hitler is sentenced to five years in prison for the Beer Hall Putsch. While there, he writes *Mein Kampf.*

December 20: Hitler is released from prison after only eight months.

1925 April 26: Paul von Hindenburg is elected president of Weimar Republic (Germany).

November 11: Adolf Hitler's personal guard, the SS (*Schutzstaffel*), is founded.

1926 September 8: Germany joins the League of Nations.

1929 January 6: Heinrich Himmler appointed Reichsführer-SS.

October 24: "Black Tuesday"—the U.S. stock market crash on Wall Street. The Great Depression begins and spreads around the world.

1930 September 14: In Reichstag (Parliament) elections, the Nazi party emerges as a serious new force in German politics, earning 107 seats in the 577-member Reichstag. In the face of massive unemployment, antisemitism in Germany intensifies and spreads throughout Eastern Europe.

1932 April 10: Paul von Hindenburg is re-elected president of Germany, defeating challenger Adolf Hitler.

July 31: In Reichstag elections, National Socialists (Nazis) become the largest party in Germany, taking 230 of 608 seats.

November 8: Franklin D. Roosevelt is elected president of the United States.

November 9: In Reichstag elections Nazis lose 2,000,000 votes and drop to 196 seats

1933 January 30: Adolf Hitler becomes the chancellor of Germany.

February 28: After a fire in the Reichstag on February 27, the Nazis declare a state of emergency, suspending freedom of speech, restricting freedom of assembly, and ending freedom of the press.

March 4: Franklin D. Roosevelt takes office for his first term as U.S. president. In his inaugural address, he says, "We have nothing to fear but fear itself."

March 23: Political prisoners arrive at Dachau.

March 24: The Reichstag approves the Enabling Act, giving Adolf Hitler dictatorial powers.

April 1: Nazis unleash a nationwide one-day boycott of Jewish businesses.

April 7: Jews are expelled from the German civil service.

April 11: Nazi definitions of "Aryan" and "non-Aryan" are adopted.

April 26: The Gestapo is established.

May 10: Nazis begin staging public book burnings, targeting works by political opponents and Jews. Eventually millions of books will be destroyed.

July 14: The Nazi Party is named the only legal political party in Germany.

July 20: An agreement (concordat) is signed between the Vatican and Nazi Germany.

October 14: Germany leaves the League of Nations.

1934 January 26: Germany and Poland sign a ten-year pact of non-aggression.

June 30–July 2: The Night of the Long Knives—also known as the Röhm Purge. Under Adolf Hitler's orders, the SS purges the SA (Storm Troopers); many SA leaders are killed.

July 20: The SS becomes an independent organization, with Heinrich Himmler as its chief.

August 2: German president Paul von Hindenburg dies.

August 3: Adolf Hitler becomes both president and chancellor. Soon all German officials and soldiers are required to swear allegiance to Hitler personally, not to the people or the country. At the September Nazi Party Congress in Nuremberg, Hitler proclaims his "Third Reich," which he says will last for one thousand years.

1935 January 13: A plebiscite in the Saarland overwhelmingly favors returning to Germany.

March 16: Hitler announces reintroduction of military conscription in violation of the Versailles treaty.

September 15: The Reichstag passes the first two "Nuremberg Laws," the Reich Citizenship Law and the Law for the Protection of German Blood and German Honor, which prohibit marriage and sexual intercourse between Germans and Jews and strip Jews of their remaining civil rights in Germany. These later serve as a model for the Nazis' treatment of Gypsies.

December 31: Jews are dismissed from the civil service in Germany.

1936 March 7: Germany sends troops into Rhineland, breaking the terms of the Treaty of Versailles.

May 9: Italy defeats Ethiopia, which it invaded in October, 1935.

July 18: A civil war erupts in Spain which will last for three years and foreshadows World War II.

August 1: The Summer Olympic Games begin in Berlin. African American runner Jesse Owens wins four gold medals during the games, but Adolf Hitler refuses to recognize the spectacular achievement.

October 25: The Rome-Berlin Axis Pact is signed, cementing an alliance between Adolf Hitler and Italian fascist leader Mussolini.

1937 March 14: In the face of increasing violence toward Jews in Europe, Pope Pius XI condemns racism and extreme nationalism in his encyclical "With Burning Concern."

July 16: Buchenwald concentration camp is opened.

September 7: Hitler declares the end of the Treaty of Versailles.

November 25: Germany and Japan sign a military and political pact.

1938 March 12–13: The *Anschluss*—Germany invades and annexes Austria.

April 26: Jews are required to register their property and financial holdings. It is now illegal for Aryans to pretend to own businesses still run by Jews; the push for "Aryanization" of businesses and property increases.

June 14: Jewish-owned businesses are forced to register with Nazi authorities.

June 15: Fifteen hundred German Jews are put into concentration camps.

July 6–13: Representatives of 32 countries meet at the Evian Conference in France to discuss the Jewish refugee and immigration problem. No solution emerges because virtually every country refuses to increase immigration quotas for Jews.

July 25: Jewish physicians are limited to treatment of Jewish patients.

August 17: Male Jews are required to add "Israel" to their names; female Jews must add "Sarah."

September 27: Jews may no longer work as lawyers.

September 29: At the Munich Conference, the Allies appease Adolf Hitler, granting Sudetenland—part of Czechoslovakia—to Germany.

October 15: Germany occupies Czechoslovakia's Sudetenland.

October 20–21: Jews are first deported to Poland from Vienna, Hamburg, and Prague.

November 9–10: The massive pogroms known as Kristallnacht explode across Germany and Austria. Synagogues are defaced and destroyed; Jewish homes and businesses are looted and vandalized.

November 15: Jewish children may no longer attend German schools.

December 3: Aryanization of Jewish businesses is mandated by law and carried out by force and intimidation.

1939 March 15–16: Germany invades Czechoslovakia.

April 22: Italy and Germany cement their alliance by signing the Pact of Steel.

May 15: The Ravensbrück concentration camp for women is established.

May 19: The MacDonald White Paper issued by the British government strengthens limits on Jewish emigration to Palestine.

August 23: The Germans and Soviets sign a non-aggression pact.

September 1: Germany invades Poland. Within the month, Poland falls.

September 2: Stutthof camp is established.

September 3: Great Britain and France declare war on Germany.

September 17: The Soviets invade eastern Poland, challenging the Germans.

September 21: SS official Reinhard Heydrich orders the creation of Jewish ghettos and Judenrate (Jewish Councils) in occupied Poland.

October 8: The first ghetto for Jews is established in Poland, in Piotrkow.

October 12: The Germans establish the Generalgouvernement in Poland.

November 23: Jews in occupied Poland are required to wear badges in the shape of the Star of David.

December 5–6: Jewish property in Poland is seized by German authorities.

1940 January 25: Nazis select the town of Auschwitz as the location for a new concentration camp.

February 12: The Nazis begin deporting Jews from Germany to occupied Poland.

April 9: Denmark and Norway are invaded by the Germans.

April 30: Łódź ghetto, established in February, is sealed; more than 200,000 Jews are not able to leave.

May 10: Germany invades the Netherlands, Belgium, Luxembourg, and northern France.

May 10: Winston Churchill becomes the prime minister of Great Britain.

May 20: Auschwitz concentration camp is established.

July 10: The Battle of Britain begins, with a major dogfight over the English Channel, and Germany's blitzkrieg bombing of London.

September 15: Battle of Britain Day—London is heavily blitzed by German bombers and fighter planes. The Luftwaffe meets with stiff resistance in the English Channel, resulting in an important Allied victory and turning point in the war.

September 27: The Tripartite Pact—Japan joins Germany and Italy in the Axis alliance.

October 16: Warsaw ghetto is established; the following month, it is sealed, holding in 400,000 Jews.

1941 March 1: Heinrich Himmler visits Auschwitz and orders an expansion that will increase capacity by at least 100,000 prisoners.

March 3: Krakow ghetto is established.

April 6: Germany invades Yugoslavia and Greece.

May 27: The German warship *Bismarck* is sunk by the British. U.S. president Franklin D. Roosevelt declares a national emergency in May because of events in Europe and Asia.

June 22: Operation Barbarossa—the Germans invade the Soviet Union.

July 8: Jews in the German-occupied Baltic countries are ordered to wear the Star of David badge.

July 21: Hermann Göring appoints Reinhard Heydrich to develop a plan for carrying out the "Final Solution of the Jewish Question"—the extermination of European Jews.

August 14: The Atlantic Charter is signed by Great Britain and the United States; the document outlines basic principles of postwar global rights and responsibilities and forms the beginnings of what will one day be the charter of the United Nations.

September 3: Zyklon B is first used in experiments at Auschwitz.

September 6: The Vilna ghettos are established with 40,000 Jews.

September 29–30: More than 33,000 Jews are massacred at Babi Yar.

October 23: Jewish emigration from Germany is prohibited.

November 24: Theresienstadt ghetto is established in Bohemia-Moravia as the Nazis' "model" Jewish ghetto. Also this month, construction begins on Bełżec extermination camp.

December 7: Japan attacks the United States at Pearl Harbor. Four days later, Germany and Italy declare war on the United States. The United States reciprocates by declaring war on the Axis powers.

December 8: The Chełmno extermination camp opens. Among its first victims are 5,000 Gypsies.

1942 January 20: At the Wannsee Conference, the Nazis coordinate plans for the "Final Solution."

January 21: The United Partisan Organization forms in Vilna.

February 23: The *Struma*, an unsafe cattle boat carrying more than 700 Jewish refugees from a port in Romania, sinks after being refused entry into Palestine.

June 1: Jews in the Netherlands, Belgium, Croatia, Slovakia, and Romania are ordered to wear the yellow Star of David badge.

March: Sobibór and Bełżec camps are established. The first transfer of French Jews to Auschwitz occurs. Marshal Petain approves French collaboration with

the Nazis. The United States starts supplying the Allies with war materials through the Lend-Lease Bill.

May 27: SS official Richard Heydrich is wounded; he dies early in June. A week later, the Nazis avenge his death by destroying the town of Lidice, in the Protectorate of Bohemia and Moravia (formerly Czechoslovakia).

June 4–6: The Allies win the Battle of Midway. Japan's eastward thrust is decisively thwarted.

June 23: Systematic gassing begins at Auschwitz.

July 19: Heinrich Himmler orders the start of Operation Reinhard.

July 23: Treblinka camp opens. The first victims and prisoners are from the Warsaw Ghetto. The Jewish Fighting Organization (ŻOB) is established in Warsaw.

August 23: The battle for Stalingrad begins. Three months later, the Soviets launch a successful counteroffensive against the Germans.

October 5: All Jews in concentration camps in Germany are to be sent to Auschwitz and Majdanek, on orders of Heinrich Himmler.

November 11: In a crucial turning point victory for Allied forces, the Germans are defeated at El Alamein, Egypt.

1943 January 18–21: A major, armed act of resistance occurs in the Warsaw ghetto.

January 29: All Gypsies in German-occupied territories are ordered arrested and sent to concentration camps.

February 26: The first transport of Gypsies is placed in the "Gypsy Camp" at Auschwitz.

March 5: Allied forces begin bombing Ruhr, a region central to Germany's coal, iron and steel industries.

April 19–30: At the Bermuda Conference, the Allies discuss the rescue of Jews in occupied Europe, but the talks are fruitless. Also this month, the Bergen-Belsen camp is opened.

April 19: The Warsaw ghetto uprising erupts and continues through May 16.

May 19: The Nazis declare Berlin *Judenfrei* (free of Jews).

June 11: Heinrich Himmler orders the liquidation of the Jewish ghettos of Poland and the Soviet Union.

June 22: German U-boats are withdrawn from the North Atlantic; the Allies win the Battle of the Atlantic.

July 5: The Sobibór extermination camp is made a concentration camp.

August 2: Prisoners at the Treblinka camp revolt; 200 escape, but the Nazis hunt them down.

October 2: The Danes rescue more than 7,200 Jews from the Nazis.

October 14: Prisoners at the Sobibór camp revolt; 300 escape. Of these, 50 survive.

November 3: Erntefest ("Harvest Festival") begins, in which 42,000 Jews are killed.

1944 January 24: War Refugee Board is created in the United States.

March 19: Germany invades Hungary; Hungarian Jews are required to wear the Star of David badge. During the next several months, more than 400,000 Hungarian Jews are deported to Auschwitz.

June 6: D-Day: The Allies land in Normandy, France. Throughout the year, Allied forces penetrate into more and more parts of Europe.

July 20: German officers fail in an assassination attempt against Adolf Hitler.

July 24: Soviet troops liberate the Majdanek camp.

July 28: The first major death march begins: Warsaw to Kutno.

August 4: Anne Frank and her family are arrested in Amsterdam and sent to Auschwitz. Anne and her sister are later sent to Bergen-Belsen.

September 1: Warsaw Polish Uprising begins and lasts until October 2 when the Polish Home Army is defeated by the Nazis.

October 6–7: Prisoners in Special Commandos (*Sonderkommandos*) at Auschwitz stage an uprising.

October 23: The Allies recognize Charles de Gaulle as the head of the provisional French government.

October 30: The last gassings at Auschwitz-Birkenau take place.

December 16–27: The Battle of the Bulge in Luxembourg and Belgium—the Germans are defeated.

1945 January 1: Germans begin full retreat on the Eastern Front.

January 17: Soviet troops enter Warsaw.

January 18: Death March from Auschwitz begins.

January 27: Soviet troops liberate Auschwitz-Birkenau.

February 4–11: Franklin D. Roosevelt, Winston Churchill, and Soviet leader Joseph Stalin meet at Yalta as the Allied forces meet with increasing success worldwide.

April 12: U.S. president Franklin D. Roosevelt dies and is succeeded by Harry S Truman.

April 12: Buchenwald and Bergen-Belsen camps are liberated. As more camps are released from Nazi control, the number of displaced persons (DPs) rises dramatically throughout Europe.

April 28: Benito Mussolini is shot by Italian partisans.

April 29: Dachau camp is liberated by American troops.

April 30: In his Berlin bunker, Adolf Hitler writes his Last Will and Testament, then commits suicide.

April–May: Allied troops liberate Dachau, Ravensbrück, Bergen-Belsen, Buchenwald, Mauthausen, and Theresienstadt camps. With liberation and the end of war in Europe, Displaced Persons (DP) camps are inundated.

May 7: Germany surrenders unconditionally to the Allies.

May 8: V-E Day—Victory in Europe.

June 5: The victorious Allies divide Germany into four occupation zones.

July 16: The first atomic bomb is tested, at Alamogordo, New Mexico.

July 17–August 2: Allied leaders Winston Churchill, Harry Truman, and Joseph Stalin meet in Potsdam.

August 6: The United States drops an atomic bomb on Hiroshima, and, three days later, on Nagasaki.

August 14: Japan surrenders. World War II is over.

November 20: The Nuremberg War Trials begin in Germany.

1946 January 7: The United Nations holds its first meeting, in London.

January 20: President Charles de Gaulle of France resigns.

October 1: The Nuremberg War Trials conclude.

October 16: The first convicted Nazi War criminals are executed by hanging at Nuremberg.

December 9: Twenty-three former Nazi doctors and scientists are tried at Nuremberg. Sixteen are found guilty; seven are executed by hanging.

1947 June 5: The Marshall Plan is instituted, to help Europe rebuild.

September 15: Twenty-one former SS Operational Squad leaders are tried at Nuremberg. Although fourteen of them are sentenced to death, only four who were group commanders are executed.

1948 May 14: The State of Israel is proclaimed.

June 25: The U.S. Congress creates a Displaced Persons Commission.

October 30: The first boatload of war refugees arrives in the United States.

1949 April 4: The North Atlantic Treaty Organization—NATO—is formed.

May 23: West Germany becomes a separate state, under occupation forces. East Germany becomes a Soviet-bloc state later in the year.

December 9: The United Nations approves the Genocide Convention.

1957 The last Displaced Persons (DP) camp closes.

1960 May 11: Adolf Eichmann is captured in Argentina. He is tried in Jerusalem starting on April 11, 1961. Found guilty, he is executed by hanging on May 31, 1962.

Sachsenhausen

Sachsenhausen was a concentration camp near **BERLIN** located on the outskirts of Oranienburg. It was built by teams of prisoners transferred to the site from small camps in the Ems area and elsewhere, beginning in July 1936. As indicated in a letter written by Heinrich **HIMMLER** to the minister of justice, Sachsenhausen, like **BUCHENWALD**, was built in anticipation of the coming war. The camp was prepared for an expected intake of large numbers of prisoners. In November 1938, following the **KRISTALLNACHT** pogrom, 1,800 Jews were sent to Sachsenhausen. About 450 of them were murdered shortly after their arrival in the camp.

The total number of persons imprisoned in Sachsenhausen was approximately 200,000. When World War II began, conditions in the camp deteriorated sharply: in 1939, more than 800 prisoners died there, and in 1940 this number increased to nearly 4,000. In 1940, 26,000 prisoners, mainly from **POLAND**, were delivered to the camp. Most of them stayed only a short while and were then transferred to other camps in the Reich. At some point, probably in August 1941, the **SS** set up an installation for mass executions by shooting, disguising it as a prisoners' examination room. In the following months, 13,000 to 18,000 Soviet **PRISONERS OF WAR**, who were not even registered in the camp's lists, were murdered there. The camp also had a gas chamber, probably installed in 1943, that was added to an existing crematorium compound (*see* **GAS CHAMBERS/VANS**). The gas chamber was used on special orders only. One such occasion, presumably, was in February 1945, when the **SS** had several thousand physically debilitated prisoners killed on the eve of the camp's evacuation. In addition to the Soviet prisoners of war executed on arrival and those prisoners who died en route to and from the camp and during its evacuation, some 30,000 persons perished in Sachsenhausen.

In the first few years, the most important work project was a brickyard that prisoners built in the spring of 1938, on the Oder-Havel canal. Some 2,000 prisoners worked daily on the project. In April 1941 a satellite camp was established for the brickyard work team. Conditions in it were exceptionally harsh, and prisoners whose assignment to it was lengthy had little chance of surviving.

From 1943 on, the prisoners were employed primarily in various branches of the armaments industry, especially in the production of engines for aircraft, tanks, and vehicles. In 1944, 7,000 prisoners were assigned to the Heinkel Works in Oranienburg. Another large group was employed at the DEMAG tank plant in Falkensee, near Berlin. Special satellite camps were put up for both these plants. The brickyard was eventually converted to the manufacture of grenades.

Prisoners of the Sachsenhausen concentration camp stand in columns under the supervision of a camp guard, 1938.

Sachsenhausen was liberated on April 27, 1945, by advance troops of the Soviet army. At that point the camp contained only 3,000 prisoners, most of whom were not fit for marching. All the other prisoners had been evacuated by the SS.

SUGGESTED RESOURCES

Preissinger, Adrian. *Death Camps of the Soviets, 1945–1950: From Sachsenhausen to Buchenwald.* Ocean City, MD: Landpost Press, 1994.

"Prisoners of War (POWs)." *Simon Wiesenthal Center Museum of Tolerance Online.* [Online] http://motlc.wiesenthal.com/pages/t062/t06234.html (accessed on September 11, 2000).

Schindler, Oskar

(1908–1974)

Oskar Schindler was a businessman who is remembered as a protector of Jews during the **HOLOCAUST**. Schindler was born a Catholic in Svitavy in the Sudetenland (a region of Czechoslovakia prior to 1938, when it became part of Germany's territory). He came to **KRAKÓW** in late 1939 in the wake of the German invasion of **POLAND**. There he took over two previously Jewish-owned firms that dealt with the manufacture and wholesale distribution of enamel kitchenware products, one of which he operated as a trustee (*Treuhänder*) for the German occupation administration.

Schindler then established his own enamel works in Zablocie, outside Kraków, in which he employed mainly Jewish workers, thereby protecting them from deportation. When the liquidation of the Kraków ghetto began in early 1943, many Jews were sent to the **PŁASZÓW** labor camp, which was noted for the brutality of its commandant, Amon Goeth. Schindler used his good connections with high German officials in the Armaments Administration to set up a branch of the Płaszów camp in his factory compound for approximately 900 Jewish workers, including persons unfit and unqualified for labor production needs. In this way, he spared them from the horrors of the Płaszów camp.

Oskar Schindler (standing 2nd from right), and a group of Jews he rescued, in Munich, Germany.

In October 1944, with the approach of the Russian army, Schindler was granted permission to reestablish his now-defunct firm as an armaments production company in Brünnlitz (Brnenc, Sudetenland) and to take the Jewish workers from Zablocie with him. In an operation unique in the history of Nazi-occupied Europe, he succeeded in transferring 700 to 800 Jewish men from the **GROSS-ROSEN** camp and approximately 300 Jewish women from **AUSCHWITZ** to Brünnlitz. In Brünnlitz, the 1,100 Jews were given the most humane treatment possible under the circumstances: food, medical care, and religious needs. Informed that a train with evacuated Jewish detainees from the Goleszow camp was stranded at nearby Svitavy, Schindler received permission to take workers to the Svitavy railway station. There they forced the ice-sealed train doors open and removed approximately 100 Jewish men and women. Nearly frozen and resembling corpses, the Jews were then swiftly taken to the Brünnlitz factory and nourished back to life, an undertaking to which Schindler's wife, Emilie, particularly devoted herself. Those whom it was too late to save were buried with proper Jewish rites.

Schindler was devoted to the humane treatment of his Jewish workers and to their physical and psychological needs. He used his good connections with friends in high government positions, as well as his jovial and good-humored disposition, to befriend and ingratiate himself with high-ranking **SS** commanders in Poland. This stood him in good stead when he needed their assistance in extracting valuable and crucial favors from them, such as making conditions better and reducing the punishments of Jews under his care. Schindler was imprisoned on several occasions when the **GESTAPO** accused him of corruption, only to be released due to the intervention of his connections in **BERLIN** ministries.

In 1949, Oskar and Emilie Schindler emigrated to Argentina. Eight years later, Schindler left his wife and returned to Germany. He began to visit his friends in Israel in 1961. In 1962, Oskar Schindler planted a tree bearing his name in the Garden of the Righteous at Yad Vashem in Jerusalem. Wanting to be buried in Jerusalem because his "children," as he called them, were there, Schindler died in 1974 and was buried in the Catholic churchyard on Mount Zion in Jerusalem.

In 1993, director Steven Spielberg released the film *Schindler's List,* a motion picture biography of Oskar Schindler that concentrated on his rescue work. The film won seven Academy Awards, including Best Picture and Best Director. It has also won awards from several other international organizations.

SUGGESTED READING

Brecher, Elinor J. *Schindler's Legacy: True Stories of the List Survivors.* New York: Dutton, 1994.

Keneally, Thomas. *Schindler's List.* New York: Simon and Schuster, 1982.

Roberts, Jack L. *Oskar Schindler.* San Diego: Lucent Books, 1996.

Schindler, Emilie. *Where Light and Shadow Meet: A Memoir.* New York: Norton, 1997.

Schindler's List [videorecording]. MCA Universal Home Video, 1993.

SCHUTZSTAFFEL. SEE SS.

SD

The SD (Sicherheitsdienst des Reichsführers-SS; Security Service of the SS) was the **NAZI PARTY**'s intelligence service and a major instrument for the implementation of the **"FINAL SOLUTION"**. In 1931 Heinrich **HIMMLER** established the nucleus of an intelligence service in the SS headquarters and appointed Reinhard **HEYDRICH** as its chief. The new section operated out of Munich, at first on a modest scale; a year later it became the Security Service of the SS. Its function was to uncover the party's enemies and keep them under surveillance; however, the relationship of the SD with similar services maintained by party organizations was not clearly defined.

In April 1934 Himmler took over the Prussian **GESTAPO**, the final link that he needed to complete his takeover of the entire political police apparatus in **GERMANY**; he appointed Heydrich as its director. Himmler and Heydrich moved to **BERLIN** and the SD headquarters moved with them. On June 9 of that year, Rudolf Hess designated the SD as the sole party intelligence service. Whereas most of the senior Gestapo men were recruited from among the professional police officers, the SD attracted an elite of ambitious intellectuals and devoted much effort to studying and formulating the political and ideological goals of the SS. The Gestapo had the status of a national political police, but the division of labor between the two intelligence branches, the SD and the Gestapo, was not clear-cut. Even though both organizations were headed by the same people, there was still rivalry between them.

The first attempt to define the respective responsibilities of each branch was made in mid-1937. Himmler announced that the SD was an intelligence and counterintelligence service whose task it was to assist the Gestapo by identifying the enemies of the state; the Gestapo's task was to deal with these enemies once they were uncovered. Further guidelines were issued on July 1, 1937, allocating areas of responsibility to either the Gestapo or the SD. Some areas, such as the "Jewish issue," remained the joint responsibility of both organizations.

These guidelines, however, failed to resolve all the existing differences regarding the coordination of work between the Gestapo and the SD. The SD chiefs also tried their hand in espionage abroad by seeking to gain control over military intelligence. This goal was achieved in July 1944, after the attempt on Hitler's life, in which the Abwehr chiefs were found to have been involved. Because it was a large organization with a network of informers who submitted regular reports, the SD was able to keep track of the changing mood of the public. In this field the SD considered itself the central branch of the intelligence service, its task being to provide the political leaders with the basic data they required for the decision-making process.

Abwehr
The intelligence service of the Wermacht—the regular German armed forces.

Jews captured by SS and SD troops during the suppression of the Warsaw ghetto uprising are forced to leave their shelter and march to the Umschlagplatz (Transfer Point) for deportation.

On September 27, 1939, Heydrich unified his command over the Gestapo and the SD by creating the **REICH SECURITY MAIN OFFICE** (RSHA; *Reichssicherheitshauptamt*). It was only after the outbreak of the war that the SD was assigned operational tasks, when it joined the **OPERATIONAL SQUADS** (*Einsatzgruppen*) that followed the invading German army into **POLAND**. Its personnel served in command positions or in the rank and file of the Operational Squads, which in the summer of 1941 launched a systematic murder campaign against Jews and other groups in the German-occupied areas of the **SOVIET UNION**. The staff organization of the civil administration centers in the German-occupied areas included officers or inspectors from the Security Police (*Sicherheitspolizei*) and the SD. The officer, a Higher SS and Police Leader, was the commander of all the SS and police units in his area. The Security Service personnel engaged in intelligence activities and in punishing and murdering the local population, chiefly the Jews.

In 1935 the Jewish Section of the SD (Section II 112) adopted a basic policy and its own independent ways of operating. The concept that the Jews, by their very nature, were enemies of the state and of the Nazi regime determined the SD's goal and methods. The "provisional goal" it set in December 1936 was "to rid Germany of the Jews." From then on the SD kept Jewish organizations and institutions under its surveillance in order to harass the Jews and exert pressure on them to leave Germany. In 1937 the section outlined the practical steps that had to be taken to achieve its goal: economic dispossession, public pressure, and terrorization.

The first director of the Jewish Section of the SD was Leopold von Milden-stein, followed in 1936 by Herbert Hagen. Adolf **EICHMANN** joined the section in early 1935 and was put in charge of subsection 112/3, which dealt with "Zionists." He entered upon his major role in the murder of the Jews when he was dispatched from the section to head the **CENTRAL OFFICE FOR JEWISH EMIGRATION** (Zentral-stelle Für Jüdische Auswanderung) in **VIENNA**. The Jewish Section of the SD had a central role in organizing and implementing the "Final Solution." On October 1, 1946, the International Military Tribunal at Nuremberg declared the SD (as well as the SS and the Gestapo) a criminal organization.

SUGGESTED RESOURCES

Breitman, Richard. *The Architect of Genocide: Himmler and the Final Solution.* New York: Knopf, 1991.

The SS. Alexandria, VA: Time-Life Books, 1989.

Williamson, Gordon. *The SS: Hitler's Instrument of Terror.* Osceola, WI: Motorbooks International, 1994.

SECRET STATE POLICE. SEE GESTAPO.

SECURITY SERVICE OF THE SS. SEE SD.

Sendler, Irena

Irena Sendler.

(b. 1916)

Irena ("Jolanta") Sendler became one of the most active members in the Polish Council for Aid to Jews known as "Zegota." This was an active underground organization in the **WARSAW** area. Sendler, a Catholic, tried to ease the suffering of her Jewish friends and acquaintances during the early days of the German occupation of **POLAND**. Her job at the Social Welfare Department of Warsaw gave her access to visit the ghetto area at all times; her official purpose was to help fight contagious diseases. She took advantage of the opportunity to provide many Jews with clothing, medicine, and money. When walking through the ghetto streets, Sendler wore an armband with the Star of David, both as a sign of solidarity with the Jewish people and so as not to call attention to herself.

At the end of the summer of 1942, Sendler was asked to join the newly founded Zegota, or Council for Aid to Jews. She was very valuable to Zegota, for she had already enlisted a large group of people in her charitable work. This group included a wide network of contacts both inside the ghetto and out.

While working with Zegota, Sendler specialized in smuggling Jewish children out of the ghetto and finding safe places for them with non-Jewish families in the Warsaw region. Each of her co-workers was made responsible for several blocks of apartments where Jewish children were sheltered. She herself oversaw eight or ten apartments where Jews were hiding under her care. Zegota provided financial support to the families who helped care for the children.

In October 1943, Sendler was arrested by the **GESTAPO**, and taken to the infamous Pawiak Prison. There she was brutally tortured to make her reveal information. The efforts to "break" her were unsuccessful, and the interrogators told her

that she was doomed. However, on the day set for her execution, she was freed, after her companions from the underground bribed one of the Gestapo agents. Officially, however, Sendler was listed on public bulletin boards as among those executed. Forced to stay out of sight for the remainder of the German occupation, Sendler continued to work undercover for Zegota. In 1965 she was recognized by Yad Vashem as **"RIGHTEOUS AMONG THE NATIONS"**.

SUGGESTED RESOURCES

Tec, Nechama. *When Light Pierced the Darkness: Christian Rescue of Jews in Nazi-occupied Poland.* New York: Oxford University Press, 1986.

Irena Sendler's rescue work was done at great risk to herself and her co-workers. Concealing Jews was a crime punishable by death in Nazi-occupied Poland. In Warsaw, Zegota sheltered at least 2500 registered Jewish children.

Seyss-Inquart, Arthur

(1892–1946)

A **VIENNA** lawyer who walked with a limp after being wounded in World War I, Seyss-Inquart became recognized as an Austrian Nazi statesman. He was active in nationalist circles and, while initially not antisemitic, he became increasingly attracted to National Socialism. Seyss-Inquart was held in high esteem by the Austrian chancellor, Kurt von Schuschnigg, who appointed him to the Council of State. Seyss-Inquart was not considered a reliable member of the **NAZI PARTY** in Austria. However, he was highly regarded by Adolf **HITLER**, who pressured Schuschnigg into appointing Seyss-Inquart as the Austrian minister of both the interior and public security on February 16, 1938.

On Hitler's ultimatum, Seyss-Inquart was appointed chancellor after Schuschnigg's resignation in March of 1938. Seyss-Inquart immediately invited the German armed forces to invade Austria. In return, Hitler appointed him the Reich commissioner of Ostmark, as Austria was now called; however, Seyss-Inquart's influence on the Austrian Anschluss was slight. On May 1, 1939, Seyss-Inquart was appointed to a government post in the central German government. In October, 1939, he was appointed deputy governor-general in **POLAND**. There, he was responsible for examining the territory to be used for the **LUBLIN** Reservation, where the Jews from the Reich were to be deported (*see* **NISKO AND LUBLIN PLAN**).

On May 19, 1940, Hitler appointed Seyss-Inquart as the Reich Commissioner of the Occupied **NETHERLANDS** and also instructed him to try to create a friendship between the Dutch and the Germans. Hitler hoped that the man who had helped in the annexation of Austria would succeed in the same way in the Netherlands. In his first months as commissioner, Seyss-Inquart acted with restraint, creating the impression that the Germans would not make life difficult for the Dutch. However, it quickly became clear to him that, apart from the small organized minority in the Dutch Nationalist Socialist movement, the Dutch would reject the efforts of the Germans to win them over. In time, the Germans began to take steps against the Dutch. Acts against the Jews, which began in late 1940 and reached a peak in February, 1941, contributed in particular to the anti-German climate. For example, Amsterdam dockworkers went on strike in reaction to what the Germans did to the Jews. Seyss-Inquart reacted sharply to these incidents, rightly seeing in them the failure of his policy. He took an active role in the anti-Jewish legislation, in the pillage of Jewish property, and in the dispatch of Jews to the **EXTERMINATION CAMPS**. Seyss-Inquart knew that the removal of the Jews from Europe was Hitler's supreme mission, and he wanted to be among the initiators of the cam-

Arthur Seyss-Inquart (2nd from left) and Konrad Henlein (3rd from left), leader of the Nazi Sudeten party, January 30, 1939.

paign rather than to allow the local **SS** to claim exclusive credit for initiating the **"FINAL SOLUTION"**. In fact, Seyss-Inquart was aware of Hitler's intentions at a very early stage. At a well-attended meeting held on May 15, 1941, Nazi officials deliberated on the confiscation of Jewish property. At this meeting, Hitler indicated that the proceeds from such confiscations should expected to provide financial resources for a "Final Solution."

In an attempt to become the one entrusted with responsibility for dealing with the Jews, Seyss-Inquart initiated several of the harshest measures that were taken against them. During the last months of the war, Seyss-Inquart began negotiations with the Allied armies in an attempt to ease the suffering of the Dutch population. After the cease-fire, he became one of the war criminals indicted for **CRIMES AGAINST HUMANITY**. Seyss-Inquart was sentenced to death at the Nuremberg Trial. Throughout all of his activities, Seyss-Inquart remained loyal to Hitler, and Hitler praised him highly on a number of occasions. A collection of speeches by Seyss-Inquart, *Vier Jahre in den Niederlanden: Gesammelte Reden*, was published in Amsterdam in 1944.

SUGGESTED RESOURCES

Conot, Robert E. *Justice at Nuremberg.* New York: Harper and Row, 1983.

Harris, Whitney R. *Tyranny on Trial: The Evidence at Nuremberg.* New York: Barnes and Noble, 1995.

Sprecher, Drexel A., *Inside the Nuremberg Trial: A Prosecutor's Comprehensive Account.* Lanham, MD: University Press of America, 1999.

SHE'ERIT HA-PELETAH. SEE DISPLACED PERSONS, JEWISH; REFUGEES, 1933–1945.

SHIPS. SEE ALIYA BET; ST. LOUIS.

SHO'AH. SEE HOLOCAUST.

SICHERHEITSDIENST. SEE SD.

Simferopol

Simferopol is a city in the Crimean peninsula; capital of the Crimean Oblast (district), in the **UKRAINE** (once part of the **SOVIET UNION**). Simferopol was founded in the eighteenth century, and Jews lived there from its inception. On the eve of World War II the city's Jewish population was more than 20,000, out of a total population of 142,678.

Simferopol was occupied by the Germans on November 1, 1941. By then most of the Jews had left on their own accord or had been evacuated, but their place had been taken by Jewish refugees from **KHERSON**, Dnepropetrovsk, and the Jewish **kolkhozy** in the Larindorf and Freidorf subdistricts. Approximately 13,000 Jews were in Simferopol when the Germans arrived, as well as 1,500 Krimchaks, the largest community of these Jews to be found anywhere. On the day after the occupation, announcements were posted ordering the Jews to form a **JUDENRAT** (Jewish Council) and to report for **FORCED LABOR**. In the following days they were ordered to register and wear a yellow badge (*see* **BADGE, JEWISH**) in the form of a Star of David.

On December 9, the Krimchak Jews were rounded up and killed. From December 11 to 13 the remaining 12,500 Jews were rounded up, put on trucks, and taken out of town to be shot to death. The murder was perpetrated by the men of **SPECIAL COMMANDO** (*Sonderkommando*) 11b, belonging to Operational Squad (*Einsatzgruppe*) D, and by German police of Reserve Ordnungspolizei Battalion No. 3. Jews who had gone into hiding and were caught were put into the local jail, and by the middle of February 1942, 300 of them were gassed to death (*see* **GAS CHAMBERS/VANS**).

Simferopol was liberated by the Soviets on April 13, 1944.

SUGGESTED RESOURCES

Gitelman, Zvi, ed. *Bitter Legacy: Confronting the Holocaust in the USSR.* Bloomington: Indiana University Press, 1997.

SIMON WIESENTHAL CENTER. SEE MUSEUMS AND MEMORIAL INSTITUTES.

Skarżysko-Kamienna

Skarżysko-Kamienna was a forced-labor camp for Jews in the town of that name in the **KIELCE** district of **POLAND**. Located next to an ammunition factory, the camp belonged to HASAG, a German corporation. **SS** officer Egon Dalski, the general manager of the HASAG factory in Skarżysko-Kamienna from 1939 to 1943, was in charge of the camp.

The harshest conditions were found at Camp C where prisoners did the deadly work of producing underwater mines and filling them with picric acid. The acid caused the skin to turn yellow, and within three months the prisoners doing this work died of poisoning.

The Skarżysko-Kamienna camp was established in August 1942, in three separate sites, identified as Factory Camps (*Werke*) A, B, and C. It existed until August 1, 1944. Most of the prisoners were from Poland. The rest were brought there from **AUSTRIA**, Czechoslovakia, **GERMANY**, the **NETHERLANDS**, and **FRANCE**. The average number of prisoners in the camp was 6,000. According to German sources, 3,241 Jews perished at Skarżysko-Kamienna between October 1, 1942, and January 31, 1943—an average of 26 deaths a day. The total number of Jews who were brought there is estimated at 25,000 to 30,000. Of those, it is believed that between 18,000 and 23,000 died.

The three camps were situated close to the factories in which the prisoners worked. The inmates worked side-by-side with free Polish laborers. Each department had a German manager, with Poles acting as his deputies and as supervisors. The camp security was in the hands of the Ukrainian factory police (*Werkschutz*), but headed by Germans notorious for the acts of robbery, murder, and rape that occurred under their watch. They reported to the factory manager.

The factories operated on two twelve-hour shifts; the prisoners were given impossible work loads. Sanitary conditions in the camp were intolerable. The food rations consisted of 7 ounces (200 grams) of bread a day and about a pint (.5 liters) of watery soup twice a day, and, occasionally, a spoonful of jam or a small portion of margarine. The prisoners had to work in the same clothes week after week. When these disintegrated—as they inevitably did, the inmates wrapped themselves in paper bags.

In all three camps, there were epidemics of dysentery, typhus, and a disease caused by weakness, which the prisoners called *hasagowka*, after the HASAG company. Medical assistance was not available in the camps until early 1944. During the spring of 1944, when the authorities faced a critical shortage of labor, living conditions in the camp improved slightly, in order to keep up the prisoners' strength. There were more food rations, medical supplies, and clothing. Some of the inmates had connections with the Jewish or Polish underground and received aid from these sources.

Prisoners who tried to escape were usually killed. In Camps A and C, any Jews caught stealing materials in the factory were hanged. In late 1943 and early 1944, mass executions took place in Camp C. The victims were prisoners of different nationalities who had been brought in from the **GESTAPO** jails in the Radom district. Shortly before the liquidation of the camp in the summer of 1944, a special unit of Jewish prisoners, under **SS** supervision, took the bodies of these victims out of the mass grave in which they had been buried in the Camp C area, in order to cremate them.

Several underground resistance groups were active in the camp, among them a cell of the **JEWISH FIGHTING ORGANIZATION** (ŻOB). Members of the Bund, a Jewish "nationalist" group, established links with the Bund leadership in **WARSAW**. Jewish prisoners smuggled arms out of the factory and gave them to Polish **PARTISANS** belonging to the Home Army (*Armia Krajowa*). Links also existed with the Polish Communist underground, the Polish Workers' Party (*Polska Partia Robotnicza*).

Two days before the liquidation of Camp C, several hundred prisoners escaped. Most of them were killed during the attempt or in the surrounding forests. In late July 1944, some 600 people were murdered on the spot. The remaining prisoners, numbering more than 6,000, were transferred to the **BUCHENWALD** camp, to camps at Częstochowa and Leipzig, and to other camps in Germany.

In 1948, twenty-five German foremen from the Skarżysko-Kamienna camp were brought to trial in Leipzig. Four were sentenced to death, two to life impris-

onment, and others to prison terms of varying lengths. The most brutal camp enforcers were never found.

Slovakia, October 1938.

SUGGESTED RESOURCES

Karay, Felicja. *Death Comes in Yellow: Skarżysko-Kamienna Slave Labor Camp.* Amsterdam: Harwood, 1995.

SLAVE LABOR. See Forced Labor.

Slovakia

Slovakia is a region in east central Europe. Until 1918 Slovakia was part of **HUNGARY**; between the two world wars, it was part of the Czechoslovak republic. Between March 14, 1939, and April 29, 1945, it was a satellite of Nazi **GERMANY**, and after World War II it became part of Czechoslovakia.

Jews had lived in Slovakia since the Roman period. During the nineteenth century, the community began to grow significantly. In 1930, 135,918 Jews (4.5 percent of the population) lived in Slovakia. More than 10,000 young Jews belonged to Zionist **YOUTH MOVEMENTS**.

At the Wannsee Conference held in January 1942, Nazi leaders noted that the Slovaks seemed sure to cooperate in facilitating the "Final Solution." In mid-February the Germans asked the Slovaks for 20,000 young Jews to "build new Jewish settlements." The Slovaks agreed, but, fearing that the Germans might leave only unproductive Jews in Slovakia, they demanded that they deport the entire community.

In September 1938, a part of Czechoslovakia, the Sudetenland, became part of Germany; the second Czechoslovak republic was established with Slovakia as an autonomous region. Germany allowed Hungary, its ally, to annex parts of Slovakia and Ruthenia. With this loss of territory, the December 1938 census showed a Jewish population of 88,951 in Slovakia. In March 1939, the Nazis invaded Czechoslovakia and made areas of **BOHEMIA AND MORAVIA** a protectorate of the Reich. Slovakia became a separate state on March 14, 1939.

A one-party totalitarian regime (the Slovak People's Party of Hlinka, known as the Ludaks) took control of Slovakia. The government aligned itself with Nazi Germany and signed a treaty that allowed Germany to interfere in Slovak internal affairs and to dictate its foreign policy.

Anti-Jewish Sentiment and Policy

ANTISEMITISM was present in Slovakia during the war years. Storm troops of the Hlinka Guard and paramilitary squads of ethnic Germans attacked Jews on the streets, looted their property, and forcibly removed Jews to the no-man's-land between Slovakia and Hungary. In July 1940, a National Socialist regime was set up in Slovakia, bringing more systematic anti-Jewish legislation. That August, the **REICH SECURITY MAIN OFFICE** (RSHA; *Reichssicherheitshauptamt*) sent Dieter **WISLICENY** to Slovakia to serve as an adviser on Jewish affairs.

The Slovaks set up the Central Economic Office to remove Jews from the economy and oversee the **ARYANIZATION** (*Arisierung*) of Jewish property. Jewish assets were estimated to be worth more than 3 billion Slovak crowns (approximately 120 million dollars), including real estate, business enterprises, and capital. This forced conversion of Jewish assets to non-Jewish ownership was completed in one year.

In the summer of 1941, anti-Jewish legislation escalated. Jews were now banned from certain public places and had to wear a yellow armband with a Star of David (*see* **BADGE, JEWISH**). Jewish apartments, as well as mail and other documents, also had to display a Star of David. The "Jewish Code," issued on September 9, 1941, classified Jews along the same lines as the **NUREMBERG LAWS**. By December 1941 Jews were forbidden to congregate and were subject to a curfew. Fifteen thousand Jews were removed from Bratislava. By March 1942, 6,700 had been resettled in Trnava, Nitra, and eastern Slovakia, or sent to labor camps.

Deportations

On March 27, the first trainload of Slovak Jews was sent to the east. By October 1942, about 58,000 Slovak Jews had been deported, most of them to **AUSCHWITZ**, **MAJDANEK**, and the **LUBLIN** area.

On May 23, 1942, the Slovak parliament passed a law that permitted the expulsion of Jews from Slovakia. As early as the autumn of 1942, rumors about the fate of Jewish deportees led some Slovak politicians to demand an end to the deportations. The Germans denied the rumors, but refused when some politicians demanded that a Slovak delegation be allowed to visit the deportees in Auschwitz. This pressure contributed to the ending of the transports in October 1942.

Jewish Response to Deportations

When Jewish leaders learned about the impending deportations several weeks before they began, an activist core group formed a committee known as the "Working Group" in an attempt to forestall them. The group's activities did not prevent

The deportation of the Jews of Stropkov, near the Czechoslovak-Polish border, took place on May 21, 1942. A Jew is subjected to a humiliating beard trimming while waiting at the railway station to be deported.

the transports, but their combined use of intervention with government and Catholic church officials, bribery, and negotiations with the Nazis contributed to ending the deportations in October 1942. Later, the **Auschwitz Protocols** came into the hands of the Working Group. Its leaders sent the reports to the West, with a plea to bomb the railway lines leading to Auschwitz and the camp itself. The Allies failed to bomb the camp, but the information contained in the protocols sparked increased internationally backed rescue activities in Hungary.

Prior to March 1944, more than 10,000 Jews escaped into Hungary. Others sought protection by converting to Christianity or by obtaining false "Aryan" papers. Some Jews who were deemed "vital" to the Slovak economy were granted "certificates of exemption" from the deportations. The five companies of Jews in the Sixth Slovak Brigade (armed forces) and most of the Jews in Slovak labor camps were usually safeguarded from deportation.

During the relatively quiet period in Slovakia between October 1942 and August 1944, the Working Group negotiated with the Nazis to save the remaining Slovak Jews, as well as other Jews slated for extermination. This bargaining (known as the Europa Plan), did not save the rest of European Jewry, but some historians believe that the contact with the Germans may have helped protect the remaining Slovak Jews until the Slovak National Uprising broke out in late August 1944.

Auschwitz Protocols
Detailed reports by four Jewish escapees from Auschwitz who reached Slovakia in the spring of 1944.

Slovak National Uprising

Efforts to oust the pro-Nazi regime and free Slovakia from its dependence on Germany led to the Slovak National Uprising (August 28 to October 27, 1944). A minority of Slovaks had never supported the regime, and **partisan units** sprang up as early as 1942. In the three labor camps, armed cells began to form during the deportations of 1942. The uprising was planned by the Czechoslovak Agrarian party, the right wing of the Social Democratic party, the Communist party, estranged Slovak nationalists, and a group of army officers. In late December 1943 the Slovak National Council (SNR) was established to coordinate the uprising. The rebels hoped their efforts would coincide with an advance by the Soviet army. If German troops attacked Slovakia, they expected their forces could hold out in central Slovakia until Soviet troops arrived.

partisan units
Organized groups of paramilitary guerrilla fighters targeting the occupying Nazi forces.

The Jews hoped that a successful uprising in Slovakia would lead to the rescue of the remaining 20,000 Slovakian Jews.

Early in 1944, contact was established between the Jewish fighting groups in the labor camps and the SNR; the Jewish groups remained part of the planning and execution of the uprising from that point on. In the spring of 1944, partisan units, most of them under Soviet command, were active in the mountains. Moscow sent guerrilla soldiers to Slovakia to engage in partisan activities, but they made little effort to coordinate with the SNR. As the Germans suffered increasing military losses, more and more Slovaks joined their own rebel forces. By the summer, the rebels controlled significant areas of eastern and central Slovakia. The government did little to stop the PARTISANS, who were operating in an area of about 5,366 square miles with a population, at the most, of 800,000. Most of the terrain consisted of mountains and valleys. The resistance forces declared a Czechoslovak republic and set up a government in the liberated area.

On August 28 and 29, to forestall further partisan gains, the Germans invaded Slovakia. The Germans had superior manpower and firepower, while the 60,000 rebels, of which 16,000 were partisans, were armed mostly with light weapons. Their heavy arsenal included only 120 cannon, 15 tanks, and 21 airplanes, which the Soviets had provided. Moreover, the rebel troops and partisans were not as experienced as the Germans. However, the Germans could not quell the uprising within a few days, as they had expected. Late in September, they brought in more SS units and within weeks, the Germans crushed the rebels. The organized military struggle ended on October 27.

More than 2,000 Jews took part in the rebellion and about 500 died in battle. During the uprising, four Jewish parachutists from Palestine reached Slovakia. Their arrival boosted Jewish morale. They worked for Jewish welfare in the "liberated" rebel territory, where most of the surviving Jews had gathered and tried to combat antisemitism in the rebel-held areas. Only one, Chaim Hermesh, survived the uprising and continued fighting with Slovak partisans until the war ended.

The uprising failed in part because of internal political differences and because of Allied reluctance to fully support it. The Western powers regarded Slovakia as part of the Soviet sphere; the Soviets gave only meager support. After the uprising collapsed, the Germans captured 5,000 Jews, mostly civilians, and about 19,000 partisans. They killed more than 1,500 of these Jews. By March 1945, the Germans had deported 13,500 Jews to Auschwitz, SACHSENHAUSEN, and THERESIENSTADT. About 10,000 Slovak Jews survived in the camps until liberation; 4,000 to 5,000 remained in hiding in Slovakian cities and towns, or with partisans in the mountains.

Including those Jews who lived in the territories that Hungary had annexed, about 100,000 Slovak Jews were lost. Between 25,000 and 30,000 Slovak Jews survived the war, but those who returned home felt unwelcome. Anti-Jewish demonstrations and violence were common, and Jews were blocked from reclaiming their own homes and other property. After the Soviet-backed regime was established in 1948, most of the remaining Jews left Slovakia; the majority immigrated to Israel in 1949.

SUGGESTED RESOURCES

"55th Anniversary of Slovak National Uprising." *Krajsk £rad Bansk Bystrica.* [Online] http://www.55snp.sk/en/ (accessed on September 11, 2000).

"Jewish Parachutists." *Simon Wiesenthal Center Museum of Tolerance Online.* [Online] http://motlc.wiesenthal.com/pages/t059/t05903.html (accessed on September 11, 2000).

"Slovak National Uprising." *Simon Wiesenthal Center Museum of Tolerance Online.* [Online] http://motlc.wiesenthal.org/pages/t071/t07147.html (accessed on September 11, 2000).

Sobibór

Sobibór was an **EXTERMINATION CAMP** near the village and railway station of Sobibór in the **LUBLIN** district of **POLAND**. Established as part of **AKTION (OPERATION) REINHARD**, the camp was built in a sparsely populated, woody, and swampy area beginning in March 1942. Local inhabitants and a group of 80 Jews from nearby ghettos built it. In April 1942, **SS** officer Franz **STANGL** was appointed camp commandant.

The camp staff included 20 to 30 German **SS** men, most of whom, like Stangl, had taken part in the **EUTHANASIA PROGRAM**. In addition, 90 to 120 Ukrainians served in the camp. Most were Soviet **PRISONERS OF WAR** who had been trained for the job at **TRAWNIKI**; some were **VOLKSDEUTSCHE**—Soviet nationals of German origin. The German staff filled most of the command and administrative positions, while the Ukrainian unit acted as guards and security personnel. Among other things, it was their job to quash any resistance offered by the Jews who were brought to the camp and to prevent escapes. Jewish prisoners also worked in the camp, performing various physical tasks.

Physical Characteristics of the Camp

The camp formed a rectangle 1,312 by 1,969 feet (400 by 600 meters) in area. It was surrounded by a barbed-wire fence 9.8 feet (3 meters) high, with tree branches intertwined in it to conceal the camp. There were three camp areas, each individually fenced in: the administration area, the reception area, and the extermination area. The administration area consisted of the *Vorlager* ("forward camp," the part of the camp closest to the railway station) and Camp I. The *Vorlager* included the railway platform, with space for 20 railway cars, and the living quarters for the German and Ukrainian staff. Camp I was fenced off from the rest. It contained housing for the Jewish prisoners and their workshops.

The reception area, also known as Camp II, was the place where Jews from the incoming transports were brought. There they went through various procedures before being killed in the gas chambers—removal of clothes, cutting of women's hair, and confiscation of possessions and valuables.

The extermination area, or Camp III, was located in the northwestern part of the camp. It was the most isolated part. It contained the gas chambers (*see* **GAS CHAMBERS/VANS**), burial trenches, and housing for the Jewish prisoners who worked there. A path 9.8 to 13 feet (3 to 4 meters) wide and 492 feet (150 meters) long, and lined on both sides with a barbed-wire fence, led from the reception area to the extermination area. The fencing here was also intertwined with branches to conceal from view this path along which the victims were herded, naked, toward the gas chambers from the shed where they had undressed.

The gas chambers were inside a brick building. Each chamber was square, measuring 172 square feet (16 square meters), with a capacity of 160 to 180 people. The chambers were entered from a platform at the front of the brick building. Each gas chamber also had another opening, through which the bodies were removed. The carbon monoxide gas was produced by a 200-horsepower engine in a nearby shed, from which it was piped into the gas chambers. The burial trenches were nearby, each 164 to 197 feet (50 to 60 meters) long, 33 to 49 feet (10 to 15 meters) wide, and 16.4 to 23 feet (5 to 7 meters) deep. From the railway platform to the burial trenches ran a narrow-gauge railway that was used to transport persons too weak to make their way to the gas chambers on their own, as well as the bodies of those who had died en route to Sobibór.

When the camp was almost finished, a test was made to verify that the gas chambers were working properly. Two hundred and fifty Jews, most of them women, were brought in from the nearby labor camp at Krychów and put to death in the chambers. All the SS men of the camp were present at this experiment.

Plan of the Sobibór extermination camp.

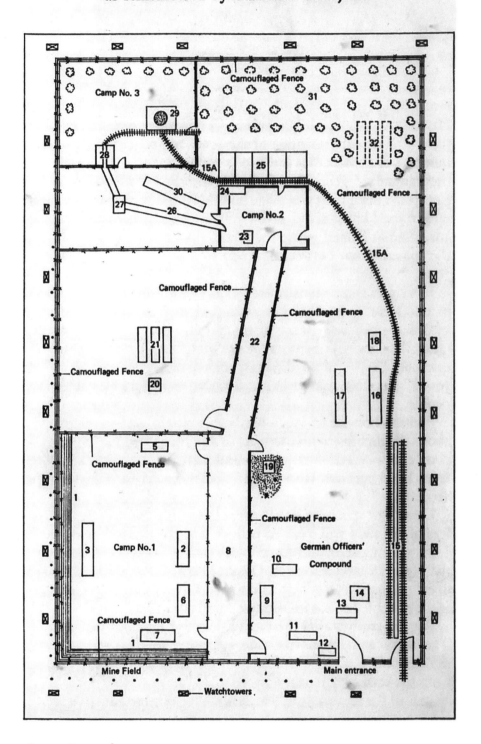

SOBIBOR EXTERMINATION CAMP
as remembered by Stanislaw Szmajzner

Camp Procedures

Several hundred able-bodied Jews were chosen from among the first few transports of prisoners to form work teams. Some worked as tailors, cobblers, carpenters, and so on, to serve the needs of the German and Ukrainian camp staff. All the other work assignments had to do with "processing" the victims along the route that led from the railway platform to the burial trenches. A total of about 1,000 prisoners, 150

of them women, were eventually put into these teams. One group of several dozen prisoners worked on the railway platform. Their job was to remove from the cars those who could not get off on their own and to remove the bodies of those who had died en route. They also had to clean out the cars. The purpose was to make sure that when the train left the camp, it would contain no trace of the human cargo it had transported. Other work teams were assigned to the reception area, to handle the clothing and luggage left there by the victims on their way to the gas chambers. These groups had to sort out the clothing and prepare it to be sent out of the camp, to search for money and other valuables that might have been left behind, and to remove the yellow patches from the clothing and any other signs that could have identified the clothes as having been worn by Jews. Yet another group in this area, the barbers, had to cut off the women's hair and package it to be sent out of the camp.

In the extermination area, 200 to 300 Jewish prisoners were held. It was their task was to remove the bodies of the murdered victims from the gas chambers, take them to the burial ground, and then clean up the chambers. A special team of prisoners, nicknamed "the dentists," was charged with extracting gold teeth from the mouths of the victims before their bodies were put into the trenches. Toward the end of 1942, in an effort to erase the traces of the mass killings, the bodies were dug up and cremated; this task too was carried out by a special team of prisoners.

Nearly every day there were *Selektionen*—"selections"—among the Jewish prisoners. In these selections, the weak and the sick were sent to the gas chambers. Their place was taken by new arrivals. Any misbehavior by a prisoner—such as the theft of food, money, or valuables found in the luggage left behind by the victims— was punished by death. Only a few prisoners survived for more than a few months.

Transports: First Stage

The process of killing trainloads of Jews was based entirely on misleading the victims and hiding the fate that was in store for them. When a train arrived, the people on board were ordered to get off. They were told that they had arrived at a "transit camp" from which they would be sent to labor camps. Before leaving for the labor camps, they were to take showers, and at the same time their clothes would be disinfected. Following this announcement, the men and women were separated (children went with the women); they were told that the sexes had to be separated for their showers. The victims were ordered to take off their clothes and hand over any money or valuables in their possession; anyone who was caught trying to conceal any item was shot. Then followed the march to the gas chambers, which had been made to look like shower rooms. Some 450 to 550 persons entered the chambers at a time. When the gas chambers were jammed full of people, they were closed and sealed and the gas was piped in. Within twenty to thirty minutes, everyone inside was dead.

The bodies were then removed from the gas chambers and buried, after the gold teeth had been taken from their mouths. The whole procedure, from the arrival of the train to the burial of the victims, took two to three hours. In the meantime, the railway cars were cleaned up and the train departed—and another 20 cars, with their human load destined for extermination, entered the camp.

The first stage of the extermination operation went on for three months, from May to July 1942. The Jews who were brought to Sobibór during this period came from the Lublin district in Poland, and from Czechoslovakia, **GERMANY**, and **AUSTRIA**. Those from countries outside Poland had first been taken to ghettos in the Lublin district, and from there were deported to Sobibór. Some 10,000 Jews were

E verything was done on the run, accompanied by shouts, beatings, and warning shots. The victims were in a state of shock and did not grasp what was happening to them.

brought from Germany and Austria, 6,000 from **THERESIENSTADT**, and many thousands from **SLOVAKIA**. In all, between 90,000 and 100,000 Jews were murdered at Sobibór in this first stage. The transports came to a temporary halt at the end of July, to enable the railway line to undergo repairs.

In Sobibór's first three months of operation, the Germans found that the gas chambers created a bottleneck in the murder program. They had a total capacity of fewer than 600 people. The halt in camp operations during August and September 1942 was therefore used to construct three more gas chambers. These were put up next to the existing chambers under the same roof, with a hallway separating the old chambers from the new. With a new capacity of 1,200 people, the rate of extermination could be doubled.

Second Stage

By the beginning of October 1942, work on the railway line was completed and the transports to Sobibór could begin again. Until early November, the arriving transports brought more Jews from towns in the Lublin district. In the winter, following the closing of the **BELŻEC** camp, and in the spring and summer of 1943, Sobibór also received transports from the region known as Eastern Galicia. The winter transports arrived bearing people who had frozen to death on the way. Some of the transports consisted of people who had been stripped naked in order to make it harder for them to escape from the train. One train carried 5,000 Jewish prisoners from the **MAJDANEK** camp. From October 1942 to June 1943, a total of 70,000 to 80,000 Jews from Lublin and the Eastern Galicia districts were brought to Sobibór. The number of victims from the **GENERALGOUVERNEMENT** was between 145,000 and 155,000.

By the end of October 1942, some 25,000 Jews from Slovakia had been killed at Sobibór. In February 1943, Heinrich **HIMMLER** paid a visit to the camp. While he was there, a special transport arrived with several hundred Jewish girls from a labor camp in the Lublin district. Himmler watched the entire extermination procedure. In March 1943, four transports from **FRANCE** brought 4,000 people, all of whom were killed. Nineteen transports arrived from the Netherlands between March and July 1943, carrying 35,000 Jews.

The last transports to arrive at Sobibór came from the **VILNA**, **MINSK**, and Lida ghettos. Approximately 14,000 Jews came on these transports in the second half of September 1943, following the liquidation of the ghettos in these cities. This brought the total number of Jews killed at Sobibór throughout the period of the camp's operation to approximately 250,000.

At the end of the summer of 1942, the burial trenches were opened and the process of burning the victims' bodies was begun. The corpses were put into huge piles and set on fire. The bodies of victims who arrived in the camp after that time were cremated immediately after gassing and were not buried.

Resistance and Escape

On July 5, 1943, Himmler ordered the closing of Sobibór as an extermination camp. It was to be transformed into a concentration camp. Throughout the camp's existence, attempts had been made to escape from it. Some of them were successful. In retaliation for these attempts, the Germans executed many dozens of prisoners. During the summer of 1943, in order to prevent escapes, and also as a safety measure against attacks by **PARTISANS**, the Germans planted land mines along the entire

---

The Dutch Jews came to Sobibón in regular passenger trains. They were given a polite welcome and were asked to send letters to their relatives in the Netherlands to let them know they had arrived at a labor camp. After they had written these letters, they were given the same treatment as all the other transports. Within a few hours they were all dead.

Before World War II, there were more than 3 million Jews in the Soviet Union. Many had lived there for generations, often in villages that were exclusively Jewish, and in Jewish areas of larger cities. In 1939 and 1940, the Jewish population expanded by nearly 2 million when the Soviet Union annexed territory including eastern **POLAND**, the Baltic states, Bessarabia, and Bukovina. In addition, Soviet Jewry during World War II included 250,000 to 300,000 Jewish refugees who had fled from Poland when it was occupied by **GERMANY** at the start of the war. In June 1941, when the Germans invaded the Soviet Union, as many as 5,250,000 Jews were under its rule, more than half the total number of Jews in Europe.

The three categories of Jews—those who had been living in the Soviet Union before 1939, those living in the territories annexed by the Soviet Union, and the refugees—differed from one another in their social makeup, their way of life, and their Jewish consciousness and identification.

In addition, the original Soviet Jewish population itself could be divided into three groups. There were Jews—between 1.25 million and 1.5 million—who were well assimilated into Soviet society, working in technical fields such as engineering and science. They lived in fairly industrialized areas, were younger than the average Soviet Jew, and had left behind the life of their parents and grandparents in small Jewish villages. Their attitude toward the Yiddish language and culture and toward religion was marked by disrespect and scorn. Many were in mixed marriages and the percentage of Communist party membership was high.

A second group, numbering between 750,000 and 1 million Jews, lived in the large cities where historically there had been centers of Jewish population. In average age and education they were not very different from the first group. The areas they inhabited, however, were less industrialized, and the population was heterogeneous (consisting of Ukrainians, Belorussians, Russians, and Poles). To some degree that factor had slowed their rate of acculturation to the Russian way of life. Many of these Jews still spoke Yiddish and spent much of their leisure time with other Jews.

A third group, numbering somewhere between 500,000 and 1 million still lived in the Jewish towns—*shtetl*—and in the Jewish agricultural areas established and encouraged by the Soviet regime in the 1920s and 1930s. This meant that at the outset of World War II, dozens of villages in the southern Ukraine and the Crimea were either exclusively Jewish or had a Jewish majority. Most of the Jews in this group were older, and their formal education was far below the average among Soviet Jews. They spent their life among other Jews, both at work and in their leisure time. The Yiddish language, Jewish jokes, and the use of Jewish metaphors were prevalent among this group, more than among any other sector of Soviet Jewry.

Refugee Jews in the Soviet Union posed a particularly difficult problem. They generally had no place to live and no employment, and had left their relatives behind in German-occupied Poland. They had no Jewish cultural network, and there was no place for them in the social structure of the territories where they lived. The Soviet authorities tried to deal with the problem by recruiting them for work in the interior of the USSR on a voluntary basis, but this attempt failed. The refugees, numbering hundreds of thousands, were given the option of accepting Soviet citizenship or returning to their homes in German-occupied Poland. If they became Soviet citizens they would be under certain restrictions, such as not being allowed to live within 62 miles (100 kilometers) of the border or in the large cities. Most of the refugees opted for returning to Poland. The Soviets took this as a mark of disloyalty to their regime, and in June and July of 1940 the refugees were exiled to the Soviet interior.

On June 22, 1941, the Germans launched Operation "Barbarossa," the invasion of the Soviet Union on a huge military scale, with the objective of ending the war

In the annexed territories, Jews were affected by a policy of forced "Sovietization" between 1939 and 1941. Jewish organizations were disbanded, Hebrew schools closed, independent Jewish newspapers were no longer published, and political parties were outlawed. Masses of Jews were arrested and exiled, because the Soviet authorities classified them as politically hostile elements.

German-occupied Soviet territory.

by that winter. Initially, the Wehrmacht (German armed forces) made rapid progress. The Red Army's lack of preparedness, the breakdown of communications, and the reluctance of the Soviet command to act without approval at the political level, brought the Soviet military position to the brink of disaster. The civilian administration was in complete disarray, as well.

Evacuation

A few days after the German invasion, the Supreme Evacuation Council was set up to organize the move of factories, employees and their families, and administrative institutions to safer territory. There was no evacuation plan, however, and the result was haphazard and chaotic. Many who escaped were highly mobile young people who held privileged positions in government offices or factories. Proximity to railway stations or other means of transportation affected one's ability to flee quickly. Generally speaking, more such opportunities were available in the large cities than in the towns.

As time went on and the pace of the German advance slackened, a proper procedure was established for moving civilians more effectively. As a result, the evacuation gradually became a planned operation. By late July 1941 the authorities began approving requests for evacuation of the general population and no longer confined themselves to the personnel of war-essential industrial plants. Those who still remained in the areas occupied by Germany early in the campaign were less likely to have opportunities to leave. The chances of getting away from larger population

For Jews, escaping to the interior of the USSR meant a chance of avoiding extermination.

centers, and from places occupied at a later date—whether on one's own or as part of an organized evacuation effort—were better.

When the Germans invaded the Soviet Union, the Soviet government initiated a military draft that was organized by age groups and geographic location. During the early months of the fighting, especially in the areas close to the front, the draft was carried out under chaotic conditions. In the annexed territories hardly any draft took place at all, because of the rapidity of the German occupation there, and in the areas west of the 1939 Soviet border, the draft was only partial, at best. The chances for a Jew to survive and fight in the Red Army depended, in large measure, on his place of residence and the timing of the Nazi occupation of that place. Since the Soviet Union was only partially occupied by the Germans throughout the war, its Jews, at least up to early 1943, were split into two groups—one group lived under Nazi occupation rule and the other under the Soviet regime.

Occupation and Extermination

The Germans divided the occupied Soviet territories into four administrative units, whose borders underwent changes resulting from developments at the front. Two of these units were under civilian administration: (1) *Reichskommissariat Ostland*, consisting of the Baltic states and western **BELORUSSIA**, including the **MINSK** district; and (2) *Reichskommissariat Ukraine* including the regions of Volhynia, Zhitomir, Kiev, Nikolayev, Tauria, and Dnepropetrovsk. Most of the occupied part of the Russian republic and part of the occupied **UKRAINE** were under a military administration. The area lying between the Dniester and Bug rivers, in which Odessa was located, was renamed Transnistria and handed over to Romanian rule. To the Jewish population, this administrative division of the German-occupied area made little difference, since it was mainly the **SS** and the **OPERATIONAL SQUADS** (*Einsatzgruppen*) that dealt with the Jews, regardless of where they lived.

During preparations for Operation "Barbarossa," German orders were issued to exterminate all the Jews. Two patterns for doing this emerged. In the areas that had been annexed by the Soviet Union in 1939 and 1940, the pattern included harassment, establishment of ghettos, starvation, and, finally, deportation to the **EXTERMINATION CAMPS**. In these areas, the total extermination of the Jews was completed within 12 to 18 months after the occupation.

The other pattern was applied in Nazi-occupied areas within the Soviet Union's pre-1939 borders. Here, the extermination of the Jews was seen as an integral element in military operations. The total annihilation of the Jews in these areas took only weeks—two to three months, at most—from the day they were occupied.

To exterminate the Jews in the occupied localities in the Soviet Union, the Germans generally used one of four methods and, in some cases, a combination of these methods:

1. The German occupation authorities appointed a three- or four-member **JUDENRAT** (Jewish Council) of prominent figures of the Jewish community; these included highly respected persons, such as doctors and engineers. A few days later an announcement was made ordering the Jews to register with the Judenrat, on pain of death. A short time later, the Jews were ordered to report at a certain spot in the town, from which they were going to be sent to a labor camp or "moved to Palestine." The Jews were told to take along only a few items, and no food at all, since it would be provided for them by the authorities. The assembled Jews were escorted by Germans and locally recruited police forces who beat and harassed the Jews and shot anyone who lagged behind or voiced any protest. The Jews then proceeded—

Very few non-Jews risked their lives to hide Jews, and only a small number of Jews were saved in this way. The majority of the population who saw the Jews being killed before their very eyes looked away; some showed outward indifference but in fact sympathized with the Jews, while others gloated over what was happening to them.

usually on foot but sometimes by truck—to nearby antitank ditches, quarries, or ravines, where they were to be killed. Just before reaching the spot, they were split up into groups of between 10 and 100 and ordered to undress. The slaughter site was surrounded by Germans armed with machine guns; the Jews were forced into the ditch, ravine, or quarry and fired at, from all directions. When one group was finished off, the next was brought in and killed in the same way.

2. In some places, especially in villages and towns with a small number of Jews who were known to all the inhabitants, the Germans did not appoint a Judenrat or register the Jews but proceeded immediately to round up and kill them.

3. In still other places, Jews were concentrated in a certain city quarter. They were ordered to move into the designated area and the non-Jewish residents were ordered to leave and move into apartments that had become available in other quarters. The result was a ghetto of sorts, into which nearly all the Jewish population was packed, under terrible conditions. The ghetto was rarely fenced in and was only loosely guarded. Its inhabitants were ordered to wear a distinctive sign, either a white armband or a badge (*see* **BADGE, JEWISH**) with a Star of David on it. Some Jews—usually the young and the skilled workers—were put to work outside the ghetto, where they also suffered from brutal mistreatment. Ghettos of this kind in the old Soviet borders lasted no longer than a few weeks or months (except for the ghetto at **MINSK**). The Jews were taken from the ghetto and shot to death at a nearby site, as described above.

4. The fourth method was to crowd the Jews into a makeshift concentration camp, in the buildings of an old factory or in an open field. The area was fenced in and put under guard. Here too, the Jews had to wear a distinctive sign. From time to time they were removed from the camp, by the thousands, and taken to slaughter sites nearby to be killed.

Resistance

There was no organized physical resistance by the Jews in the Soviet Union, during or after the extermination campaign. However, in many instances individual Jews resisted spontaneously, with acts ranging from spitting in a German's face to snatching his gun away and killing him. The only effective resistance option available to Jews was to join the forest-based partisan units (*see* **PARTISANS**). The forests and other remote areas became rallying points for Soviet army officers and political commissars whose units had disintegrated, for a few Communist officials who had not managed to escape, and for Jews who had fled from German harassment and murder in their villages. The forests also became places of refuge for entire Jewish refugee families. The emergence of partisan groups was a spontaneous phenomenon and it was natural for some of the units to be made up largely of Jewish fighters. As these Jewish partisan groups made contact with the Soviet partisan organization, many of the units lost their distinctly Jewish character, and the Jewish officers were replaced by non-Jews.

Jews in the Soviet Army

The Jews who lived under the Soviets during the **HOLOCAUST** included roughly 2 million civilians and hundreds of thousands, mostly men, who served in the Red Army. Most men, Jew and non-Jew alike, were drafted into the Soviet army. Thousands more Jews volunteered for military service, and the percentage of Jews in the army was higher than their percentage in the overall population. Jews served in every branch of the service. Since they were, on the average, more educated, relatively more served in the specialized branches, such as the air force, the armored corps, the engineering corps, the artillery, and the medical corps. Many Jews served as generals in senior command positions of the Soviet army. Jewish soldiers fought willingly in the Soviet army, inspired by devotion to the country and a desire to avenge, as best they could, the murder of their families and their people.

After the War

Beginning in 1944, and even earlier, when most of the occupied areas of the Soviet Union were liberated, the Jews began to return to villages and cities. Their Jewish communities had been destroyed and the territories that had been under German control had become huge burial grounds for Jews. Every city and town had its mass graves. From non-Jews and the few Jewish survivors, the returning Jews learned that many of their neighbors had helped the Germans, either directly, or by seizing Jewish property. Many who had collaborated with the Germans were now reinstated in the Soviet administration. Jewish appeals to the authorities to take action against the collaborators were unsuccessful. The apartments in which Jews had lived—those that the war had spared—were occupied, and many Jews had to resort to long and exhausting litigation to get them back. Despite the general shortage of experienced manpower, the authorities preferred not to reinstate Jews in some of the positions and posts they had held before the war. The many Jews who had fought and suffered on behalf of the Soviet Union, and who had endured severe persecution by the Germans, were now faced with renewed ANTISEMITISM in the villages and cities they had once called home.

In a single decade, from 1939 to 1948, the Jews of the Soviet Union underwent far-reaching change and upheaval. The Jewish population was diminished by half; the Jewish villages ceased to exist; the greater part of the Yiddish-speaking population was annihilated; the belief in the brotherhood of the Soviet peoples was shaken to the core; the possibility of assimilation with the general population was put in doubt; and popular antisemitism was again revived.

The Holocaust has been a major factor in the reorientation of Soviet Jewry since 1948. The Holocaust and the rise of the state of Israel have played a crucial role in the awakening of Jewish religious and national consciousness among Soviet Jewry. Despite efforts by the government to disguise the Jewishness of the victims of the Nazis and their helpers, memory of those terrible years has not been erased.

SUGGESTED RESOURCES

Gitelman, Zvi, ed. *Bitter Legacy: Confronting the Holocaust in the USSR.* Bloomington: Indiana University Press, 1997.

Pomerantz, Jack. *Run East: Flight from the Holocaust.* Urbana: University of Illinois Press, 1997.

Porter, Jack Nusan, ed. *Jewish Partisans: A Documentary of Jewish Resistance in the Soviet Union During World War II.* Washington, DC: University Press of America, 1982.

Zipperstein, Steven J. *Imagining Russian Jewry: Memory, History, Identity.* Seattle: University of Washington Press, 1999.

Special Commando

Special Commando, or *Sonderkommando*, is a term that could refer to one of three groups of people:

1. A German unit, mainly of the **SS**, gathered for special duties or assignments. The Special Commandos took part in the **"FINAL SOLUTION"** of the "Jewish question" in Europe. Along with the **OPERATIONAL SQUADS** (*Einsatzgruppen*) that operated in the occupied Soviet territories, there were about ten Special Commandos. One of them, first known as the Lange Kommando and later as Special Commando Bothmann, carried out the extermination operation at the **CHEŁMNO** camp. The designation "Sonderkommando 1005" was given to the units whose task it was to obliterate the traces of mass slaughter by opening the burial pits and burning the corpses they contained (*see* **AKTION (OPERATION) 1005**).

2. The designation of Special Commando was also given to units made up of Jewish prisoners, mainly those assigned to the death installations—the gas chambers and crematoria. Such Special Commandos worked at **AUSCHWITZ**-Birkenau; they were themselves put to death and replaced every few months with new prisioners. One of these Special Commandos staged an uprising in the Birkenau camp in 1944.

3. There was also a Jewish Special Commando in the **ŁÓDŹ** ghetto. It dealt with criminal offenses and functioned as part of the **JEWISH GHETTO POLICE** (Jüdischer Ordnungsdienst).

SUGGESTED RESOURCES

Fromer, Rebecca. *The Holocaust Odyssey of Daniel Bennahmias, Sonderkommando.* Tuscaloosa: University of Alabama Press, 1993.

Good Evening Mr. Wallenberg [videorecording]. Orion Home Video, 1994.

MacLean, French. *The Cruel Hunters: SS-Sonderkommando Dirlewanger, Hitler's Most Notorious Anti-partisan Unit.* Atglen, PA: Schiffer, 1998.

Sporrenberg, Jacob

(1902–1952)

Jacob Sporrenberg was an **SS** officer. He was born in Düsseldorf, **GERMANY**, was raised Catholic, and studied at a vocational school. Sporrenberg volunteered for the border guard and for the army (the Reichswehr). In 1923 the French occupation authorities sentenced him to two years' imprisonment on a charge of underground activity for the **NAZI PARTY** in the Ruhr region, but he was released on bail.

In 1925 Sporrenberg joined the Nazi party, in 1929 he joined the *Sturmabteilung* (Storm Troopers), and in 1930 the **SS**. He was a delegate to the Reichstag (parliament) in 1933. From 1933 to 1936 Sporrenberg was SS commander in the Schleswig-Holstein sector, and from 1936 to 1939, regional commander in East Prussia. Subsequently he occupied various posts in Wiesbaden and Königsberg. In 1940 he served in the SS Germany Brigade on the western front, where he was appointed *Gruppenführer* (lieutenant general). In August, 1941 he was sent to lead the struggle against the **PARTISANS** in the east and was appointed SS and Police Leader in **MINSK**, **BELORUSSIA**. Later he served in the Second Police Regiment in the fight against the partisans.

In August 1943 Sporrenberg became SS and Police Leader in the **LUBLIN** district. That November he organized Aktion **ERNTEFEST** ("Harvest Festival"), which resulted in the slaughter of 42,000 to 43,000 Jews interned in the camps of **MAJDANEK**, **TRAWNIKI**, and Poniatowa.

After the German retreat from the Lublin area in July 1943, Sporrenberg was sent to organize the defense fortifications on the Vistula-Nida line in the Radom district. In November he was sent to Norway. On May 11, 1945, several days after the German surrender, Sporrenberg was arrested by the Allies. The British extradited him to **POLAND**, where he stood trial on a charge of collective punishment, imposition of a rule of terror by mass murders, and organization of Aktion "Erntefest." Sporrenberg was sentenced to death and hanged.

SUGGESTED RESOURCES

Bronowski, Alexander. *They Were Few.* New York: Peter Lang, 1992.

Goldstein, Arthur. *The Shoes of Majdanek.* Lanham, MD: University Press of America, 1992.

Sprachregelung

During the Nazi years, language was manipulated to serve the purposes of the regime. Idioms coined by the Nazis served as an official language and as a language of propaganda and camouflage. The term *Sprachregelung* ("language regulation") refers to this specific application of language. It was in this language that Joseph **GOEBBELS**, the propaganda minister, communicated through the Nazi-controlled press. An example is the use of the word *Gleichschaltung* (coordination), which in actuality meant the elimination of political opponents and Nazi control of the German state agencies and public organizations.

Sprachregelung was employed particularly in the implementation of anti-Jewish policy, and here it was designed to fill a variety of roles. Words and expressions with generally neutral or positive meanings were used to camouflage acts of terror and destruction. The intention was to hide the nature of those acts from the world and even from the German public, and also to mislead the Jews, who, failing to understand what awaited them, would take no preventive actions. Thus an apparently normal situation was created in which those who issued an order had an exact knowledge of its true content but were not obliged to call it by name. As acts of murder became routine and were explained and discussed in written reports, the use of *Sprachregelung* gradually decreased for a time. Hitler saw the need to issue a special order on July 11, 1943 instructing that official **SS** reports use only the term **"FINAL SOLUTION"** when discussing the resolution of the Jewish problem, and not the straightforward term "destruction."

The expression "Final Solution," which was accepted as a term by all those dealing in the **HOLOCAUST**, is one of the outstanding and typical examples of *Sprachregelung*. In many contexts the Nazis used the term "solution" or even "final solution" to note a way or means to overcome a difficulty. This was also true of the prefix "special" (*sonder-*), which designated exceptional cases or actions. The first to use the term "special treatment" (*Sonderbehandlung*) with regard to the Jews was apparently, and most ironically, the German president, Paul von Hindenburg. He asked Hitler not to apply the discriminatory laws of April 1933 to Jewish civil servants (and other civil servants considered undesirable by the Nazis) who had been wounded as soldiers in World War I or who had a family member wounded in that war—essentially requesting exemptions in cases where there was a "reason for special treatment." However, in the language of the Nazis, "special treatment" meant execution. On more than one occasion, with overt cynicism, Nazi policies and practices

were nominally based on (and presented as) acts undertaken for the common good. For instance, they justified shutting Jews in ghettos by explaining that this would prevent the spread of typhus; and they claimed that Jews were sent to forced-labor camps for "work education." In fact, when they first rose to power in **GERMANY**, the Nazis had declared that the **CONCENTRATION CAMPS** were set up for "reeducation."

DEPORTATIONS and transfers were camouflaged by a number of special expressions. The word *Abwanderung* ("leaving [a place]") originally indicated internal migration, as in a move of villagers to the town; in other words, it expressed free population movement. The Nazis used this word to indicate emigration of Jews and forced migration. The deportations of the Jews and Poles from the Warthegau to the **GENERALGOUVERNEMENT** were called *Umsiedlung* ("change of residence"). To indicate deportation, two expressions were used. *Aussiedlung* ("evacuation") was supposed to arouse the delusion that the Jews deported to the **EXTERMINATION CAMPS** were being sent to a place of resettlement. In contrast, the term *Abschiebung* ("removal") denoted that they were being removed from the place of their abode, without indicating the destination to which they were being sent. This term was for internal use only.

The expression *Verjudung* ("Judaization") was in common usage among many antisemites, for whom it indicated the destructive influence, as it were, of the Jews on the people among whom they lived. The counteraction was called "removal of the Jews" or "purification from Jews" (*Entjudung*). This term was used by the Nazis to indicate the removal of Jews from the German economy, and it appears in different combinations in the relevant legislation. In euphemistic language the ghetto was called the "Jewish residential area" (*jüdischer Wohnbezirk*), and deportation to the **THERESIENSTADT** ghetto was described as "transfer of residence." One of the most widely used words, and one also used by the Jews in the ghetto, was *Aktion* ("action"), meaning organized hostile action against the Jewish populace such as disturbances, arrests, property confiscations, deportations, and concentration in the ghetto, or for sending to extermination camps. In the use of such seemingly benign terms, Nazi acts of oppression and the annihilation of the Jews could be masked and hidden from immediate view of the world outside, as well as from the oppressed themselves.

SUGGESTED RESOURCES

Reuth, Ralf Georg. *Goebbels.* New York: Harcourt Brace, 1993.

SS

The *SS* (*Schutzstaffel*; Protection Squad) were Hitler's bodyguard, **NAZI PARTY** police, and, later, the most "racially pure" elite guard of the Third Reich as well as the main tool of Nazi terror and destruction.

Early History

As Adolf **HITLER'S** personal bodyguard, recruited from the SA (*Sturmabteilung*; Storm Troopers) in March 1923, the SS was distinguished by a black cap with a death's-head emblem, and later by their entirely black uniforms. The two dozen bodyguards participated in Hitler's unsuccessful Beer-Hall Putsch of November 1923 in Munich, when he tried to overthrow the government. They were outlawed, as was the rest of the Nazi party, following the failed coup. When the party was legalized again at the end of 1924, Hitler reestablished the unit and created several

more such "commandos." In contrast to the SA, which tended to consider itself a semi-independent, paramilitary mass organization, the SS and its new commandos were an exclusive elite, subject directly to Hitler's authority.

In November 1926, the SA High Command was created, and in spite of numerous protests, it took over the SS headquarters. This move threatened the special status of the fledgling SS. On January 6, 1929, Heinrich **HIMMLER** assumed control of the SS as the *Reichsführer-SS* (Reich Leader of the SS).

Between 1929 and 1933, the SS grew and was entrusted with the security of party headquarters and the personal security of most of the party leaders, especially at Hitler's public appearances. An embryonic secret intelligence, the **SD** (*Sicherheitsdienst*; Security Service), was founded under the command of Reinhard **HEYDRICH**, as was the SS Race and Resettlement Main Office (RuSHA; *Rasseund Siedlungs-Hauptamt*), the bureau responsible for the racial purity of the SS and the eventual settlement of inhabitants of conquered eastern territories.

SS officers had to prove their own and their wives' "racial purity" back to the year 1700, and membership was conditional on "Aryan" appearance. Traditional symbols and pre-Christian myths were combined with an aura of fearlessness to create an SS mystique. This mystique was reflected in the wearing of the black uni-

R acial ideology and mythology was institutionalized in the SS.

The state's political police were unified as the Gestapo and fully amalgamated with the SS in 1936. The Security Police (Sipo) was divided into the Gestapo, under Reinhard Heydrich, and the Criminal Police (Kripo) under Arthur Nebe. The Order Police (Orpo) was encompassed within the SS as a separate SS outfit. Heydrich encouraged bureaucratic competition between the Gestapo and SD, which led to ever-harsher police tactics and methods.

form, black cap, death's-head emblem, death's head "ring of honor," and officer's dagger bearing the SS motto, "Meine Ehre heisst Treue" ("Loyalty Is My Honor"). Later, pagan ceremonies were practiced and pilgrimages were made to ancient Teutonic "sacred sites." The regional organization also bore traditional titles and was first divided into squads (*Schar, Trupp*), platoons (*Sturm*), companies (*Sturmbann*), and battalions (*Standarte*), which in late 1932 were put together into county SS sections under regional command. The regional commanders were directly responsible to Himmler and were often rotated to avoid grass-roots power-base building.

In contrast to the vague and yet far-reaching goals of the SA, Himmler aimed after Hitler's rise to power to gain control over the political police (**Gestapo**) while establishing the **concentration camps** of the SS. The first model of that kind was **Dachau**, built early in March 1933. Himmler managed to maintain exclusive control over Dachau. By mid-1934 the SS took over all the political police and concentration camps. The Dachau commandant, Theodor **Eicke**, was made inspector of the concentration camps and SS guard formations on July 4, 1934.

Himmler maintained the concentration camp system separately as a totally SS branch under Eicke, in which guards were trained in a savage killer outfit called the **SS Death's-Head Units** (*Totenkopfverbände*). This was the source of the militarized SS units later known as the Waffen-SS, who were trained for civil war duties, and later were transferred as SS frontline units fighting under the army's operational control. Young officers schools were established to train and indoctrinate young cadets, some already the products of the Nazi youth movement, the **Hitler Youth** (*Hitlerjugend*), as the new fighting and pitiless racial elite. Special SS police units, the **Operational Squads**(*Einsatzgruppen*), were established to enter invaded territories. The regional SS was reorganized under Higher SS and Police Leaders, who acted as Himmler's personal representatives in each military district from the outset of World War II. The plan was expanded to enforce the "Germanization" of the occupied territories.

Special institutions were created in cooperation between Himmler's personal office and the RuSHA. These included *Lebensborn* (Fountain of Life)—a system of SS stud farms that were the brainchild of Himmler's program for the development of a pure Aryan race—and Ancestral Heritage (*Ahnenerbe*). The official functions of the latter were to adopt "suitable" children for childless SS families, to nurture "racially sound" pregnant women and their offspring, and to conduct "racial research" that eventually culminated in **medical experiments** with the "racially inferior," mainly Jews, in concentration camps. This was done in cooperation with the chief SS physician and his own bureaucracy, which also played a major role in the **Euthanasia Program**.

The SS in World War II

The war led to enormous growth in the SS as a whole and increased the murderous level of its activities. The cruel, inhuman regime of the SS was encouraged from the top down. Sipo commanders in the occupied territories competed with SS head offices to implement increasingly harsh official policies. The SS headquarters itself was reorganized in 1939, with the establishment of the **Reich Security Main Office** (RSHA; *Reichssicherheitshauptamt*), and again in 1942, when eleven main offices emerged. During the war, the Waffen-SS grew into Hitler's personal multinational brigade. Himmler saw them as an assurance of SS domination in the Nazi postwar order.

In 1941 the first implementation of the "Final Solution," during the invasion of the **Soviet Union**, was carried out primarily by the *Einsatzgruppen*, which conducted

mass killings by firing squads and, later, mobile gas vans (*see* **GAS CHAMBERS/VANS**) as well. The men of the *Einsatzgruppen* had been recruited from the Gestapo and the SS and had undergone special training. Their operations were made possible by a formal agreement between the SS, represented by Heydrich, and the **Wehrmacht** High Command that was concluded in the spring of 1941, together with the final preparations for the invasion of the Soviet Union. The SS was aided in the killings by various police units, Wehrmacht forces, and numerous local collaborators.

In the occupied countries of western and southeastern Europe, the SS, in cooperation with the SD, Gestapo, local police, and local officials, organized the mass extermination of the Jews in camps in the east from 1942 to 1944. A special terminology (*see* **SPRACHREGELUNG**) was perfected to mislead the victims. The process of killing by gas in the **EXTERMINATION CAMPS**, as well as the camps' structure and management, were organized and overseen by SS officers, most of whom had been trained by Eicke in Dachau.

The SS **ECONOMIC-ADMINISTRATIVE MAIN OFFICE** (*Wirtschafts-Verwaltung-shauptamt*), later known as the WVHA, planned to use the concentration camps as sources of slave labor that would also serve the enterprises of the SS under Oswald **POHL**. Since Pohl was entrusted at the same time with the factory-like destruction of the Jews in the extermination camps, his role, like this phase of SS policy, was inherently contradictory. Nonetheless, special procedures were invoked in the camps to select Jews for immediate mass killings or for slave labor (which usually resulted in death anyway).

When Nazi Germany's final collapse became inevitable, Himmler ordered the termination of the "Final Solution," apparently hoping to use the remnants of European Jewry as trump cards in negotiations with the West against the Soviets. The SS in pointless marches drove the survivors of the now-evacuated camps outside the Reich to Germany. Many perished on these **DEATH MARCHES** or died at the hands of the SS guards, until the latter fled from the approaching armies of the Allies.

In the charter of the International Military Tribunal at Nuremberg, the SS was designated a criminal organization. Thus, everyone who participated in the SS was to be considered a war criminal subject to court action at Nuremberg and in other proceedings.

SEE ALSO **NAZI PARTY; TRIALS OF THE WAR CRIMINALS.**

SUGGESTED RESOURCES

MacDonald, C. A. *The Killing of Reinhard Heydrich: The SS "Butcher of Prague."* New York: Da Capo Press, 1998.

Rempel, Gerhard. *Hitler's Children: The Hitler Youth and the SS.* Chapel Hill: University of North Carolina Press, 1989.

The SS. Alexandria, VA: Time-Life Books, 1989.

Williamson, Gordon. *The SS: Hitler's Instrument of Terror.* Osceola, WI: Motorbooks International, 1994.

Wehrmacht
Regular German armed forces.

To the very end, the SS remained the backbone of the Nazi regime. It involved hundreds of thousands of Germans in its crimes: Gestapo policemen, uniformed police, who were used as firing-squad killers or helped carry out deportations, private firms, which supplied equipment to extermination camps and used SS forced labor, and Wehrmacht units, which provided the military framework of occupation and control necessary for the SS massacres.

SS Death's-Head Units

The SS Death's-Head Units (SS-*Totenkopfverbände*) were units of the **SS** (*Schutzstaffel*) originally formed to guard **CONCENTRATION CAMPS**. The SS

Death's-Head Units developed from the Upper Bavarian Guard Troop of the General SS, the DACHAU guard unit. They were developed starting in 1934 by Theodor EICKE, the Inspector of Concentration Camps and Commander of SS Guard Formations. Eicke wanted the Death's-Head Units to be an elite unit within the elite SS.

In March 1935 the Dachau unit and the guard units of the concentration camps were reorganized into six units under Eicke:

1. Oberbayern (Upper Bavaria), at Dachau

2. Ostfriesland (East Friesland), at Esterwegen

3. Sturmbann Elbe (Elbe Company), at Lichtenburg

4. Sachsen (Saxony), at Sachsenburg

5. Brandenburg, at Oranienburg and Columbia Haus

6. Hansa, at Fehlsbüttel

In September, 1935, Adolf HITLER publicly recognized the Death's-Head Units, making the Reich assume the cost of their operation, and thereby allowing for their expansion. In March 1936, Heinrich HIMMLER authorized an expansion from 1,800 to 3,500 men, and on March 29 the formations were officially designated as a separate SS unit named *Totenkopfverbände*, removed from the authority of the General SS, and given distinctive dark brown uniforms. Three SS-*Totenkopfstandarten* (SS Death's-Head Regiments) were established:

1. Oberbayern (Upper Bavaria), at Dachau

2. Brandenburg, at SACHSENHAUSEN

3. Thüringen, at BUCHENWALD

Following the Anschluss (annexation) of AUSTRIA in March 1938, a fourth regiment, Ostmark (Austria), was set up for the MAUTHAUSEN camp.

On August 17, 1938, Hitler declared that in order to fulfill special domestic tasks of a political nature, the Death's-Head Units, the SS Special Service Troops (reserve troops), and the SS Cadet Schools were to be armed, trained, and organized as military units, outside the structure of both the army and the police. In the event of mobilization, the Death's-Head Units would be transferred to the Special Service Troops. By the outbreak of World War II the Death's-Head Units and their reserves numbered some 24,000 men. Nine days after German forces invaded POLAND, the three original Death's-Head Regiments, followed by some of the newer regiments, were sent. Acting with the cruelty they had been trained to use, they perpetrated acts of terror that would be repeated again and again throughout Nazi-controlled Europe.

On August 15, 1940, Himmler transferred the Death's-Head Units that had been designated as reserves for the Totenkopfdivision to the Command Office of the Waffen-SS. In April 1941, in the course of preparing for the campaign against the SOVIET UNION, the remaining *Totenkopfverbände* officially became part of the Waffen-SS, completing their transition into the German army and closing the chapter of the autonomous *Totenkopfverbände*, or Death's-Head Units.

In this new context the Death's-Head Units and their reputation for brutality continued to expand. The number of men in the Death's-Head Units grew constantly; according to official SS figures, there were 40,000 men and women in its units on January 15, 1945, guarding 714,211 camp inmates.

WAITING

This is a time of lightning without thunder,
This is a time of unheard voices,
Of uneasy sleep and useless vigils.
Friend, do not forget the days
Of long easy silences,
Friendly nocturnal streets,
Serene meditations.
Before the leaves fall,
Before the sky closes again,
Before we are awakened again
By the familiar pounding of iron footsteps
In front of our doors.

—PRIMO LEVI, 2 JANUARY 1949

Primo Levi, Collected Poems, *translated by Ruth Feldman and Brian Swann (London: Faber and Faber Ltd.), 1984.*

Concise History of the Death's-Head Units

The following summary outlines the development of the *Totenkopfverbände* from 1934 to 1941:

July 1934. Theodor **EICKE** institutes the Death's Head (*Totenkopf*) insignia for the Upper Bavarian Guard Troop of the General SS in Dachau.

March 1935. Under Eicke the Guard Troop is reorganized into six units, all remaining under the General SS. The units are posted as guards at concentration camps.

March 1936. The six units under Eicke are officially designated as SS-Totenkopfverbände, and they are independent of the General SS.

September 1937. Still under Eicke, the Totenkopfverbände are reorganized into three *Standarten* (regiments).

August 1938. The *Totenkopfverbände* begin their expansion. By September 1939, eight new regiments are established and the number of men, including reserves, reaches 24,000.

October 1939. (1) Eicke establishes and commands the Totenkopfdivision, a part of the new Waffen-SS. The division includes the original three Totenkopf Standarten. (2) SS-*Oberführer* Alfred Schweden takes command of the remaining Totenkopfverbände. There is a flow of men between the Totenkopfverbände and the Totenkopfdivision.

April 1941. The Totenkopfverbände are completely incorporated into the Waffen-SS and lose their autonomy. Near the end of the war, they number about 40,000.

SUGGESTED RESOURCES

Hohne, Heinz. *The Order of the Death's Head; the Story of Hitler's S.S.* New York: Coward-McCann, 1970.

The SS. Alexandria, VA: Time-Life Books, 1989.

Sydnor, Charles W. *Soldiers of Destruction: The SS Death's Head Division, 1933-1945.* Princeton, NJ: Princeton University Press, 1990.

Williamson, Gordon. *The SS: Hitler's Instrument of Terror.* Osceola, WI: Motorbooks International, 1994.

Stahlecker, Franz Walter

(1900–1942)

Franz Walter Stahlecker was an **SS** officer who served as commander of an Operational Squad (*see* **OPERATIONAL SQUADS**). Born in Sternenfels, Stahlecker joined the **NAZI PARTY** in 1932, served in the police, and in 1934 was appointed police chief of the Württemberg region. He was then assigned to the **SD** (*Sicherheitsdienst*; Security Service) main office, and in 1938 became the SD chief of the Danube district (**VIENNA**), retaining this post even when he became the Higher SS and Police Leader of the Protectorate of **BOHEMIA AND MORAVIA**. In 1940 Stahlecker was sent to Norway, where he held the same position, and was promoted to *SS-Oberführer* (brigadier general). In June 1941 he became a *Brigadeführer* (major general) in the SS and the police force, and was appointed the commanding officer of Einsatzgruppe (Operational Squad) A, which operated in the Northern Command, including the Baltic states and the area west of Leningrad, killing Jews and other Soviet nationals. At the end of November 1941, Stahlecker was also made Higher SS and Police Leader of **Reichskommissariat Ostland**. He was killed on March 23, 1942, in a clash with Soviet **PARTISANS**.

Reichskommissariat Ostland
The civil (non-military) administration of occupied Soviet territories of Estonia, Latvia, Lithuania, and Belorussia which were among the easternmost areas held under Nazi control.

SUGGESTED RESOURCES

Gitelman, Zvi, ed. *Bitter Legacy: Confronting the Holocaust in the USSR.* Bloomington: Indiana University Press, 1997.

Stangl, Franz

(1908–1971)

Franz Stangl was a Nazi police officer. He was born in Altmünster, **AUSTRIA**, the son of a former soldier who brutalized him throughout his childhood. Initially a master weaver, Stangl joined the Austrian police in 1931. His talent for organization soon became evident, and he was shortly appointed criminal investigation officer in the political division, which at that time was charged with investigating antigovernment activities.

In November 1940, Stangl became police superintendent of the Euthanasia Institute at the Hartheim castle, near Linz. In March 1942 he became commandant of the **SOBIBÓR** extermination camp in **POLAND**, and from early September 1942 to August 1943 he was the commandant of **TREBLINKA**. In less than a year there, he supervised the mass killing of at least 900,000 Jews.

In September 1943, after the inmates' revolt in Treblinka, Stangl and most of his staff were transferred to Trieste. There, aside from a brief stint at the San Sabba concentration camp, he was largely employed in organizing antipartisan measures for Odilo **GLOBOCNIK**, the Higher **SS** and Police Leader of the Adriatic seaboard area.

At the end of the war Stangl made his way back to Austria, where he was eventually interned by the Americans for belonging to the SS, although they knew noth-

Franz Stangl, sitting in court at witness stand.

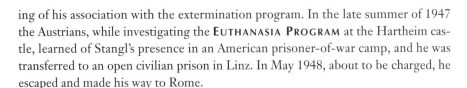

ing of his association with the extermination program. In the late summer of 1947 the Austrians, while investigating the **EUTHANASIA PROGRAM** at the Hartheim castle, learned of Stangl's presence in an American prisoner-of-war camp, and he was transferred to an open civilian prison in Linz. In May 1948, about to be charged, he escaped and made his way to Rome.

With assistance from Bishop Alois Hudal, rector of Santa Maria del Anima, Stangl obtained a Red Cross pass, money, and a job as an engineer in Damascus, Syria, where his family soon joined him. In 1951 the family moved on to Brazil, where, registering under their own names at the Austrian consulate, they were soon established in the city of São Bernardo do Campo, near São Paulo. There, Stangl worked at the Volkswagen factory.

Sixteen years later, Stangl's presence in Brazil became known. He was arrested on February 28, 1967, and extradited to **GERMANY** that June. His trial in Düsseldorf lasted one year; in December 1970 he was sentenced to life imprisonment for joint responsibility in the murder of 900,000 people during his tenure as commandant of Treblinka. He died in prison on June 28, 1971.

SUGGESTED RESOURCES

Arad, Yitzhak. *Belzec, Sobibor, Treblinka: The Operation Reinhard Death Camps.* Bloomington: Indiana University Press, 1987.

Sereny, Gitta. *Into That Darkness.* New York: Vintage Books, 1983.

Starachowice

Starachowice was a labor camp in **POLAND**. Before World War II, Starachowice, a town in the **KIELCE** subdistrict of Poland, was the site of armament factories and an iron-ore mine. Under the German occupation of Poland, these enterprises were renamed the Hermann Göring Works (Hermann Göring Werke). Jews were sent there for **FORCED LABOR**.

Starachowice was occupied on September 9, 1939, soon after **GERMANY**'s invasion of Poland. Jewish males between ages 17 and 60 were put to work in the town's factories for very little pay, plus a bowl of soup during working hours. In February 1941 an "open" ghetto was established in Starachowice. Jews living in the area were sent there, as well as Jews from Płock and **ŁÓDŹ**. On October 27, 1941, the Starachowice ghetto was liquidated. Some 200 Jews were shot to death on the spot. The physically fit were moved to a nearby camp that had been prepared in advance (Julag I—the name came from the German word *Judenlager*, meaning "Jewish camp"). The rest were deported to **TREBLINKA**, an **EXTERMINATION CAMP**. The Jews working in the armament factories were also moved to Julag I.

Some 8,000 Jews passed through Starachowice camp. Records show that 9 percent of them died in typhus epidemics or were shot to death following a selection. The camp population averaged 5,000; from time to time the camp was replenished with prisoners from **MAJDANEK**, **PŁASZÓW**, and other places.

In the summer of 1943, the prisoners employed in the factories were moved to another camp, Julag II. Five thousand prisoners passed through Julag II, and 7 percent of them died of typhus or were murdered outright. The average number of prisoners in Julag II was 3,000.

In July 1944, steps were taken to liquidate Starachowice camp. When the prisoners became aware of what was happening, they began destroying the camp's installations and fence and tried to escape. The Ukrainians guarding the camp opened fire and threw hand grenades at the desperate inmates, killing 300 of them on the spot. Those who escaped were captured and murdered. The rest of the camp's prisoners—1,500 of them—were deported to **Auschwitz**-Birkenau.

SUGGESTED RESOURCES

Browning, Christopher R. *Nazi Policy, Jewish Workers, German Killers.* New York: Cambridge University Press, 2000.

State Department. See United States Department of State.

Sterilization. See Euthanasia Program; Medical Experiments.

St. Louis

The *St. Louis* was a German ship carrying Jewish refugees whose entry into Cuba was denied because their landing permits to Havana were invalidated by the Cuban government.

Owned by the Hamburg-America Line, the *St. Louis* departed from Hamburg for Cuba on May 13, 1939. It carried 936 passengers, of whom 930 were Jews carrying landing certificates for Havana. Arranged by the Cuban director general of immigration, Manuel Benitez González, these certificates were to replace the usual immigration visas. According to Cuban law, such certificates required no fee. However, González sold them for personal gain, for as much as $160.00. Cuban government officials became jealous of González's illicit wealth. This jealousy, combined with local sentiment against the influx of additional Jewish refugees and the government's pro-fascist leanings, led the Cuban government to invalidate the landing certificates and to curtail the authority of the director general (May 5, 1939). The government decreed that the certificates would be honored only until May 6. Apparently, both the Hamburg-America Line and its passengers were aware of the decree, but they believed that the certificates, which were bought well before the decree, would be honored. Only 22 of the Jewish refugee passengers actually met Cuba's new visa requirements.

When the *St. Louis* reached Havana on May 27, its passengers were denied entry. The American Jewish **Joint Distribution Committee** (JDC) dispatched Lawrence Berenson to Havana to negotiate the disembarkation of the refugees. Berenson arrived in Havana on May 30. Cuban president Federico Laredo Bru insisted that the ship leave the Havana harbor: he claimed that because the shipping line and the JDC had both known in advance that the certificates were invalid, they should be taught a lesson about respect for Cuban law. The *St. Louis* left Havana on June 2. The ship's captain, Gustav Schroeder, steered the *St. Louis* in circles in the areas off Florida and Cuba while the negotiations continued.

American immigration officials announced that the refugees would not be allowed to enter the **United States**. However, an agreement was reached on June 5 that allowed them to land in Cuba for a $453,000 bond ($500.00 per refugee), to be deposited by the following day. The JDC could not meet the deadline, and the

Jewish refugees, aboard the SS *St. Louis,* off the shore of Havana, Cuba, June 3, 1939.

ship sailed for Europe on June 6. Twenty-nine passengers had been permitted to land, of whom twenty-two were Jews with valid Cuban visas. Max Loewe, a Jew without a valid visa, was hospitalized after a suicide attempt. Six of those permitted to land were not Jewish.

While the *St. Louis* was en route to Europe, four countries—**GREAT BRITAIN, BELGIUM, FRANCE,** and the **NETHERLANDS**—agreed to take in the refugees. After the ship reached Antwerp on June 17, 287 of the refugees entered Britain, 214 entered Belgium, 224 entered France, and 181 entered the Netherlands. Most of the passengers who received temporary refuge in European countries were later victims of the **"FINAL SOLUTION"**.

SEE ALSO **ALIYA BET; REFUGEES, 1933–1945.**

SUGGESTED RESOURCES

Bachrach, Susan D. *Tell Them We Remember: The Story of the Holocaust.* Boston: Little, Brown, 1994.

Thomas, Gordon. *Voyage of the Damned.* New York: Stein and Day, 1974.

Streicher, Julius

(1885–1946)

Julius Streicher was a Nazi politician whose specialty was inciting antisemitic sentiment. Born in Augsburg, Bavaria, Streicher taught elementary school and fought in World War I. He helped to found the German Socialist Party in 1919;

shortly thereafter he merged it with the **NAZI PARTY**. He held several political posts, including *Gauleiter* (district leader) of Franconia (1928–1940); member of the Bavarian provincial legislature (1924–1932); and member of the **Reichstag**, beginning in 1932. He was also a general in the SA (*Sturmabteilung*; Storm Troopers).

Reichstag
German Parliament.

One of the most rabid anti-semites in the Nazi party, Streicher founded *Der Stürmer* (The Attacker) in Nuremberg in 1923, becoming its editor and, as of 1935, its owner as well. He gave the newspaper its special antisemitic-pornographic character. It was crude and aggressive, with simple language that made it easy to comprehend. Antisemitic cartoons by Philipp Rupprecht ("Fips") featured caricatures of Jews, designed to make them look ugly and revolting. Articles accused Jews of terrible crimes and claimed there was an international "Jewish conspiracy." At times, the paper was so extreme that even the Nazi authorities disassociated themselves from it and closed it down. The papers were heavily advertised in public places, such as bus stops, busy streets, parks, and factory canteens. After 1933, nine special editions were published, often timed to appear at the annual Nuremberg rally.

During the early 1930s, Streicher urged municipalities in Franconia to ban Jews from restaurants and cafes and even to establish Jewish ghettos. After he was appointed to the Central Defense Committee against Jewish Atrocity and Boycott Propaganda in 1933, he helped to organize the April 1 economic boycott of Jewish businesses (*see* **BOYCOTT, ANTI-JEWISH**). He helped initiate and write the **NUREMBERG LAWS**. As early as 1938, in an article entitled "War against the World Enemy," he called for the total destruction of the Jewish people.

Julius Streicher.

In March 1940 Streicher was suspended from his post as *Gauleiter* of Franconia, after the supreme court of the Nazi party investigated him for bribery. Even so, Streicher remained one of the leading proponents of militant **ANTISEMITISM**. Circulation of *Der Stürmer* dropped sharply after 1940, owing partly to wartime paper shortages but mainly because Jews had disappeared from everyday life in Germany. The final issue appeared on February 1, 1945, denouncing the invading Allies as tools of the international Jewish conspiracy.

When the war ended, Streicher tried to hide out, disguised as a housepainter, but he was recognized and American soldiers arrested him on May 23, 1945. He was among the major Nazi criminals tried by an International Military Tribunal at Nuremberg. The court said, "For twenty-five years [Streicher] incited to hatred of the Jews, in speeches and in writing, and became widely known as the 'Number 1 enemy of the Jews.'" The tribunal sentenced Streicher to death; he was executed by hanging, on October 16, 1946.

SUGGESTED RESOURCES

Bytwerk, Randall L. *Julius Streicher.* New York: Stein and Day, 1983.

Dutch, Oswald. *Hitler's 12 Apostles.* Freeport, NY: Books for Libraries Press, 1969.

Showalter, Dennis E. *Little Man, What Now? Der Stürmer in the Weimar Republic.* Hamden, CT: Archon Books, 1982.

Stroop, Jürgen

(1895–1951)

Jürgen Stroop was the SS and police chief who crushed the **WARSAW GHETTO UPRISING** and destroyed the **WARSAW** ghetto. Josef Stroop (he changed his first name to the more "Aryan"-sounding Jürgen in 1941) was born in Detmold, in cen-

The front page of an issue of Julius Streicher's infamous *Der Stürmer* shows the blood of innocent Germany pouring into the platters of the Jews.

tral **GERMANY**, into the family of a Catholic policeman from the lower middle class. Educated in a nationalist and militarist spirit, he volunteered for the army in World War I, was wounded three times, and in 1918 was promoted to the rank of captain. After the war, Stroop was employed in the Detmold municipal administration. In 1932 he joined the **NAZI PARTY** and the SS, attracted by both the nationalist views and the uniforms. He quickly rose in the ranks of the SS and by 1939 was an SS-*Oberführer* (brigadier general) and commander of a police unit.

Upon the outbreak of war between Germany and the **SOVIET UNION** in June 1941, Stroop was sent to the front at his own request. After being wounded, he was transferred to police functions in the occupied Soviet territories, where he specialized in persecuting the population and harassing local **PARTISANS**. On April 17, 1943, on the eve of the liquidation of the Warsaw ghetto, he was summoned by the Higher SS and Police leader of the **GENERALGOUVERNEMENT**, Friedrich Wilhelm **KRÜGER**. The SS and police chiefs apparently rushed Stroop to Warsaw, doubting the ability of the local police commander, Ferdinand Sammern-Frankenegg, to

Jürgen Stroop (2nd from left), SS General, "Conqueror of the Ghetto," surrounded by SS men under his command; Warsaw, Poland, 1943.

carry out the liquidation of the ghetto. Sammern-Frankenegg's helplessness became apparent shortly after the liquidation began; during the outbreak of the ghetto uprising on April 19, 1943. Stroop assumed command.

Stroop conducted the action against the insurgent ghetto as a military campaign; his methods consisted of unrestrained and indiscriminate killing and destruction. He had under his command about 2,000 men from different units, equipped like frontline troops. Stroop sent daily reports on the campaign in the ghetto to **KRAKÓW**, the capital of the Generalgouvernement. In his concluding report at the end of the campaign, which he called the "Great Operation"(*Grossaktion*), he wrote:

> After the first days it was clear that the Jews would not think of being deported of their own free will, but had definitely decided to defend themselves in all possible ways and with the arms in their possession.... The number of Jews taken from their homes in the first days and captured was relatively small. The Jews were apparently hiding in the sewers and in specially prepared bunkers.... Twenty- to thirty-member combat units made up of Jewish youths eighteen to twenty-five years old, with a certain number of women, spread the revolt and renewed it periodically. These combat units had been ordered to defend themselves with arms to the end, and when necessary to commit suicide rather than be taken alive.... In this armed revolt there were women in the combat units, armed like men, some of them members of the He-Haluts movement. The women often fired from guns in both hands.... The Jewish opposition and rebels could be broken only by the energetic and constant use of strike forces day and night. On April 23, 1943, the order was given by the SS-*Reichsführer* [Heinrich

HIMMLER], through Wilhelm Krüger, to effect the evacuation of the Warsaw ghetto with the greatest rigor and unrelenting diligence.... The Great Operation terminated on May 16, 1943, at 8:15 p.m., with the blowing up of the Warsaw synagogue. There is no longer any activity in the former Jewish residential quarter … all the buildings and everything else have been destroyed; only the Dzielna [Pawiak] security prison was spared.

In his last daily report, dated April 16, Stroop reported that out of 56,065 Jews caught, 13,929 were exterminated and about 5,000 to 6,000 were killed in the shelling and burning.

After putting down the uprising, Stroop continued to serve as SS and Police Leader in the Warsaw district. In September 1943, he was appointed Higher SS and Police Leader in Greece, with promotion to the rank of SS-*Gruppenführer*. That November, Stroop was transferred to serve in the same capacity in the Twelfth Army District in the Reich, which included the areas of Wiesbaden, Darmstadt, and Luxembourg. He remained in this post until the end of the war.

Soon after the war's end, Stroop was discovered attempting to change his identity, in the Wiesbaden area, which was in the hands of the United States army. When military officials searched his home, they found a meticulously organized album, containing his reports from the Warsaw ghetto campaign and a series of photographs taken by the Germans during the uprising. In January 1947 Stroop was tried by the American military court in **DACHAU** (Trial No. 12-3188, *United States* v. *Stroop*) and charged with responsibility for war crimes perpetrated in the Twelfth Army District. Of the 22 people accused in this trial, which concluded in March, 13 were sentenced to death, including Stroop. The verdict was not carried out, and Stroop was extradited to Poland as a war criminal wanted in the Polish People's Republic.

The prosecution presented the photographs, together with parts of Stroop's reports, at the **NUREMBERG TRIAL** of the principal Nazi criminals. This constituted one of the most shocking and condemning documents in the entire trial. During his interrogation in a Polish prison, Stroop provided clarifications and supplementary information to the reports he had written during the Warsaw ghetto uprising in April and May 1943.

In July 1951 Stroop was tried at the Warsaw district court. He was executed by hanging that September in Warsaw.

Stroop was held in prison in Warsaw with Kazimierz Moczarski, a member of the Polish underground Home Army (Armia Krajowa). Their lengthy conversations were later the subject of Moczarski's book *Gespräche mit dem Henker* (Conversations with an Executioner).

SUGGESTED RESOURCES

Landau, Elaine. *The Warsaw Ghetto Uprising.* New York: Macmillan, 1992.

Moczarski, Kazimierz. *Conversations with an Executioner.* Englewood Cliffs, NJ: Prentice-Hall, 1981.

Stroop, Jurgen. *The Stroop Report: The Jewish Quarter of Warsaw Is No More!* New York: Pantheon Books, 1979.

STRUTHOF. SEE NATZWEILER-STRUTHOF.

Stuckart, Wilhelm

(1902–1953)

A Nazi politician and jurist, Wilhelm **STUCKART** was responsible for the drafting of the **NUREMBERG LAWS** and their subsequent implementation orders.

Stuckart was born in Wiesbaden and studied law in Frankfurt am Main and Munich. He joined a **Freikorps** group in the aftermath of World War I and was twice imprisoned by the French for his oppositionist activities. Already a right-wing extremist, Stuckart joined the **NAZI PARTY** in 1922, became its legal adviser in 1926, and a judge in 1930. He had to resign in 1932 because of his political affiliations, but his career revived when the Nazis seized power in January 1933. He became, successively, state secretary in the Prussian Ministry of Culture, Education, and Church Affairs (June 1933), a member of the Prussian State Council (September 1933), and secretary of state in the Reich Ministry of the Interior (March 1935).

Stuckart headed the department for constitutional and legislative matters, and in this capacity was instrumental in helping to draft the Nuremberg Laws (1935). He joined the **SS** in 1936. Together with Hans Globke, he edited a commentary on German racial legislation in 1936; he also published a number of works on Nazi legal theory. In 1942 he participated in the **WANNSEE CONFERENCE**, at which he warmly endorsed plans for the **"FINAL SOLUTION"**, the compulsory sterilization of all "non-Aryans," and the dissolution of mixed marriages. In racial matters Stuckart was even more extreme than Reinhard **HEYDRICH**.

Arrested in 1945, Stuckart was sentenced to four years' imprisonment by the International Military Tribunal at Nuremberg. He claimed to be ignorant of the **EXTERMINATION CAMPS**. He was released in 1949 and died near Hannover in an automobile accident that was rumored to have been the work of a group taking revenge on Nazi war criminals.

SUGGESTED RESOURCES

Newman, Amy. *The Nuremberg Laws: Institutionalized Anti-semitism.* San Diego, CA: Lucent Books, 1999.

Noakes, Jeremy, and Geoffrey Pridham. *Documents on Nazism 1919–1945.* New York: Viking Press, 1974.

"The Nuremberg Laws." *American-Israeli Cooperative Enterprise.* [Online] http://www.us-israel.org/jsource/Holocaust/nurlaws.html (accessed on September 11, 2000).

Stutthof

Stutthof was a concentration camp 22 miles (36 kilometers) east of Danzig (Gdańsk), at the mouth of the Vistula River. It was first designated as a "camp for civilian war prisoners" and officially became a concentration camp on January 8, 1942.

The camp remained in existence from September 2, 1939, to May 9, 1945. About 115,000 prisoners passed through Stutthof; of these, 65,000 perished and 22,000 were moved to other **CONCENTRATION CAMPS**. In the early period of its existence, several thousand prisoners were released from Stutthof. At the end of the war a few hundred survivors were set free when Stutthof and its satellite camps were liberated by Soviet and Polish forces.

Stutthof had several dozen satellite camps, spread over what is now northern **POLAND** and the Kaliningrad district of Russia. The largest of the satellite camps were at Thorn and Elbing; each had 5,000 Jewish women prisoners. The camp staff consisted of **SS** men and a group of Ukrainian auxiliary police (*see* **UKRAINIAN MILITARY POLICE**). The total number of SS men stationed at Stutthof during the

CHRISTMAS EVE, STUTTHOF

On Christmas Eve of 1944, on the main roll call ground of the old camp, the Germans put up a beautiful Christmas tree. It was big and decorated with colored candles. All the prisoners of the old and the new camps were called to roll call late in the evening. This roll call lasted for hours. Suddenly a young Pole was brought into the middle of the square. Only then did we realize that a gallows had been erected next to the festively decorated tree.

After the officers had conversed for a long time and had abused the youth over and over, he was hanged in front of all eyes. On the eve of that high Christian holiday the prisoners were made to view the hanging—as if the Germans wanted to let us know that the cruelty would not stop, despite the holiday. The young man had been condemned to death for the theft of bread.

—SCHCHANA RABINOVICI

Schchana Rabinovici, Thanks to My Mother *(Puffin Books, 2000), p. 199.*

years of its existence was 3,000. Initially, the prison population was made up of Poles from Danzig and Pomerania; later, Poles from all parts of northern Poland and from **WARSAW** joined them. The camp also contained a considerable number of Soviet prisoners, as well as large groups of Norwegians, Danes, and others. In the early stage the number of Jewish prisoners was quite small.

At first, Stutthof was in effect an "extermination" camp because the hard labor and harsh conditions caused the death of many prisoners. In 1943 conditions improved slightly, as far as the non-Jewish prisoners were concerned. The prisoners were put to work in various plants and arms factories. They were accommodated, at the beginning, in the camp's old wooden barracks. In 1943 concrete barracks were put up in the new camp. Relatively few prisoners attempted to escape from Stutthof. Executions took place quite frequently; the victims were mostly activists in the resistance movement. In 1944 large transports of Jews, mostly women, were brought to the camp from the Baltic countries and **AUSCHWITZ**. They were put through a *Selektion* and some were sent to the camp's gas chambers (*see* **GAS CHAMBERS/VANS**).

In January 1945 the prisoners in most of the satellite camps and the main camp itself were evacuated westward toward the vicinity of Lębork, in dreadful winter conditions. Tens of thousands perished in these **DEATH MARCHES**. Some groups of prisoners were evacuated by sea in small boats; many of these prisoners drowned. Stutthof was liberated on May 9, 1945.

SUGGESTED RESOURCES

Birger, Trudi. *A Daughter's Gift of Love: A Holocaust Memoir.* Philadelphia: Jewish Publication Society, 1992.

Rabinovici, Schoschana. *Thanks to My Mother.* New York: Puffin Books, 2000.

Yla, Stasys. *A Priest in Stutthof; Human Experiences in the World of the Subhuman.* New York: Manyland Books, 1971.

TWELVE-YEAR-OLD AT STUTTHOF

These thoughts and memories were recorded soon after the liberation of Stutthof by Werner Galnik, a young boy who survived the **HOLOCAUST,** *but lost most of his family.*

On September 25, 1944, when the Red Army was not far from Riga, the Germans sent us Jews to the Stutthof concentration camp near Danzig....

Everything was taken away from us at Stutthof. We were allowed only the prison clothes we had on our backs. We had to come to assembly and be counted. Then we were shown our sleeping quarters. Four people had to sleep on a cot six feet long and 20 inches wide. I was here only with my brother. My mother was in the women's camp, and I was in the men's camp. I could see my mother only through a fence.

When I got a piece of bread for a present because I was small, I would carefully throw a piece of bread to my mother over the barbed wire. When a woman guard saw it, my mother would be hit with a belt. Once, a woman guard saw that I gave my mother a little piece of bread. My mother was terribly punished. I begged them not to hit my mother, but they hit her even more....

[When the Russians came]....I was very happy. I became a free person. I ran back and cried to the Jews, "Come, come, the Russians are here, we are free people."

....Now I would like to have my parents, and I would like to live again like we lived before with my parents.

—WERNER GALNIK, RECORDED AT RIGA, AUGUST 26, 1945

Children in the Holocaust and World War II: Their Secret Diaries, *Laurel Holliday, editor (New York: Pocket Books/Simon & Schuster) 1995, pp. 61–65.*

SUBSEQUENT NUREMBERG PROCEEDINGS. SEE TRIALS OF THE WAR CRIMINALS.

Sugihara, Sempo

(1900–1986)

Sugihara was a Japanese consul general in **KOVNO**, Lithuania, who actively assisted Jewish refugees in 1940. In early August of that year, three weeks before the Soviet authorities intended to remove all foreign consular representatives from

Kovno, Sugihara was approached by Dr. Zorah Warhaftig, a representative of the Jewish Agency Palestine Office in Lithuania. Warhaftig asked Sugihara to grant Japanese transit visas to Polish Jewish refugees stranded in Kovno as a means for them to obtain Soviet visas. Warhaftig outlined a plan to Sugihara: the refugees would travel to the Dutch-controlled island of Curaçao in the Caribbean, which did not require an entry permit; the refugees would get to the island by way of the USSR and Japan. The Soviets made their approval of this plan contingent on whether the refugees obtained transit visas from Japan.

Though his government rejected the proposal, Sugihara decided to grant visas to any Jewish refugees who requested them. Scheduled to leave Kovno on August 31, Sugihara devoted most of his time in the weeks before his departure to granting visas. Many rabbinical students, such as those of the famed Mir academy, took this opportunity to leave Lithuania. After spending time in China and other countries, they eventually reached the United States and Israel. It appears that at least 1,600 visas were issued (Sugihara estimated the figure at some 3,500).

At the end of the year, Sugihara was reassigned to other Japanese diplomatic posts in Europe. Upon his return to Tokyo in 1947, he was asked to submit his resignation for his insubordination seven years earlier. In 1984, Yad Vashem awarded him the title of **"RIGHTEOUS AMONG THE NATIONS"**.

Years later, while recalling the dramatic and tense days of August, 1940, Sugihara explained his predicament: "I really had a hard time, and was unable to sleep for two nights. I thought as follows: 'I can issue transit visas … by virtue of my authority as consul. I cannot allow these people to die, people who had come to me for help with death staring them in the eyes. Whatever punishment may be imposed upon me, I know I should follow my conscience'" (Ryusuke Kajiyama, in *Sankei Shinbun Yukan Tokuho*, January 24, 1985).

Sempo Sugihara.

SUGGESTED RESOURCES

Gold, Alison Leslie. *A Special Fate: Chiune Sugihara, Hero of the Holocaust.* New York: Scholastic Press, 2000.

Lyman, Darryl. *Holocaust Rescuers: Ten Stories of Courage.* Springfield, NJ: Enslow, 1999.

Passage to Freedom: The Sugihara Story [sound recording]. Live Oak Media, 2000.

Sakamoto, Pamela Rotner. *Japanese Diplomats and Jewish Refugees: A World War II Dilemma.* New York: Praeger, 1998.

Survivors, Psychology of

The **HOLOCAUST** remains a trauma for all mankind and a monstrous enigma which severely challenges optimistic views of mankind. Research in psychology, sociology, and psychiatry has not been able to fully explain how or why the idea of systematically exterminating human beings made its appearance in the twentieth century. Nonetheless, scientists who have studied the psychology of survivors of the Holocaust, with all its trauma, note that this appalling episode in human history also illustrates the victory of life over death and destruction, as shown by research on later effects among survivors and their families in Europe, Israel, and the **UNITED STATES**.

Early ideas about the psychology of survivors were based on early observations of injured survivors. But in order to comprehend the full impact of the Holocaust,

HOLOCAUST 1944

To my mother
I do not know
In what strange far off earth
They buried you;
Nor what harsh northern winds
Blow through the stubble,
The dry, hard stubble
Above your grave.

And did you think of me
That frost-blue December morning,
Snow-heavy and bitter,
As you walked naked and shivering
Under the leaden sky,
In that last moment
When you knew it was the end,
The end of nothing
And the beginning of nothing,
Did you think of me?

Oh I remember you my dearest,
Your pale hands spread
In the ancient blessing
Your eyes bright and shining
Above the candles
Intoning the blessing
Blessed be the Lord....

And therein lies the agony,
The agony and the horror
That after all there was no martyrdom
But only futility—
The futility of dying
The end of nothing.
I weep red tears of blood.
Your blood.

—ANNE RANASINGHE

Holocaust Poetry, *compiled and introduced by Hilda Schiff (London: Fount Paper-backs), 1995.*

one must observe survivors in relation to their families, not just as individuals. In addition, one must consider the diverse experiences of survivors both during and after the Holocaust.

Nazi **RACISM** and persecution affected both individuals and the Jewish community, but also the specific culture that was a part of each individual. Because the traumatization was both individual and collective, most individuals made great efforts to create a "new family" to replace the nuclear family they had lost. Small groups of friends gathered during the years of the Holocaust, sharing all basic necessities. Through their common experiences—shared stories about the past, fervent hopes for the future, and joint prayers—as well as through creative expression

in poetry, art, and diary records that reveal continued aspirations of hope and love, victims sought to resist dehumanization and find support.

Some of the defenses were traditional, including black humor or sharp irony directed at the victims themselves and at the aggressor; identification with martyrs of the past; identification with religious or political ideologies; the formation of mutually supportive systems with a special character; and the creation of fantasy. Imagination was an important way to escape from the frustrations of reality, and fantasies also allowed the self-image to transform itself from victim to hero. Examining these elements helps one to understand the survivors.

Studies of Jewish survivors reveal some common features and similar psychophysiological patterns in their responses to the Holocaust. They often experienced several phases of psychosocial response, including attempts to actively master the traumatic situation, then, finally, passive compliance with the persecutors. These phases may be understood as trial periods, in which victims tried to adapt and cope with the tensions and dangers they faced.

Later research showed that the adaptation and coping mechanisms of survivors were influenced by their childhood experiences, developmental histories, family structures, and emotional family bonds. Behavioral scientists have asked specific questions in their studies: What was the duration of the trauma? During the Holocaust was the victim alone or with family and friends? Was he in a camp or in hiding? Did he use false "Aryan" papers? Was he a witness to mass murder in the ghetto or the camp? What were his support systems—family and friends—and what social bonds did he have? Studies show that those who were able to actively resist the oppressor, whether in the underground or among the **PARTISANS**, had vastly different experiences than the survivors of **EXTERMINATION CAMPS**.

Survivors faced many difficulties in re-entering society after the war. Often, they aroused ambivalent feelings of fear, avoidance, guilt, pity, and anxiety in others. However, it seems that most survivors managed to rejoin the paths their lives might have taken prior to the Holocaust. This is especially true for those who were adolescents or young adults during the Holocaust.

Survivors of Ghettos and Camps

The Jews arrested and brought to **CONCENTRATION CAMPS** during World War II were under sentence of death, whether they were murdered immediately after their arrival or were kept alive to work. Their chances of surviving the war were minimal. Personal qualities, qualifications, and attitudes meant nothing. Jewish prisoners could hardly avoid feeling constantly threatened by the brutal treatment that was their fate.

After spending months or years in ghettos, with continuous persecution and arbitrary selections, many Jews developed chronic insecurity and anxiety; others felt apathy and hopelessness. This mental state was complicated by overcrowding, infectious diseases, lack of facilities for basic hygiene, and continuous starvation. The extreme brutality used to transport Jews to camps augmented the helplessness and confusion felt by prisoners.

The fear of death was very real. People could see that the camp was the last stop in the prisoner's life; the farewells that took place on the train ramps were forever. The sentence of death by labor might take longer than the gas chamber, but it was equally ominous.

Clearly, a uniform picture that depicts Holocaust survivors as having suffered from a static concentration camp syndrome (as it was described from 1945–1955), is not valid. The descriptions of the survivors' syndrome in the late 1950s and 1960s created a new means of diagnosis in psychology and the behavioral sciences and served as a model in examining the results of catastrophic stress situations.

Many survivors described themselves as incapable of living life fully, often barely able to perform basic tasks.

Indescribable living conditions, filth and lack of hygiene, diseases and extreme nutritional insufficiency, continuous harassment and physical abuse, perpetual psychic stress caused by the recurrent macabre deaths—all combined to deeply influence the attitudes and mental health of inmates. Yet some former prisoners describe mainly resignation, curtailment of emotional and normal feelings, weakening of social standards, regression to primitive reactions, and, finally, "relapse to the animal state." Others observed comradeship, community spirit, humanity, and extreme altruism—even moral development and religious revelation. Such differences are inevitable considering the vast numbers of prisoners—about a million at any one time—and various nationalities and religions.

Liberation and After

When liberation came, most of the Jewish inmates were too weak to move or understand what was happening. People died by the hundreds in the first weeks after liberation. After the first physical improvement, the ability to feel and think returned and many felt completely isolated, no longer about to repress what had actually happened. Studies of survivors living in Israel show that 80 percent to 90 percent had lost most of their closest relatives, and three out of four had lost their entire family.

Survivors clung to the hope of finding some family member still alive in the new DISPLACED PERSONS' camps. The massive scale of the effort to assist displaced persons contributed, inadvertently, to the sense of disorientation among survivors. International organizations cared for them and tried to put new meaning into their lives, but within the mechanics of these organizations the individual was of very little consequence.

Most of the survivors wanted to be independent and to leave the countries that symbolized persecution and destruction. Most hoped to reach Palestine, seeing immigration there as the solution to their problems. After the state of Israel was founded, those who were among the new settlers integrated quickly into the new society. The struggle for the young country, and the tasks of building it up, required survivors to suppress their own problems. The majority adapted to newly founded families, jobs, and kibbutz life. Many, however, still endured chronic anxiety, sleep disturbances, nightmares, emotional instability, and depression. The survivors who went to the United States, Canada, and Australia, some of them extremely traumatized, faced more problems. They had to face strange new surroundings, a new language, and new laws, in addition to building new lives without the cultural and religious camaraderie shared by those building new lives in Israel.

When the West German government decided to compensate victims for physical damage suffered during Hitler's regime, many were examined intensively by medical specialists. In most cases no ill effects directly attributable to detainment in the camps were found. This was not surprising because anyone who showed signs of physical disease had already been eliminated and killed in the ghettos and camps and during the infamous DEATH MARCHES. The Jews who survived both the camps and the marches were an extremely select group. Their main problems were emotional, which the Germans did not deem worthy of restitution.

Many survivors described themselves as barely able to perform basic tasks in daily lives lacking a sense of joy or hope. It often took many years, following such

extreme trauma, before self-confidence and a sense of personal value returned and before they fully adjusted to the life of their communities.

Despite their ability to adjust to life's challenges after their Holocaust experiences, rigorous investigation shows that these survivors suffered deep wounds that have healed very slowly; a half century later the scars are present. Holocaust survivors show long-term consequences in the form of psychological stress, associated with heightened sensitivity to **ANTISEMITISM** and persecution. Normal people before the Holocaust, these survivors endured extreme stress and psychic trauma. Their reactions were "normal"—because not to react to this previously unheard-of kind of treatment would be abnormal.

Survivors in Israel

In 1964 researchers compared Jewish Holocaust survivors then living in Israel and non-Jewish Norwegians who returned to Norway after being deported and imprisoned during the war. The results showed that Jewish survivors suffered more from the total isolation in the camps, from the danger of death, which was greater for the Jews, and from "survivor guilt," than did the Norwegians.

A study of Israeli Holocaust survivors in **kibbutzim** revealed that survivors who could not mourn their losses immediately after the war began mourning and working through their grief as they adjusted to life in the kibbutz. This study showed that many survivors had a low threshold for emotional stress that surfaced as depression and tension in stressful situations.

Surveys made in Israel more than 30 years after World War II did not show significant differences in the extent of psychological damage between people who survived by hiding during Nazi occupation and those who were former concentration camp inmates. However, the latter experienced more pronounced emotional distress than those who survived the occupation outside the camps.

Research on elderly Holocaust survivors in Israel showed that they encountered particular difficulties adjusting after the war because of the serious problems they had to overcome (loss of family and of the social and cultural background they had known before the Holocaust).

A controlled study carried out in a university psychiatric hospital in Jerusalem 40 years after the end of the war revealed a difference between hospitalized depressive patients who had been inmates of Nazi concentration camps and a matched group of patients who had not been persecuted. Concentration camp survivors were more belligerent, demanding, and regressive than the control group—traits that may, in fact, have helped them to survive.

Children of Survivors

Research and experience reveal that survivors' children born after the Holocaust bear its legacy. Much of the published research on these psychological problems consists of in-depth studies of individual cases. Some of the literature, however, focuses on the whole family. Researchers in Canada, the United States, Israel, the **NETHERLANDS**, **FRANCE**, and Eastern Europe have shown a growing interest in the psychosocial problems of the second generation, as documented in a survey of research done worldwide on the subject, conducted by Tikva Nathan in 1981. This study shows that children of survivors may develop psychological problems, which are rooted in the atmosphere of anxiety, bereavement, and loss prevailing in their homes. They show family dynamics characterized by fear of separation, overprotec-

> Despite the many difficulties faced by Holocaust survivors in Israel, their overall adjustment, both vocationally and socially was generally more successful than that of Holocaust survivors in other countries.

kibbutzim
Collective settlements or communities in Israel.

tiveness, ongoing bereavement reactions, and mutual guilt feelings in both parents and children.

Not all of these investigations have been controlled, but the validity of the clinical findings is supported by the fact that most were conducted independently, in places far removed from one another, and with no contact between the researchers. The findings also conform with the descriptions that members of the second generation give of themselves, especially when they have themselves become professionals in the field. However, since these findings are based on research conducted in clinical settings, they are thus not applicable to the general population of survivors' children. Only a few studies have been carried out on the psychological and social adjustment of the latter group. For instance, surveys on attitudes conducted outside of Israel report that second generation children have feelings of shame and embarrassment with regard to their survivor parents, whereas the children of Holocaust survivors growing up in Israel demonstrate empathy and identification with their parents.

Research results also demonstrate that the relationships between survivor parents and their children bear distinctive characteristics stemming from the Holocaust experience and contain unique psychodynamic phenomena. But there is no evidence of the existence of a psychopathological syndrome, or of pathological patterns of adjustment. On the contrary, a study conducted by Tikva Nathan in 1988 among secondary school students in Israel showed that the offspring of Holocaust survivors were just as healthy mentally as their peers in school, and that they coped successfully both in school and socially. Such children even manifested a certain resilience to stressful life events.

Investigators throughout the world agree that certain patterns of parent-child relations are typical in survivor families, including overprotection and separation difficulties. The parents often expect levels of achievement and of solace that their children find difficult to fulfill. Their sense of obligation, along with feelings of guilt at not being able to oblige at all times, may alternate with outbursts of aggression and sorrow.

These children of survivors sometimes have to fulfill the difficult role of compensating their parents for all the losses and suffering sustained by the latter. This special position of a child in survivor families has been noted by Tikva Nathan, who uses the term "the precious child." In the words of Judith S. Kestenberg, the birth of a child to a survivor constituted "the undoing of GENOCIDE."

SEE ALSO **DISPLACED PERSONS; RESCUE OF CHILDREN; UNITED STATES ARMY AND SURVIVORS IN GERMANY.**

SUGGESTED RESOURCES

Facing Hate with Elie Wiesel and Bill Moyers [videorecording]. Mystic Fire Video, 1991.

Fremont, Helen. *After Long Silence: A Memoir.* New York: Delacorte Press, 1999.

Landau, Elaine, ed. *We Survived the Holocaust.* New York: Franklin Watts, 1991.

Langer, Lawrence L. *Holocaust Testimonies: The Ruins of Memory.* Neew Haven, CT: Yale University Press, 1991.

Whiteman, Dorit Bader. *The Uprooted: A Hitler Legacy; Voices of Those Who Escaped Before the "Final Solution".* New York: Insight Books, 1993.

A variety of psychological phenomena are shared among members of the second generation, including problems of communication with their parents and problems of adaptation to the social environment, as expressed in loneliness or strong dependency needs, a search for affection, and outbursts of aggression.

ONE-TWO-THREE

This is the last poem of Hannah Szenes, written in 1944 while she was in
prison in Budapest. It was translated from the Hungarian by Peter Hay.

One-two-three …

eight feet long,
Two strides across, the rest is dark …

Life hangs over me like a question mark.

One-two-three …
maybe another week,
Or next month may still find me here,

But death, I feel, is very near.

I could have been
twenty-three next July;
I gambled on what mattered most,

The dice were cast. I lost.

—HANNAH SZENES

Hannah Senesh: Her Life and Diary, *translated by Marta Cohn (London: Vallentine,*
Mitchell and Co. Ltd.), 1971.

Szenes, Hannah

(1921–1944)

One of a group of Palestinian Jews who parachuted into German-occupied Europe, Hannah Szenes (Senesh) was a poet. Born into a Jewish family from Budapest that produced a number of poets, writers, and musicians, Szenes displayed creative talent at an early age. She kept a diary and composed poems—first in Hungarian, and later, when she became an ardent Zionist, also in Hebrew. In 1939, Szenes emigrated to Palestine (present-day Israel). Two years later, she joined a kibbutz. There she wrote some of her most moving poems, including "To Caesarea" (*see* **YOUTH MOVEMENTS**).

In Palestine, Szenes joined the British Army and volunteered in 1943 to parachute into occupied Europe in order to aid Jews under Nazi oppression. She underwent training for the mission in Egypt. In March 1944, about a week before the German occupation of Hungary, Szenes was dropped into Yugoslavia. Together with fellow parachutists from Palestine, she spent three months there with anti-Nazi partisans under the leadership of Josef Broz Tito (later the president of Yugoslavia). Szenes hoped that with the partisans' help she would be able to get into Hungary. She was convinced that even if she and her associates did not succeed in rescuing Jews, their personal sacrifice would be a symbol and inspiration to the Jews of Europe. A chance meeting with a Jewish woman **partisan** inspired her to compose a poem, "Ashrei ha-Gafrur" (in English, "Blessed Is the Match"). She left the text with Reuven Dafni, a fellow parachutist.

In early June 1944, Szenes crossed the border into Hungary. She was immediately captured by the Nazis, and found to have a radio transmitter in her possession.

partisan
A paramilitary guerrilla fighter.

51

Hannah Szenes, sitting in a field at the Kibbutz Sdot Yam, Israel.

She was then taken to Szombathely, put into prison, and tortured. But no physical torture, and not even the threat that her mother's life was at stake, could extract the code for the forbidden transmitter from her. After five months in jail, Szenes was brought to trial, at which she forcefully and proudly defended herself. She was convicted of treason against Hungary and shot to death by a firing squad. She refused to wear a blindfold, choosing to look her executors in the face.

Hannah Szenes has been the subject of novels, plays, and a movie; she has become a symbol of courage, steadfastness, and moral strength. Her writings have been published in many editions. In 1950, Szenes's remains were brought to Israel and buried on Mount Herzl in Jerusalem. A village, Yad Hannah, commemorates her name.

SUGGESTED RESOURCES

Hay, Peter. *Ordinary Heroes: Chana Szenes and the Dream of Zion.* New York: Putnam, 1986.

Schur, Maxine. *Hannah Szenes: A Song of Light.* Philadelphia: Jewish Publication Society of America, 1986.

Senesh, Hannah. *Hannah Senesh: Her Life and Diary.* London: Vallentine, Mitchell, 1971.

"Women of Valor: Partisans and Resistance Fighters" [Online] http://www.interlog.com/%7 Emighty/valor/bios.htm (accessed on September 11, 2000).

TARNOPOL. SEE TERNOPOL.

Tarnów

interwar period
The years between the end of World War I and the beginning of World War II.

Tarnów is located in southern **POLAND**, east of **KRAKÓW**, and it is one of the oldest cities in the country. The presence of Jews in Tarnów was first recorded in the mid-fifteenth century. Under Austrian rule (1772–1918), Tarnów became an important trade center, in which the Jews played the leading role. In independent Poland during the **interwar period**, Tarnów Jewry was impoverished as a result of the government's discriminatory policy, but there was much educational and cultural activity in the community. On the eve of World War II, 25,000 Jews were living in Tarnów, representing 55 percent of the city's total population.

After World War II broke out in September 1939, thousands of Jewish refugees from western Poland converged on Tarnów, but as the Germans advanced eastward, the Jews of Tarnów itself fled to the east. The Germans occupied the city on September 8. From the first day of the occupation, Wehrmacht troops harassed the Jews, seizing them for **FORCED LABOR** and robbing them of their belongings. On September 9, most of the city's synagogues were set on fire. In early November a **JUDENRAT** (Jewish Council) was established. At first its members, while carrying out the German orders, sought also to provide relief to the community, by organizing economic support for the needy, attempting to have hostages set free, and offering medical aid. The Judenrat also helped the Jewish refugees in the city find places to stay. On Passover of 1940, several Judenrat members were arrested for their devoted services to the community. They were replaced by persons of lesser standing, whose behavior came to be sharply criticized by members of the community.

In the spring of 1940 the Germans subjected the Jews of Tarnów to increasingly harsher decrees: a collective fine was imposed; Jews were apprehended on the

street for forced labor; they had to hand over valuables in their possession; and they had to evacuate apartments in designated streets. During the first half of 1941, the **GESTAPO** seized Jewish refugees whose presence in the city was "illegal" and killed them. That December, following the outbreak of war between **GERMANY** and the **UNITED STATES**, more than one hundred Jews were arrested and many of them were put to death.

On June 11, 1942, 3,500 Jews were deported to **BEŁŻEC**, and several hundred others were murdered in the streets of the city or in the Jewish cemetery. On June 15 the Germans resumed this operation and within three days another 10,000 persons were deported to Bełżec. Many others were murdered in the cemetery or in huge pits that had been prepared near the city.

On June 19 a ghetto was established, and sporadic killings took place within its walls. On September 10 all the ghetto inhabitants had to assemble in a city square and were subjected to a *Selektion*. Persons possessing a document that showed them to be working at jobs of importance to the German economy were separated out, while the rest, some 8,000 in all, were taken to Bełżec to be killed. In October, Jews from nearby areas were imprisoned in the Tarnów ghetto, whose population increased to 15,000. The wave of **DEPORTATIONS** to the **EXTERMINATION CAMPS** continued, and in mid-November another train left for Bełżec, carrying 2,500 Jews.

Against the background of this liquidation process, a Jewish underground group was organized in Tarnów in the fall of 1942. Members of the Zionist youth movement Ha-Shomer ha-Tsa'ir were among those who took the lead. Later, the members of other political movements joined them. Some members of the **JEWISH GHETTO POLICE** also took part, and helped the underground acquire weapons. One group of underground members left the ghetto for the forests in order to take part in armed struggle against the Germans, but most of them fell in battle against **SS** units. Others remained active in the ghetto and concentrated on trying to arrange border crossings into **HUNGARY**, where they hoped they would find refuge. Only a few, however, managed to escape in that way.

During the course of 1943 more killings took place in the ghetto, and the final liquidation was launched on September 2. Approximately 7,000 Jews were deported to **AUSCHWITZ**, and 3,000 to **PŁASZÓW**. Three hundred were left behind in Tarnów to sort out the belongings of the deported Jews. They too were deported to Płaszów in late 1943, when Tarnów was declared *judenrein* ("cleansed of Jews").

SUGGESTED RESOURCES

Kornbluth, William. *Sentenced to Remember: My Legacy of Life in Pre-1939 Poland and Sixty-Eight Months of Nazi Occupation.* Bethlehem, PA: Lehigh University Press, 1994.

Tenenbaum, Mordechai

(1916–1943)

Mordechai Tenenbaum was a key leader of the Jewish underground movements in **VILNA**, **WARSAW**, and **BIAŁYSTOK**. In Białystok he was also in command of the uprising. Born in Warsaw, Mordechai Tenenbaum (Tamaroff) was the seventh child in a family of moderate means. He attended a secular school in which Hebrew was the language of instruction. In 1936, he was accepted as a student in the Warsaw Oriental

kibbutz
A Jewish communal farm or settlement.

Institute; the Semitic languages he learned there later gave him the ability to work in the Jewish underground movement throughout **POLAND** by posing as a Tatar.

Tenenbaum was active in Jewish youth organizations. He trained for **kibbutz** life and attended a course for Hebrew tutors in Vilna. Late in 1938, Tenenbaum was called to Warsaw to join the staff of the He-Haluts-Pioneer Jewish Youth head office. He was a regular contributor to the movement's periodicals.

In September 1939, before the fall of Warsaw, Tenenbaum and his co-workers left the city and made their way to Kovel and Vilna, hoping to reach Palestine. The number of immigration "certificates" for Palestine was severely limited, and Tenenbaum provided his comrades with forged documents. Instead of going with them to Palestine, however, he chose to stay behind in Vilna and continue his work.

In June 1941, Vilna was taken by the Germans. Attacks against Jews began immediately. Tenenbaum tried to help his fellow members by providing them with forged work permits, but many were caught. In an effort to save his peers, Tenenbaum moved the survivors of the He-Haluts kibbutz from Vilna to the **BIAŁYSTOK** ghetto, which was still relatively quiet, with the help of Anton Schmid, an anti-Nazi Austrian sergeant in the German army.

On January 1, 1942, the youth of the Vilna ghetto issued a call to the Jews not to permit themselves "to be led like sheep to the slaughter," to refuse to cooperate, and to resist deportation by all available means. Tenenbaum added a comment of his own to a copy of this appeal and hid it safely inside the ghetto; the document was recovered years later, when the city was liberated. To continue the work of the underground movement, Tenenbaum left Vilna with forged documents identifying him as a Tatar by the name of Yussuf Tamaroff. He went by train to the **GRODNO** and Białystok ghettos.

In March of 1942, Tenenbaum returned to Warsaw and reported on the situation in Vilna and the other ghettos he had visited, trying in vain to convince the He-Haluts leadership that the Germans intended to exterminate all the Jews under their control. Shortly thereafter, reports came in of the mass murder of Jews in **LUBLIN** and its vicinity and of the gassing of Jews in the **CHEŁMNO** extermination camp, which the Germans had put into operation in December 1941.

One of the founders of the **JEWISH FIGHTING ORGANIZATION** (ŻOB; Żydowska Organizacja Bojowa) in July 1942, Tenenbaum was active in acquiring arms from outside the ghetto and teaching others how to use the weapons. In November 1942, Tenenbaum went to Białystok to organize and led a resistance movement there. When he arrived, he found the ghetto sealed and surrounded by Germans. Tenenbaum tried to reach Grodno, but he was stopped by Germans, who discovered that his papers were false. Though shot in the leg, he escaped, and eventually he reached the one Grodno ghetto that was still in existence.

After recovering from his wounds, Tenenbaum traveled to Białystok, where he worked to unify all the underground movements in the ghetto and help them gather weapons. Tenenbaum then assumed yet another task: the establishment of an underground archive. He collected German documents; evidence concerning Białystok, Grodno, and other towns in the area; the minutes of **JUDENRAT** meetings and copies of the announcements it had made; and folklore items and songs composed in the ghetto. He also kept a diary and urged others to do so, and wrote articles, letters, and manifestos. He preserved this archive as a memorial to the Jews, their sufferings, and their struggle against the Nazis, and as a means to indict the Germans in the course of history for their unspeakable crimes against the Jews. His writings represent an extraordinary testimony of the era, unparalleled among underground leaders. Only Emanuel **RINGELBLUM**'s archive can be compared with the record that Tenenbaum assembled.

Mordechai Tenenbaum.

Early in 1943, the Germans began deporting Jews from Białystok. Because weapons were scarce, Tenenbaum decided to keep his forces intact and hold back, but to intensify efforts to obtain more arms and train his men. He sent emissaries into the forests to make contact with the **PARTISANS** and to search for arms. Jews employed in German factories were instructed to sabotage the products on which they were working. Weapons were stolen from the Germans; food was stockpiled. Tenenbaum issued a call for resistance: "Let us fall as heroes, and though we die, yet we shall live." In July 1943, Tenenbaum managed to unify all the underground movements in the ghetto—only a few weeks before the ghetto's liquidation.

On August 16, 1943, anticipating action by the Germans, Tenenbaum gave the signal for the uprising. He had hoped to break the German blockade of the ghetto, thereby enabling Jews to escape to the forests and continue the fighting from there. But the German forces surrounding the ghetto were too strong; masses of Jews were seized with panic and despair and did not join the fight. Nevertheless, groups of fighters held out for a month and even harassed the German forces at night; some small groups that had been caught jumped from moving trains or fought their way through the German lines and joined the partisans.

All trace of Tenenbaum was lost during the uprising and it is not known when or where he died, although there were rumors that he and a deputy committed suicide. After the liberation, the Polish government posthumously gave Tenenbaum the award of Virtuti Militari. Most of Tenenbaum's archive is kept by Yad Vashem, in Jerusalem; a small part is preserved by the Jewish Historical Institute in Warsaw, and another portion is held in a museum near Naharia, in Israel.

SUGGESTED RESOURCES

The Ghetto Fighters' House Museum of the Holocaust and Resistance. [Online] http://www. amfriendsgfh.org/Docs/gfh.html (accessed on August 30, 2000).

Rescue and Resistance: Portraits of the Holocaust. New York: Macmillan Library Reference USA, 1999.

A Teacher's Guide to the Holocaust: Resisters. [Online] http://fcit.coedu.usf.edu/holocaust/ people/resister.htm (accessed on August 30, 2000).

TEREZÍN. SEE THERESIENSTADT.

Ternopol

Ternopol (in Polish, Tarnopol) is a city in the Ukrainian SSR, which was founded by Poles in 1540. During the period from 1772 to 1918 the city was in the province of Galicia, then under Austrian rule. Between the two world wars it was part of **POLAND**. In 1939 it was annexed by the **SOVIET UNION**. Jews lived there from the time of its foundation and for a long period constituted a majority. In 1939 there were 18,000 Jews living in Ternopol.

On July 2, 1941, Germans conquered the city. Two days later a pogrom was begun that lasted more than a week (July 4–11). Both Germans and Ukrainians participated and some 5,000 Jews were murdered. In July and August of that year, the Germans issued decrees against the Jews: their movement inside and outside the city was restricted; they were forbidden to change their places of residence; many of

I n a meeting of the Dror underground group at Białystok on February 27, 1943, Tenenbaum proclaimed, "We are the last. It is not … particularly pleasant …: it involves a special responsibility. We must decide today what to do tomorrow. There is no sense in sitting together in a warm atmosphere of memories! Nor in waiting together, collectively, for death. Then what shall we do…? We can see to it that not one German leaves the ghetto, that not one factory remains whole … we will fight to the last, till we fall."

ghetto
A restricted part of a city where Jews were required to live under Nazi supervision.

their homes and valuables were confiscated; and hundreds were taken out daily for **FORCED LABOR**. In September, the Germans issued an order to set up a **ghetto**. The concentration of the Jews in the ghetto and the fencing of its area continued until the beginning of December. The **JUDENRAT** (Jewish Council) allocated the houses in the ghetto, conducted a census, and supplied forced laborers. In the fall and winter of 1941–42, the Judenrat was compelled to send groups of young people to the labor camps set up in the area.

On March 23, 1942, the Germans carried out an operation (*Aktion*) that ended with the killing of 700 Jews in the Yanovka Forest. That spring the Judenrat opened several workshops in the ghetto to perform work vital to the German economy, hoping they would gain a certain immunity in the event of further operations (*Aktionen.*). In July the sporadic killings increased, and from August 27 to 30, the Germans carried out another *Aktion*. In a *Selektion*, more than 3,000 persons, most of them aged and sick, were deported to the **BEŁŻEC** extermination camp. A few hundred men were sent to the labor camp in the area. At the beginning of September, the Germans reduced the area of the ghetto and living conditions deteriorated.

Another *Aktion* came on September 30, 1942. The Germans ordered the Judenrat to gather 1,000 Jews, but when the Jewish leaders did not provide that number, the Germans conducted their own manhunt. They put 800 Jews onto a train destined for Bełżec. During the first half of November there were two further *Aktionen* in Ternopol, and an additional 2,500 Jews were sent to Bełżec.

At the beginning of 1943, the Germans established a labor camp in the area of the ghetto. They assembled Jews classified as "useful" and employed them in factories vital to the German economy. Jews from other parts of the ghetto attempted to infiltrate the camp in the belief that its inmates would remain unharmed. In the operation of April 8 and 9, 1943, a total of 1,000 persons were removed from the ghetto and killed in pits adjacent to the city.

In April and May 1943, the murders in the ghetto continued, culminating in the final operation on June 20. The Germans killed the sick and the aged on the spot, while the others were murdered in fields in the vicinity of the city. The labor camp was closed on July 22, when all its inmates were put to death, except for a group of workers who were kept alive for another two weeks to sort out the belongings of the victims. At the beginning of August, they too were killed. The Germans and the Ukrainians continued to hunt Jews hiding in the city and the neighboring forests. Many fell into their hands up to the last days of the German occupation.

SUGGESTED RESOURCES

Kahana, David. *Lvov Ghetto Diary.* Amherst: University of Massachusetts Press, 1990.

Marshall, Robert. *In the Sewers of Lvov: A Heroic Story of Survival from the Holocaust.* New York: Maxwell Macmillan International, 1991.

T4 OPERATION. SEE EUTHANASIA PROGRAM.

Theresienstadt

Theresienstadt (in Czech, Terezín) was a ghetto established in northwestern Czechoslovakia. Theresienstadt was founded as a garrison town in the late eigh-

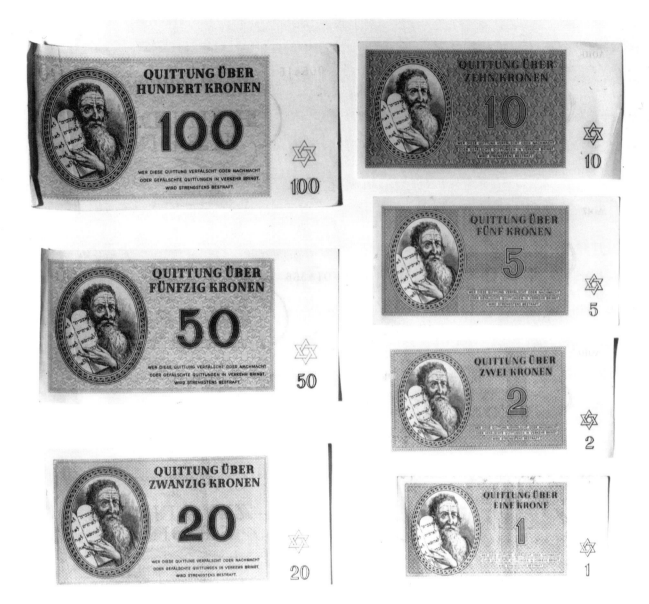

Examples of currency produced by the Nazis as part of their effort to deceive the world into believing that Theresienstadt was an autonomous Jewish city. In reality, it was a ghetto and a transit station for Auschwitz and other places.

teenth century during the reign of Emperor Joseph II and named after his mother, Empress Maria Theresa. In World War II, the town served as a ghetto to which the Nazis expelled 140,000 Jews from the protectorate of **BOHEMIA AND MORAVIA** and from central and western Europe. Control of the ghetto was in the hands of the Central Office for the Solution of the Jewish Question in Bohemia and Moravia, which came under the **REICH SECURITY MAIN OFFICE** (RSHA; Reichssicherheitshauptamt). It was run by the **SS**. Czech police served as the ghetto guards, and with their help the Jews in the ghetto were able to maintain contact with the outside world. The "small fortress," which was near the ghetto, was used as an internment camp for political prisoners, non-Jews and Jews, mainly from the protectorate.

The Nazi plan to establish a ghetto in Theresienstadt is first mentioned in a document dated October 10, 1941. The plan was (1) to concentrate in Theresienstadt most of the Jews of the protectorate as well as certain categories of Jews from **GERMANY** and western European countries: prominent persons, persons of special merit, and old people; (2) to transfer the Jews gradually from Theresienstadt to **EXTERMINATION CAMPS**; and (3) to camouflage the extermination of European Jews from world opinion by presenting Theresienstadt as a "model Jewish settlement."

Barracks in the women's camp at Theresienstadt, Czechoslovakia.

The leaders of Czechoslovak Jewry supported the plan hoping it would mean that the Jews would not be deported to the east and would stay in their country throughout the war.

The first group of Jews, from Prague, came to Theresienstadt at the end of November 1941, and by the end of May 1942, 28,887 Jews had been deported to the ghetto, one-third of the Jewish population of the protectorate. In the first few months, conditions in Theresienstadt were similar to other Nazi **CONCENTRATION CAMPS**. However, it did not take long to dispel the hope that Theresienstadt would save Jews from deportation to the east; the first deportation, of 2,000 Jews to **RIGA**, took place in January 1942. From then on, for as long as the ghetto existed, deportation and the threat of deportation cast a pall of fear over the ghetto population.

In September 1942 the ghetto population reached its peak, 53,004 people, living in an area of 125,770 square yards (115,004 sq m). In that month, 18,639 persons arrived in Theresienstadt, and 13,004 were deported to the extermination camps; 3,941 died in the ghetto. **DEPORTATIONS** to Theresienstadt came to an end in the first half of 1943. By then approximately 90 percent of the Jews of the protectorate and nearly all the Jews left in Germany and **AUSTRIA** had been brought into the ghetto. In 1943 and 1944 the remaining Jews of **THE NETHERLANDS** and **DENMARK** were also taken to Theresienstadt. Deportations to the east—to ghettos in **POLAND** and the Baltic states and, as of October 1942, to the **TREBLINKA** and **AUSCHWITZ** extermination camps—were continued. The final phase began in the fall of 1944 and continued for as long as the gas chambers in the east were still in operation. By then, only 11,068 people remained in the ghetto.

The majority of the Theresienstadt ghetto population were assimilated Jews, reflecting the religious practices of central and western European Jewry. There were also smaller groups of Orthodox Jews and ardent Zionists. There were a few groups of Protestants and Catholics who under the Nazi racial laws were classified as Jews. The Zionists, especially the members of the Zionist **YOUTH MOVEMENTS**, made efforts to carry on educational and cultural activities, and represented the most active, enterprising, and influential element in the ghetto population.

TEREZÍN

That bit of filth in dirty walls,
And all around barbed wire,
And 30,000 souls who sleep
Who once will wake
And once will see
Their own blood spilled.

I was once a little child,
Three years ago.
That child who longed for other worlds.
But now I am no more a child
For I have learned to hate.
I am a grown-up person now,
I have known fear....

—HANUS HACHENBURG, IN A COLLECTION OF WORKS BY CHILDREN
BETWEEN TEN AND SIXTEEN.

I Never Saw Another Butterfly ...: Children's Drawings and Poems from Terezín Concentration Camp, 1942–1944, (Schocken Books), 1978, p. 22.

The internal affairs of the ghetto were run by a Council of Elders, to which Jewish leaders from among the prisoners were appointed. As in other ghettos, the Jewish leadership had the terrible task of making up the lists of those to be deported. It was also responsible for assigning the work to be done in the ghetto, distributing the food, providing housing for new arrivals, and overseeing sanitation and health services, the care of the old and the young, cultural activities, and the maintenance of public order. In all the areas of which it was in charge, the council also exercised judicial authority.

Education, which was the Jewish leadership's chief concern, was primarily in the hands of youth counselors who had been members of youth movements. The atmosphere in the youth hostels (*Jugendheime*), which housed a substantial part of the children of school age (up to the age of sixteen), was almost totally divorced from the harsh reality of the ghetto. Although schooling was prohibited, regular classes were held, clandestinely. The educational effort made in Theresienstadt was an outstanding example of moral resistance to the Nazi regime.

Thanks to the large number of artists, writers, and scholars in the ghetto, there was an intensive program of cultural activities, with several orchestras, an opera, a theater troupe, and both light and satiric cabarets. Lectures and seminars were held, and a 60,000-volume library was established, with special emphasis on Jewish subjects. For many, this library provided their first opportunity to gain an understanding of their Jewish identity. Every week there were dozens of performances and lectures. Religious observance had to contend with difficult conditions, but it was not officially banned.

The Nazis used the multifaceted activities in the Theresienstadt ghetto for their own purposes. They even printed special currency for use within the ghetto. At the end of 1943, when word spread in the outside world of what was happening in the extermination camps, the Nazis decided to allow an International Red Cross investigation committee to visit Theresienstadt. In preparation for the visit, more prisoners were deported to Auschwitz, to reduce the ghetto population of its congestion. Dummy stores were put up, as well as a café, a bank, kindergartens, a

Children in the Theresienstadt concentration camp, the Nazis "model camp."

school, and flower gardens—all the trappings of a place in which human beings lead normal lives. The Red Cross committee's visit took place on July 23, 1944; the meetings of the committee members with the prisoners had all been prepared in advance, down to the last detail. In the wake of the "inspection" the Nazis made a propaganda film showing how the Jews were leading a new life under the benevolent protection of the Third Reich. When the filming was completed, most of its "cast," including all the members of the internal leadership group and nearly all the children, were deported to the gas chambers in Auschwitz.

As a result of the intolerable conditions in the ghetto—overcrowding, a total lack of sanitation facilities, and appalling nutritional shortages—diseases of epidemic proportions broke out and took a fearful toll. In 1942, 15,891 persons died in Theresienstadt, equal to 50.4 percent of the average total population. By the end of 1943 the ghetto health department had managed to set up a network of hospitals, with 2,163 beds, and a beginning was made in regular medical checkups and inoculations against contagious diseases. That year the mortality rate dropped to 29.4 percent, and the following year, 1944, to 17.2 percent.

In the last six months of the ghetto's existence, the Jewish population was increased; 1,447 from **SLOVAKIA**, 1,150 from **HUNGARY**, and 5,932 (persons of "mixed blood") from the protectorate, Germany, and Austria. Before the war came to an end, the International Red Cross succeeded in transferring some of the survivors to neutral countries: 1,200 Jews to Switzerland on February, 5, 1945, and 413 Danish Jews to Sweden on April 15 of that year. At the end of April the ghetto experienced its final shock, when the Germans brought in thousands of prisoners who had been evacuated from concentration camps. As a result there was a new outbreak of epidemics in Theresienstadt; many died, both new arrivals and veterans of

Theresienstadt. On May 3, five days before the Red Army liberated the ghetto, the Nazis handed Theresienstadt over to a Red Cross representative, putting him in charge of the ghetto and its prisoner population. The last Jew left Theresienstadt on August 17, 1945.

According to a number of statistical sources (which differ slightly), between November 24, 1941, and April 20, 1945, 140,000 Jews had been expelled from their homes and taken to Theresienstadt. Of these, 33,000 died there, 88,000 were deported to extermination camps, and 19,000 were alive (either in Theresienstadt or among the two groups that had been transferred to Switzerland and Sweden) when the ghetto was liberated; 3,000 of those deported survived the extermination camps. By national origin, the people who had been taken to Theresienstadt came from Czechoslovakia (75,500), Germany (42,000), Austria (15,000), the Netherlands (5,000), Poland (1,000), Hungary (1,150), and Denmark (500).

SUGGESTED RESOURCES

Bondy, Ruth. *"Elder of the Jews": Jakob Edelstein of Theresienstadt.* New York: Grove Press, 1989.

I Never Saw Another Butterfly; Children's Drawings and Poems from Theresienstadt Concentration Camp, 1942–1944. McGraw-Hill, 1964. Reprint, New York: Schocken Books, 1993.

Roubickova, Eva Mandlova. *We're Alive and Life Goes On: Theresienstadt Diary.* New York: Henry Holt, 1998.

Rubin, Susan Goldman. *Fireflies in the Dark: The Story of Friedl Dicker-Brandeis and the Children of Terezin.* New York: Holiday House, 2000.

Theresienstadt, Gateway to Auschwitz [videorecording]. Ergo Media, 1993.

Transfer Point (Umschlagplatz)

The *umschlagplatz*, or "transfer point," was the area separating the **WARSAW** ghetto from the Polish part of the city, on the corner of Zamenhof and Niska streets. From this location, hundreds of thousands of Jews were deported to **EXTERMINATION CAMPS** and **CONCENTRATION CAMPS**, mostly to **TREBLINKA**, between July and September of 1942 and January and May of 1943.

The Warsaw *Umschlagplatz* (or *Umschlag*, as many referred to it) was, until the mass deportation in the summer of 1942, the only official transit point for the transfer of manufactured goods and commodities to and from the ghetto. It had a railway siding and a special 120-man Transferstelle (transfer office), run by the Germans, who supervised the movement of individuals and goods through the junction.

When the **DEPORTATIONS** were launched on July 22, 1942, the place ceased to function as a link between the ghetto and the outside world and became the *Umschlag*, the spot where the deportees from the ghetto were assembled for deportation. Karl **WOLFF**, an **SS** general on Heinrich **HIMMLER**'s staff, was responsible for providing a daily train for the deportations from Warsaw. In a letter dated July 28, 1942, Theodor Ganzenmüller, the director general of the Reich Ministry of Transportation, stated: "Since July 22, a freight train with five thousand Jews has been making its way daily from Warsaw to Treblinka via Malkinia." Next to the *Umschlag* was a courtyard surrounded by a high fence, and in its center was a vacant building that had once served as a hospital. The Jews designated for deportation

were rounded up in the streets of the ghetto and marched, under guard, to the *Umschlag*, where they were kept sitting on the ground in the courtyard or on the floor inside the building, pending the arrival of the daily train. When the train arrived, they were packed in, 100 to 120 in each freight car. SS men, Ukrainian and Baltic forces, the Polish auxiliary police, and the **JEWISH GHETTO POLICE** (Jüdischer Ordnungsdienst) were on guard during the process.

In the spring of 1988 a monument was unveiled at the *Umschlagplatz* to mark the place where some 300,000 Warsaw Jews were sent to their death.

SUGGESTED RESOURCES

Roland, Charles G. *Courage Under Siege: Starvation, Disease, and Death in the Warsaw Ghetto.* New York: Oxford University Press, 1992.

"The Umschlagplatz" [photographs]. *A Teacher's Guide to the Holocaust.* [Online] http://fcit.coedu.usf.edu/holocaust/resource/gallery/umschlag.htm (accessed on August 31, 2000).

Trawniki

Two members of the Warsaw underground smuggled ŻOB activist Emanuel Ringelblum out of Trawniki in 1943 and took him to Warsaw, disguised as a railway worker. With his family and other Jews, he went into hiding and continued writing the archives known as Oneg Shabbat until he and his family were killed in 1944.

Trawniki was a labor camp established in a town of that name, southeast of **LUBLIN, POLAND**, in the fall of 1941. Located in what had once been a sugar factory, the camp was used to house Soviet **PRISONERS OF WAR** and Polish Jews. It was also a training site for Ukrainian camp guards. Trawniki belonged to the network of camps under the control of Odilo **GLOBOCNIK**, the Higher **SS** and Police Leader in the Lublin district. In the spring of 1942, Jews from **GERMANY, AUSTRIA**, and Czechoslovakia were brought to Trawniki. Many of them died as a result of starvation and disease. Others were deported to **BEŁŻEC**, an **EXTERMINATION CAMP**, or were shot to death in the nearby forest.

Late in 1942, a brush factory that had been in operation in the Międzyrzec Podlaski ghetto was moved, together with its crew, to Trawniki. After the liquidation of the Warsaw ghetto in the wake of the **WARSAW GHETTO UPRISING** in 1943, the Fritz Schulz Works in Warsaw was moved to Trawniki. It had 10,000 workers, with workshops for tailors, furriers, and broom makers. Among the arrivals from Warsaw were Dr. Emanuel **RINGELBLUM** and 33 members of the **JEWISH FIGHTING ORGANIZATION** (Żydowska Organizacja Bojowa; ŻOB). The ŻOB members set up an underground organization in the camp. They were able to acquire a few arms, and made plans for an uprising.

Important factories supplying goods for Germany's war effort, such as army uniforms, were moved to Trawniki in 1943. In May of that year, Jews from **THE NETHERLANDS** and from **BIAŁYSTOK, MINSK**, and Smolensk were taken to Trawniki. The Jewish prisoners in the camp worked in the war-supplies factories as well as in peat mining and in earth-moving operations outside the camp.

After the uprising that took place in the **SOBIBÓR** camp on October 14, 1943, the Nazis became alarmed about the possibility of more such rebellions breaking out. Heinrich **HIMMLER** soon ordered the liquidation of all the Jewish camps. This order led to the **ERNTEFEST ("HARVEST FESTIVAL")** *Aktion*, an SS "operation," of early November 1943, in which 43,000 thousand Jews were killed. Trawniki's population was liquidated on November 5. On that day, 10,000 Jews were taken out of the camp, brought to pits that had been prepared in advance, and murdered. The

Jewish underground members were taken by surprise, but they resisted, and all fell in battle. In the spring of 1944, the remaining prisoners in the camp were transferred to the **STARACHOWICE** camp, in the Radom district. Some 20,000 Jewish prisoners passed through Trawniki during its existence.

SUGGESTED RESOURCES

"Soviet Prisoners of War." Simon Wiesenthal Center Museum of Tolerance Online. [Online] http://motlc.wiesenthal.org/pages/t062/t06261.html (accessed on August 31, 2000).

Treblinka

Treblinka was an **EXTERMINATION CAMP** in the northeastern part of the **GENERALGOUVERNEMENT**, a region of **POLAND** under German occupation. The camp was located in a sparsely populated area, 2.5 miles (4 km) northwest of the village and railway stop of Treblinka. The site was heavily wooded and well hidden from view.

A penal camp, known as Treblinka I, had been set up nearby in 1941. Poles and Jews were imprisoned there, working in quarries to extract materials for the German war effort. The extermination camp was established as part of **AKTION (OPERATION) REINHARD**. Work began in May 1942 and was completed on July 22 of that year. The project was carried out by German firms. For labor, they used prisoners from Treblinka I as well as Jews brought in from neighboring towns. In addition to the camp structures and gas chambers, a branch railway track was built. It led from the camp to the nearby railway station. Huge pits were dug within the camp grounds to be used as mass graves.

Physical Layout of the Camp

The camp was laid out in a rectangle, 1,312 feet wide by 1,968 feet long (400 x 600 m). It resembled the **SOBIBÓR** camp, which had already been built. Two barbed-wire fences surrounded the camp; the inner one had tree branches entwined in the wire to block any view of the camp and its activities. Watchtowers, each 26 feet (8 m) high, were placed along the fence and at each of the four corners. The camp was divided into three parts: the living area, the reception area, and the extermination area.

The living area contained housing for the German and Ukrainian staff. The camp offices, clinic, and storerooms were also located there. One section, set off by its own fence, held the barracks that housed the Jewish prisoners who worked in the camp. The workshops where they labored as tailors, shoemakers, and carpenters were also there.

In the reception area, the prisoners were taken off the incoming transport trains. They then had to go through a variety of procedures before being forced into the gas chambers (*see* **GAS CHAMBERS/VANS**). In addition to the railway siding and platform, this area contained the "deportation square," a fenced-in section with two barracks in which the new arrivals had to undress. Near the railway platform were two large storerooms where the clothes and other possessions taken from the victims were sorted and stored.

The extermination area, called the "upper camp" by the Germans, was in the southeastern part. Covering an area of 656 by 820 feet (200 x 250 m), it was com-

ADMINISTRATION AND STAFF LIVING AREA

1. Entrance to the camp and Seidel street
2. Guard's room near the entrance
3. SS living quarters
4. Arms storeroom
5. Gasoline pump and storeroom
6. Garage
7. Entrance gate to Station square
8. Camp Command and Stangl's living quarters
9. Services for SS — barber, sick bay, dentist
10. Living quarters of Domestic Staff (Polish and Ukrainian girls)
11. Bakery
12. Foodstore and supply storeroom
13. The barrack in which "Gold Jews" worked
14. Ukrainian living quarters and latrines — "Max Bialas barracks"
15. Zoo
16. Stables, chicken coop, pig pen
17. Living quarters for Capos, women, tailor shop, shoe-repairs, carpentry shop and sickroom
18. Prisoners' kitchen
19. Living quarters for men prisoners, prisoners' laundry and tool room
20. Locksmithy and smithy
21. Latrine
22. Roll-call square

RECEPTION AREA

23. Station platform (ramp) and square
24. Storeroom for belongings taken from victims — disguised as a station
25. Deportation square
26. Barrack in which the women undressed and relinquished their valuables
27. Room in which women's hair was cut
28. Barrack in which men undressed, also used as a storeroom
29. Reception square
30. "*Lazarett*" — execution site
31. "The Tube" — the approach to the gas chambers

EXTERMINATION AREA

32. New gas chambers (10 chambers)
33. Old gas chambers (3 chambers)
34. Burial pits
35. "The Roasts" for burning bodies
36. Prisoners' living quarters, kitchen, and latrines

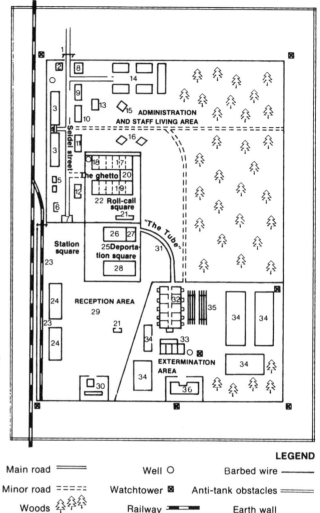

LEGEND

Main road	═══	Well ○	Barbed wire ————
Minor road	═════	Watchtower ⊠	Anti-tank obstacles ═══
Woods	🌲🌲🌲	Railway ▅▅▅	Earth wall

Plan of the Treblinka extermination camp, spring 1943.

pletely fenced in and separated from the rest of the camp. In this area was a brick building containing three gas chambers, each measuring 13 by 13 feet (4 x 4 m). An adjoining shed housed a diesel engine, which produced the carbon monoxide gas for the chambers. The gas was fed into the gas chambers by way of pipes that ended in what looked like shower heads, to create the impression that the chambers were merely shower rooms. A hallway led to each of the three gas chambers. Inside each, facing the entrance, was a second door through which the dead bodies were removed. The huge trenches in which the bodies were buried lay 492 to 656 feet (150–200 m) from the gas chambers, to the east of the building. A narrow path, fenced in on each side and camouflaged with tree branches, led from the reception area to the extermination area. It was along this path, nicknamed the "pipe," or "tube" (*Schlauch*), that the Jews, now naked, were driven to the gas chambers.

Camp Staff and Administration

In August 1942, Franz **Stangl**, the former commander of Sobibór, became the commander at Treblinka. The German staff numbered between twenty and thirty **SS** men, all of whom had taken part in the **euthanasia program**. They held the command and administrative positions in the camp—the most powerful jobs. A

Surviving Treblinka

Very few prisoners lived to tell of their experiences in the four death camps: Bełżec, Chelmo, Treblinka and Sorbibór. Some who did were participants in the Treblinka rebellion of August 2, 1943.

In Leni Yahil's *Holocaust,* Stanislaw Kon recalls the events that began with a pistol shot "exactly at four in the afternoon" on that day: ". . .hands are stretched out to grasp the longed-for rifles, pistols, and hand grenades. . . . the chief murderers in the camp are being attacked. Telephone contact is immediately cut off. The guard towers are set alight with petrol." He goes on to describe the prisoners' state of readiness: "The weapons are divided up among the comrades. We have two hundred armed men. The remainder attack the Germans with axes, spades, and pickaxes."

Kon remembers that the burning of the camp and the sound of gunfire brought to the site "Germans from all around. SS men and gendarmes from Kosov, soldiers from the nearby airfield, and even a special SS unit from Warsaw. . . . Most of our warriers fall, but Germans fall as well. Few of us are left."

Sixteen camp guards were killed in the effort. Although 150 of 700 prisoners managed to escape, most were caught and killed outside the camp by Nazis who hunted them down. The camp was closed down by the end of September.

Ukrainian company consisting of between 90 and 120 men served as camp guards and security personnel. They had the tasks of making sure that no Jews escaped and putting down any attempt at resistance. Some of the Ukrainians were given other duties, including the operation of the gas chambers. Most were Soviet **PRISONERS OF WAR** who had volunteered to serve the Germans, and had been trained for their duties at the **TRAWNIKI** camp. Some of them were of ethnic German extraction (**VOLKSDEUTSCHE**), and the majority of these were appointed platoon or squad commanders. There were also between 700 and 1,000 Jewish prisoners in the camp. They did all the manual labor, including work that was part of the extermination process. In addition, they had to take care of the personal needs of the German and Ukrainian staff.

Groups of Jewish prisoners did construction work as well, which went on even while the extermination process was in operation. They were also kept busy with such jobs as cutting tree branches in the nearby woods and using them for camouflage. These prisoners were taken from the incoming transports, put to work for a few days or weeks at the most, and then "selected" out and killed. Their places were taken by new arrivals. In September 1942, the camp commanders decided to introduce more efficient methods, to reduce the time required to kill the people in each transport. The plan was to establish a permanent staff of Jewish prisoners (rather than one that was constantly replaced). These inmates would each specialize in one particular phase of the process. Such a permanent staff did come into being, but the prisoners did not last long under the harsh conditions of the camp—the frequent

selections (*Selektionen*) for death, execution for the slightest offense, illness, epidemics, and suicides all took their toll. Among the Jewish prisoners, fifty women were used for help in the laundry and the kitchen. Some were also put to work in the extermination area.

Railway Transports

The Treblinka extermination process was based on experience the Germans had gained in the **BEŁŻEC** and Sobibór camps. An incoming train, usually with 50 to 60 cars (containing a total of 6,000 to 7,000 people), first came to a stop in the Treblinka village railway station. Twenty of the cars were brought into the camp; the rest waited behind in the station. As each part of a transport was due to enter the camp, Ukrainian guards took their posts on the camp railway platform and in the reception area. When the cars came to a stop, the doors were opened and SS men ordered the Jews to get out.

A camp officer then announced to the arrivals that they had come to a "transit camp," and from there they would be sent to various labor camps. For hygienic reasons, they would now take showers and have their clothes disinfected. Any money and valuables in their possession were to be handed over for safekeeping and would be returned to them after they had been to the showers. Following this announcement, the Jews were ordered into the deportation square.

At the entrance to the square, the men were ordered into a barrack on the right, and the women and children to the left. This was done with the prisoners on the run—the guards shouted at them, drove them on, and beat them. In the barracks, they had to undress. Beginning in the fall of 1942, the women's hair was cut off at this point. Naked, they then entered the "pipe" that led to the gas chambers. Women and children were gassed first, while the men were kept in the deportation square, standing naked and waiting until their turn came. Once the victims were locked inside the gas chambers, the diesel engine was started and the carbon monoxide poured in. In less than thirty minutes, all had suffocated. Their bodies were removed and taken to the trenches for burial. In the initial stage of the camp, it took three to four hours for all the people in the twenty railway cars to be liquidated. But with time, the Germans gained expertise and reduced the length of the killing process to an hour or two.

While the killing was going on, the railway cars were cleaned. The corpses of people who had died en route and articles that had been left behind were taken off the cars. This work was done by a team of some fifty male prisoners. The empty twenty-car segment of the train then pulled out to make room for another twenty cars, with their human load, to enter the camp from the station. At this time, another team of prisoners of fifty men collected the clothes and other articles that had been left in the deportation square barracks and transferred them to the sorting area. There, a team of 100 prisoners searched the clothing and articles for any money or valuables. They also removed the yellow badges (which Jews were forced to wear) from the clothing and any other identifying signs, destroyed all passports and identity cards, and prepared the items to be sent out of the camp.

The Germans soon realized—as they had at Bełżec and Sobibór—that the bottleneck in the speed of the extermination process at Treblinka was the limited capacity of the gas chambers, which covered an area of no more than 57 square yards (48 sq m). Ten more gas chambers were built between the end of August and the beginning of October 1942, with a total area of 383 square yards (320 sq m).

A group of 200 to 300 prisoners, kept apart from the other Jewish inmates, worked in the extermination area, removing the corpses from the gas chambers, cleaning the chambers, extracting the victims' gold teeth, and burying their bodies. After the practice of cremating the bodies began in the spring of 1943, these prisoners also performed that task.

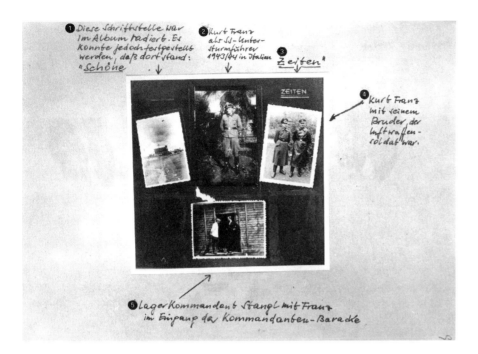

A page from deputy camp commander Kurt Franz's photo album about life in Treblinka.

They were inside a brick building that had a hallway down the center and five doors on each side, each leading to a gas chamber. A second door in each chamber could be opened only from the outside and was used to remove the corpses. The capacity of the new gas chambers was more than sufficient for the entire human load of twenty railway cars at one time.

Another efficiency measure in the extermination process was the introduction of what was called the "infirmary." When a transport arrived, those too weak to reach the gas chambers on their own were told that they would be put into the sick bay. They were taken to a closed-in, camouflaged area with a Red Cross flag flying over it. Inside was a large ditch where SS men and Ukrainians were waiting for the sick Jews. They murdered them on the spot.

Extermination Program

The mass extermination program at Treblinka went into effect on July 23, 1942. The first transports to reach the camp were made up of Jews from the **WARSAW** ghetto. By September 21, some 254,000 Jews from Warsaw and 112,000 from other places in the Warsaw district had been murdered at Treblinka, making a total of 366,000 from the area. From the Radom district, 337,000 Jews were murdered, and 35,000 from **LUBLIN**, most of them before the winter of 1942–43. The total number of victims who had been residents of the General-gouvernement was 738,000. More than 107,000 Jews from the **BIAŁYSTOK** district were taken to Treblinka to be killed, most of them between November 1942 and January 1943.

A total of 29,000 Jews from outside Poland were also killed at Treblinka. Seven thousand Jews from **SLOVAKIA** were murdered in the summer and fall of 1942. Five transports brought 8,000 Jews from **THERESIENSTADT** in Czechoslovakia in October 1942. From Greece, more than 4,000 Jews who had first been deported from their homes came in March 1943. From Macedonia, a part of Yugoslavia that Bulgaria had annexed, 7,000 Jews were murdered in Treblinka in March and April 1943. And at least one transport of 2,800 Jews came from Salonika in March 1943.

Two thousand **GYPSIES** (Romani) were also among the victims of Treblinka. The mass extermination program continued until April 1943, after which only a few isolated transports arrived; the camp had fulfilled its function.

In late February and early March of 1943, SS head Heinrich **HIMMLER** visited Treblinka. He ordered an operation to burn the bodies of the victims, in an effort to erase traces of the murders. The mass graves were opened and the corpses were taken out, to be consumed by the flames of huge pyres (the "roasts"). The bones were crushed and, together with the ashes, were reburied in the same graves. This burning of corpses continued until the end of July. Upon its completion, the camp was shut down, in the fall of 1943. A total of 870,000 people had been murdered there.

Escape and Resistance

Hundreds of attempts to escape were made as the trains were on their way to the camp. Some of those who tried to escape died from the jump from the train, or were shot to death by the transport escorts. Others were caught by railway guards or were handed over to the police by local inhabitants. Some of the escapees managed to reach ghettos, only to be sent to their death when it was the turn of the Jews in those ghettos to be deported to the camps.

There were also many attempts to escape from the camp itself, especially in the first few months of its existence, when order and security had not been fully established. Most attempts were made at night. Prisoners tried to get through fences or hide in the railway cars that had been loaded with the victims' clothing and valuables and were about to leave the camp. Another method was to dig an underground passage leading to a point beyond the camp perimeter, but all those who tried this means of escape were caught. Not many survived of those who were able to escape from trains to or from the camp. Anyone who was caught in an escape attempt was hanged. As time went by, more stringent security measures were taken in the camp.

Several efforts at resistance were made in Treblinka, both by individuals and by entire transports, in which SS men and Ukrainians were killed or wounded. At the beginning of 1943, a resistance group was formed among the inmates, led by people who held the top posts entrusted to prisoners; one of them was Dr. Julian Chorazycki, who was the SS men's physician. At a later stage, the chief **KAPO**, Marceli Galewski, and other Kapos and work-team leaders also joined. Attempts were made to obtain weapons with the help of the Ukrainians, but these efforts failed and led to Chorazycki's death.

Prisoners from both the main camp and the extermination area belonged to the underground resistance group. In the extermination area, the resistance was led by a Jewish officer from the Czech army, Zelo Bloch. The group's plan, which took form in April 1943, was based on taking weapons from the SS armory and then seizing control of the camp, destroying it, and fleeing to the forests to join the **PARTISANS**. Fifty to seventy men were members of the resistance, but it was expected that all the prisoners would join in an uprising if it were to break out.

When the burning of the bodies was nearing completion and it was clear that the camp was about to be closed and the remaining prisoners murdered, the leaders of the underground resolved that the rebellion must take place in the afternoon of August 2, 1943. Initially the uprising went according to plan. With the help of a copied key, the armory was opened. Weapons were taken out and handed to the resistance members. At this point, the resistance men began to suspect that one of the SS officers, Kurt Küttner, had noticed unusual activities and was about to alarm

F or every prisoner who escaped, ten of those left behind were executed. Measures of this kind discouraged escape attempts.

the camp guard; the SS man was shot at once. The gunshot alerted the guards and put an end to the removal and distribution of weapons from the armory, and the plan to seize control of the camp was abandoned. Instead, resistance members who had weapons opened fire at the SS men and set some of the camp buildings on fire. Masses of prisoners now tried to storm the fence and escape from the camp. They were fired at from all the watchtowers, and most of them were hit, falling in or near the fence area. Those who managed to get out of the camp were caught and shot by German security forces called to the scene. Of the approximately 750 prisoners who had tried to make their escape, seventy survived to see liberation.

Most of the camp structures, except for the gas chambers, were made of wood and were burned. Of the prisoners who were left, some were killed on the spot. The rest were made to demolish the remaining structures and erase all traces of the activities that had taken place at the camp. When this work was done, these prisoners were shot. The grounds were plowed under and trees were planted. The land was turned into a farm, and a Ukrainian peasant family was settled there.

After the War

Two trials were held of SS men who had served in Treblinka. In the first trial, which lasted from October 1964 to August 1965, there were ten defendants, including the deputy camp commandant, Kurt Franz. Of the ten, one was acquitted. Five were sentenced to prison terms ranging from three to twelve years, and four were given life sentences. The second trial was that of Franz STANGL, the camp commandant, who had escaped to Brazil but was extradited to GERMANY. His trial, conducted from May to December 1970, resulted in a sentence of life imprisonment.

The area of the Treblinka camp was made into a Polish national monument, in the form of a cemetery. Hundreds of stones were set in the ground, inscribed with the names of the countries and places from which the victims had originated.

SUGGESTED RESOURCES

Arad, Yitzhak. *Belzec, Sobibor, Treblinka: The Operation Reinhard Death Camps.* Bloomington: Indiana University Press, 1987.

Donat, Alexander, ed. *The Death Camp Treblinka: A Documentary.* New York: Holocaust Library, 1979.

Steiner, Jean-François. *Treblinka.* London, Weidenfeld & Nicolson, 1967. Reprint, New York: MJF Books, 1996.

Willenberg, Samuel. *Surviving Treblinka.* New York: Basil Blackwell, 1989.

Trials of the War Criminals

General Survey

At the end of World War II, men and women accused of war crimes against Allied citizens stood trial in a variety of courts. Military or political leaders whose crimes had no particular geographical location were classified as "major" war criminals. They were brought to Nuremberg or Tokyo, where they were tried before courts established by Allied international agreement. Numerically these trials were a small part of a very large picture. The overwhelming majority of post-1945 war crimes trials were those of "minor" war criminals. They were civilians or former

John Demjanjuk, surrounded by guards in courtroom, 1988.

members of enemy armed forces whose crimes were committed in specific locales, as in **CONCENTRATION CAMPS**. Minor war crimes trials were conducted by military courts in the British, American, French, and Soviet zones of occupied **GERMANY**; in **ITALY** and **AUSTRIA**; and by courts established for that purpose in Allied countries. The new governments installed in the former occupied and satellite countries also tried war criminals, and after the creation of the Federal Republic of Germany, German courts began prosecuting war criminals on their own. Two war criminals, Adolf **EICHMANN** and John (Iwan) Demjanjuk, were brought to Israel, where they were tried for their crimes in 1961–62 and 1988–89, respectively.

The term "Nuremberg trials" is often used to describe four different criminal proceedings. The first, which focused on 24 indicted "major" German and Austrian war criminals, was conducted by the International Military Tribunal (IMT) between October 18, 1945, and October 1, 1946. Only 22 suspects were actually tried: Robert Ley committed suicide, and Gustav Krupp von Bohlen was too ill to

stand trial. Judges from **GREAT BRITAIN**, **FRANCE**, the **SOVIET UNION**, and the **UNITED STATES** presided over the IMT, which tried defendants on charges of conspiracy, crimes against peace, war crimes, and **CRIMES AGAINST HUMANITY**. Nuremberg was also the site of 12 later trials of 177 members of organizations and groups alleged to have been of a criminal character. Former members of the **GESTAPO** and the **SS**, as well as civil servants and industrialists, were among those tried. American lawyers served as judges in these proceedings. The third type of "Nuremberg trial" was held in Tokyo. A multinational panel of 11 judges, who comprised the IMT in East Asia, presided over the trials of Japanese military and political leaders. The trials of "minor" war criminals conducted by military and national courts were the fourth type of Nuremberg proceeding. These trials were held variously in the zones of former Axis territory occupied by the victorious powers, in the liberated territories, and at or near the scenes of the crimes.

The first trial of Nazi war criminals took place in July 1943, nearly two years before the war ended.

Krasnodar Trial

The first trial of Nazi criminals was held in the Soviet city of Krasnodar from July 14 to 17, 1943, before the Soviet military tribunal of the North Caucasian Front. The trial dealt with the crimes committed by the Nazis in the city, involving 7,000 acts of murder.

Thirteen Soviet citizens were brought to trial; all had served in the auxiliary unit of Sonderkommando 10a (from Einsatzgruppe D), under the command of Dr. Kurt Christmann. They were charged with annihilating all the patients in the Krasnodar municipal hospital, in the Berezhanka convalescent home, and in the regional children's hospital by means of lethal gas. In their testimony, the accused described the set-up and methods used for these murders (*see* **GAS CHAMBERS/VANS**).

Twenty-two local witnesses testified, including Ivan Kotov, who survived the gas van by breathing through a piece of material soaked in urine. On July 17, 1943, eight of the accused were sentenced to death by hanging, and three others to twenty years' imprisonment with **FORCED LABOR**. This was the first trial in which the mass murders of the **OPERATIONAL SQUADS** (Einsatzgruppen) and the use of gas vans were made known to the world.

Nuremberg Trial

The Nuremberg Trial—designed to punish the leaders of a regime, a government, and an army for crimes committed in the framework of their policy and its implementation by means of an independent court of law of an international character—was the first of its kind in history. This court would try the accused in accordance with the principles of justice and the rules of law, with the accused having every opportunity to defend themselves.

The judges appointed to the tribunal were urged to follow the law and their conscience, notwithstanding the fact that they were nationals of the countries that had won the war—the United States, the Soviet Union, Great Britain, and France— and that it was the governments of these countries that had appointed them.

The Nuremberg court's purpose was to sit in judgment on the men and women who were guilty of crimes against humanity and peace (by planning, executing, and organizing such crimes, or by ordering others to do so) during World War II. The term "international" was included in the IMT's official designation to underline the universal validity of its judgment and its importance for the entire world.

The International Military Tribunal (IMT) intended to hold the trial of the major Nazi war criminals in Berlin, and the opening session, on October 18, 1945, did indeed take place there. The ruins of the German capital could not accommodate such a large-scale event, however, so the trial was moved to Nuremberg—a location selected, among other reasons, because of what it symbolized as a Nazi stronghold that had gained infamy for the racist laws named after it (see Nuremberg Laws).

The IMT tried 22 of Nazi Germany's political, military, and economic leaders: Hermann Göring, Rudolf Hess, Joachim von Ribbentrop, Wilhelm Keitel, Ernst **KALTENBRUNNER**, Alfred **ROSENBERG**, Hans **FRANK**, Wilhelm Frick, Julius **STREICHER**, Fritz Sauckel, Alfred Jodl, Martin **BORMANN**, Franz von Papen, Arthur **SEYSS-INQUART**, Albert Speer, Konstantin Freiherr von Neurath, Hjalmar Schacht, Walther Funk, Karl Dönitz (the commander of the navy, whom Adolf **HITLER**, on the eve of his suicide, appointed as his successor); Erich Raeder (the commander of the navy prior to 1943); Baldur von Schirach (leader of the **HITLER YOUTH** and district leader of **VIENNA**); and Hans Fritzsche (in charge of radio propaganda).

The individual defendants were indicted under Article 6 of the charter, as follows:

Article 6. The Tribunal established by the Agreement referred to in Article 1 hereof for the trial and punishment of the major war criminals of the European Axis countries shall have the power to try and punish persons who, acting in the interests of the European Axis countries, whether as individuals or as members of organizations, committed any of the following crimes:

The following acts, or any of them, are crimes coming within the jurisdiction of the Tribunal for which there shall be individual responsibility:

(a) Crimes against peace: namely, planning, preparation, initiation or waging of a war of aggression.

(b) War crimes: namely, violations of the laws or customs of war.

(c) Crimes against humanity: namely, murder, extermination, enslavement, deportation, and other inhumane acts.

Leaders, organizers, instigators, and accomplices participating in the formulation or execution of a common plan or conspiracy to commit any of the foregoing crimes are responsible for all acts performed by any person in execution of such plan.

The judgment, which was delivered on September 30 and October 1, 1946, sentenced 12 of the defendants to death: Bormann, Göring, Ribbentrop, Keitel, Kaltenbrunner, Rosenberg, Frank, Streicher, Sauckel, Jodl, Bormann, and Seyss-Inquart. Bormann, who was not captured, was sentenced *in absentia*, and Göring committed suicide; the other ten were hanged, on October 16, 1946. Hess, Funk, and Raeder were sentenced to life imprisonment; Speer, Neurath, Dönitz, and Schirach were given sentences ranging from ten to twenty years; and von Papen, Schacht, and Fritzsche were acquitted.

Both the indictments and the judgments of the IMT stressed the legal definition of a "war of aggression." A formal state of war exists as soon as such a state is declared, but this is not always accompanied by an act of aggression. On the other hand, aggression, in the form of an armed attack, can be carried out without being preceded by a declaration or announcement, and without the victim putting up any resistance or being able to defend himself. This was the case in Austria and Czechoslovakia, which the IMT cited as examples of states victimized by Nazi planning and preparing for wars of aggression.

The tribunal determined that the **NAZI PARTY** leadership, the SS, the Gestapo, and the **SA** could all be charged with criminal activity, but they excluded the Reich government, the German General Staff, and the high command of the German armed forces among the organizations declared as criminal. The prosecuting team excluded certain categories from the charge of criminal participation in criminal organizations, including persons holding strictly administrative posts in the police

Military officers and judges inside the Nuremberg Trial courtroom.

and members of certain party or official bodies, so as to remove the slightest suspicion of trying anyone under the principle of collective responsibility.

The IMT determined that wars of aggression, in any form, are prohibited under a great number of international treaties. The tribunal, however, disregarded the charges in the indictment of conspiracies to commit war crimes, and dealt only with the defendants' common plan to prepare and conduct a war of aggression. The tribunal considered that all the other crimes were derived from the crimes against peace. The crime of participation in a criminal organization was included in the IMT charter so that none of those who participated in planning or carrying out Nazi atrocities could escape justice, even if their responsibility for any specific criminal act could not be proved. In adopting the rule that participation in a criminal organization was a crime, the IMT had in mind the members of several Nazi frameworks classified by its charter as criminal organizations, and it planned to indict them, unless they could prove that despite their membership in such criminal organization or conspiracy they bore no personal responsibility for the criminal acts. The basis of this decision was the fact that these were voluntary organizations whose members had joined them in full knowledge of their criminal aims and methods.

The IMT, like the courts of many countries, also held to the principle that persons committing a criminal violation of international law are individually responsible for violations and that the official position of such criminals does not absolve

them from punishment. In addition, the tribunal took a clear stand on the issue of responsibility for crimes carried out on orders from above; the following of superior orders was not an excuse for the perpetration of a crime.

The testimony given at the Nuremberg Trial, the documents presented by the prosecution, and the entire record of its proceedings constitute an incomparable source for the study of the **HOLOCAUST**, and for understanding how to prevent its recurrence in any form, and especially to prevent the resurgence of **ANTISEMITISM** and of discrimination against foreigners.

The conclusions arrived at by the IMT were also applied to the drafting of (1) the international convention for the prevention of the crimes of **GENOCIDE** (the Genocide Convention), adopted by the United Nations on December 9, 1948; (2) the Human Rights Declaration of December 10, 1948; (3) the Convention on the Abolition of the Statute of Limitations on War Crimes and Crimes against Humanity of November 26, 1968; and (4) the Geneva Convention on the Laws and Customs of War of 1949, and its supplementary protocols of 1977.

The principle that the only legal wars are wars in self-defense or against aggression—a fundamental rule of present-day international law—also derives from the United Nations Charter, the IMT charter, and the IMT judgment.

Bergen-Belsen Trial

The trial of the **BERGEN-BELSEN** camp staff was held from September 17 to November 17, 1945, before a British military tribunal at Lüneburg, Germany. The accused were on trial for crimes committed in the **AUSCHWITZ** and Bergen-Belsen camps. They were charged with planning and conspiring to torture and murder prisoners, committing acts of murder, and meting out inhuman treatment and punishment with their own hands.

Among the accused in this trial were Josef **KRAMER**, who had been a commandant of concentration camps from 1943 on; Dr. Fritz Klein, who took an active part in making *Selektionen* and sending people to their death; and prisoners who collaborated with the Nazis and were given the status of agents of the camp administration, such as Stanisława Staroska, a Polish woman known as "Stana the Flogger." Forty-five persons stood trial, twenty-one of them women.

Kramer, Klein, and nine others—among them two women, Irma Grese and Elisabeth Volkenrath, who were charged with torturing and assaulting prisoners— were sentenced to death by hanging. Erich Zoddel, the camp's chief **KAPO**, was sentenced to life imprisonment, Staroska to ten years, and others to periods of one to three years. Fourteen of the accused were acquitted.

Zyklon B Trial

In March 1946 the trial of Bruno Tesch, Joachim Drösihn, and Karl Weinbacher was held before a British military tribunal in Hamburg. The accused were owners and executives of a Hamburg factory that from January 1, 1941, to March 31, 1945, manufactured poison gas used to kill concentration camp prisoners. The gas, called **ZYKLON B**, was manufactured by the Tesch and Stabenow Company. It was used by the SS, **SS DEATH'S-HEAD UNITS** (*Totenkopfverbände*) stationed in Auschwitz, and the other **EXTERMINATION CAMPS**.

The defendants in the trial claimed that they did not know what their product had been used for, a claim that was rebutted by Tesch's official company reports of his trips to Auschwitz. Tesch and Weinbacher (the executive manager of the "facto-

When the British liberated Bergen-Belsen in April 1945, they found hundreds of rotting corpses on the ground and in the barracks. Among the survivors, many were too weak to move unassisted. Prisoners had been beaten, tortured, or starved to death, or had died of diseases such as typhus. The barracks for the prisoners were deplorable, each crammed beyond a tolerable limit; many prisoners became ill or died due to dreadful sanitary conditions.

ry for means of death") were sentenced to death and executed; Drösihn, an employee of the factory, was acquitted. The Zyklon B Trial established for the first time that the manufacture of gas for killing prisoners was a war crime.

Subsequent Nuremberg Proceedings

On December 20, 1945, four weeks after the opening of the trial of the major war criminals by the International Military Tribunal, the Allied Control Council announced its Law No. 10. This law empowered the commanding officers of the four zones of occupation to conduct criminal trials on charges of aggression, war crimes, crimes against humanity, and membership in an organization aiming at such crimes.

Under the charge of crimes against humanity, persecution of the citizens of any country on political, religious, and racial grounds was declared punishable under the principles of international law. To carry out Law No. 10, the Office of the United States Government for Germany (OMGUS) established six military tribunals, composed of civilian judges recruited from among state supreme court judges in the United States. In 1,200 sessions of 12 trials known as the Subsequent Nuremberg Proceedings, which were held between December 1946 and April 1949, 177 persons were tried, including representatives of the leadership of the Reich ministries, the Wehrmacht, industrial concerns, the German legal and medical establishment, and the SS.

All the judgments rendered at Nuremberg claimed to enforce statutory law or international common law, and widespread petitions to administer retroactive or *ad hoc* special law were rejected by the courts. As a result, the **"FINAL SOLUTION"** was classified among the conventional crimes—murder, maltreatment, abduction, enslavement, and robbery—committed on racial grounds. Since it was the tribunals' task to prove the criminal nature of many of the activities carried out by the pillars of the German state, each of the twelve cases dealt with a specific sphere. The destruction of the Jews as a crime therefore appears in the Nuremberg Proceedings not as a single entity but split up into detailed component parts, next to and in conjunction with other criminal pursuits.

Chronologically, the stages of the persecution of the Jews are distributed among the Subsequent Nuremberg Proceedings in the following pattern:

1. *Preparation of the Nuremberg Laws* and their decrees of implementation.

2. *Application of the Law for the Protection of German Blood and Honor by Rassenschande (race defilement) tribunals.*

3. *Forced "ARYANIZATION"* of Jewish-owned capital.

4. *Forced "Aryanization" of agricultural property.*

5. *Abduction and mass shooting of Jews* in concentration camps maintained by the Wehrmacht in Serbia, in retaliation for partisan attacks.

6. *The extermination campaign by the Einsatzgruppen* in the war against the Soviet Union.

7. *Logistic support for the Einsatzgruppen,* direct orders to them, and responsibility for their actions under the law of war.

8. *The deportation of Jews* from western Europe.

9. *Events relating to the deportations from Denmark, Slovakia, Croatia, Serbia, France, Italy, and Hungary.*

10. *Deportations from Greece.*

11. *Antisemitic indoctrination* of the population and dulling of their conscience during the extermination process.

The International Military Tribunal (IMT) declared that all the leaders, organizers, inciters, and accessories to a criminal act who participated in the decision or implementation of a common plan, or a conspiracy to commit crimes, were guilty not only of their own acts but also of the crimes carried out by any other person in the execution of the common plan or conspiracy.

12. *Pillage of the property left behind by the Jews who were abducted from Germany.*

13. *Administration of concentration camps and the Vernichtung durch Arbeit (annihilation through work) system* in the SS-run companies Ostindustrie Gbmh (Osti) and Deutsche Erd- und Steinwerke (German Earth and Stone Works; DEST).

14. *The enslavement of Jews* by private industry, through forcing them to work under conditions like those in concentration

15. *The government-sponsored slave economy.*

16. *Sale of* Zyklon B *(prussic acid) to the SS and construction of industrial plants in Auschwitz.*

17. *Medical experiments on human beings in concentration camps,* including sterilization experiments for future application to *Mischlinge.*

18. *Hoarding of dental gold from Auschwitz.*

With the exception of the Reichsbahn (the national railway system) and the **REICH SECURITY MAIN OFFICE** (RSHA; Reichssicherheitshauptamt), the Subsequent Nuremberg Proceedings exposed the principal agencies involved in the extermination of the Jews, determined the culpability of their personnel, and passed sentences on a few of their leading figures. The courts next turned their attention to the personnel who had been directly engaged in carrying out the liquidation process in the extermination camps and the killing squads.

Contrary to the expectations of those who initiated them, the Subsequent Nuremberg Proceedings had no influence on the way the German people viewed their recent history. The Germans exerted constant organized pressure on United States High Commissioner John J. McCloy to suspend the sentences. By 1951, primarily at the urging of the German churches and political parties, a hurried pardoning policy was introduced. Many ex-convicts resumed their interrupted careers or retired, usually keeping entitlements to pensions for their official services.

Germany

As early as 1943, the Allies in the war against Germany agreed that they would punish officials of the Nazi regime who were responsible for its crimes. On the basis of that agreement, Allied military tribunals convicted and sentenced an estimated 60,000 Germans and Austrians of war crimes and crimes against humanity.

Until late 1950, the crimes related to the Nazi regime that were tried by German courts in the Federal Republic of Germany dealt mainly with relatively minor transgressions. Some grave crimes, however, were also within the jurisdiction of German courts in that period, such as crimes committed in the concentration camps, murders during the course of the **EUTHANASIA PROGRAM**, and the so-called final-phase crimes. Almost all these criminal trials resulted from charges brought by the victims or their heirs against participants in the crimes who were known or who had been discovered by chance, rather than through any deliberate investigative process.

In 1950, shortly after the establishment of the Federal Republic of Germany in the three Western zones of occupation, prosecutors were free to embark upon a systematic investigation of all Nazi crimes and to prosecute the criminals involved in them. Due to a lack of personnel and adequate material resources, however, investigations were difficult to organize. German attention and resources were, not surprisingly, focused on post-war rehabilitation and the restoration of the country's economic strength.

The destruction of Jews was not classified as a separate criminal offense at Nuremberg, a fact that has since often been deplored. In legal terms, this offense was one of the several atrocities summarized as "crimes against humanity."

According to the statute of limitations of May 8, 1950, the operative date for Nazi crimes, as distinguished from other crimes, was the day the war ended, rather than the date on which the crime was committed, since prosecution of these crimes had not been possible during the Nazi regime. The statute thus made it possible to inaugurate a series of trials for crimes committed in the Auschwitz and TREBLINKA extermination camps, in the BUCHENWALD, NEUENGAMME, GROSS-ROSEN, Flossenbürg, and SACHSENHAUSEN concentration camps, in the THERESIENSTADT camp, and in the Sajmište (Semlin) detention camp.

However, from 1951 to 1955 the number of proceedings conducted in the courts of the Federal Republic was sharply reduced, because by the time the statute was issued, five years after the end of the war, offenses that bore a maximum sentence of five years could no longer be prosecuted. Most of the investigations of these offenses had originated with complaints filed by victims of the crimes or their heirs, and, sometimes, against suspects who had been discovered by chance.

On May 8, 1955, the statute of limitations was to go into effect for Nazi-related crimes with a maximum sentence of ten years. As far as the prosecution of Nazi crimes was concerned, this meant, for all practical purposes, that henceforth only acts of premeditated murder could be prosecuted. At about the same time, on May 3, 1955, the "transition agreement" between Germany and the United States, Britain, and France went into effect, containing the following provision:

> Persons who have been tried for a crime by the American, British, or French authorities in their respective zones of occupation and the proceedings against them [having] terminated, will not be tried again for the same crime by the German public prosecution, regardless of the outcome of the trial under the Allied occupation authorities—conviction, acquittal, or dismissal of the case because of lack of evidence; this provision also applies to cases in which new evidence has come to light against persons who have been either acquitted or have had their case dismissed.

Nevertheless, 1955 marked the beginning of a change in the prosecution of Nazi crimes.

It began with an investigation into the murder of Jews in the German-Lithuanian border region by members of an Einsatzkommando (mobile killing sub-unit). In this case, the prosecution pursued all leads that came to light during the investigation of other crimes committed by Einsatzgruppen and Einsatzkommandos, and added these criminal charges to the initial complaint. The mass of information gathered by this process made it clear that some of the worst crimes committed by the Nazi regime had yet to be prosecuted.

In the fall of 1958 the ministers of justice of all the states (*Länder*) of the Federal Republic established the Central Office of the Judicial Administrations of the *Länder* for Investigation of Nazi Crimes (Ludwigsburger Zentralstelle), in Ludwigsburg. The new office was assigned the task of finding all available sources of information on Nazi crimes and instituting criminal proceedings against the responsible persons.

In the first year, the Ludwigsburger Zentralstelle initiated 400 extensive investigations. The most significant had to do with the crimes committed by Einsatzgruppen and Einsatzkommandos in the Soviet Union and POLAND; by the Sicherheitspolizei (Security Police), Ordnungspolizei ("order" police), and the so-called Ethnic Germans' Self-Defense Force in the occupied territories; and in the Auschwitz, BEŁŻEC, SOBIBÓR, Treblinka, and CHEŁMNO extermination camps.

The Germans, for the most part, felt that the Nuremberg sentences were arbitrary and unfair decisions made by the victorious powers.

For political reasons, the government of the German Federal Republic would not establish contact with the Eastern European countries—most of which were still without diplomatic relations with the Federal Republic—even though many documents necessary for the investigation and prosecution of Nazi criminals were available only through these countries.

protocols
Written records, for example, interview transcripts or minutes of meetings.

On May 8, 1960, fifteen years after the war had ended, the statute of limitations on the Nazi-influenced crimes of manslaughter, deliberate physical injury leading to death, and deprivation of liberty with lethal results went into effect. Political figures active in the Social Democratic party of the Federal Republic of Germany had attempted to introduce a law that would block the statute of limitations from going into effect, but the majority of the Bundestag (the German parliament) were in favor of the statute being applied. Henceforth, only murder could still be prosecuted by the courts.

Even the charge of murder, according to the law existing at the time, would be subject to a statute of limitations on May 8, 1965, unless criminal proceedings were instituted against suspects before that date. Accordingly, the Ludwigsburger Zentralstelle and the prosecuting attorneys in the various German states made efforts to collect all available evidence as quickly as possible and use it in time to institute criminal proceedings against persons known to be, or suspected of being, participants in a crime of murder under the Nazi regime.

Since most of the available documentary evidence at that time was kept in archives of countries outside Germany, the Ludwigsburger Zentralstelle appealed to the Western countries for their assistance. The authorities, especially in the United States, gave the Zentralstelle broad access to the material held in their archives. Most of the relevant documents, however, were held by the Communist countries of Eastern Europe, and were therefore not accessible to German investigators.

In late 1964, it became clear that despite all the efforts being made, the perpetrators of the majority of Nazi acts of murder would benefit from the statute of limitations when it went into effect the following May 8. At this point, the Federal Republic of Germany requested that all foreign governments make available all evidence in their possession on Nazi war crimes. As a result, German prosecuting attorneys and Zentralestelle officials were able to examine the contents of additional archives containing hundreds of thousands of documents and **protocols** of interrogations and investigations.

In March 1965, the Bundestag legislated a postponement of the date for the statute of limitations on Nazi acts of murder to December 31, 1969. It was hoped that by then, with additional staff on the job, it would be possible to have investigated the Nazi murder charges.

The Zentralstelle staff was subsequently increased. German consular officials and local authorities in many countries gathered evidence from witnesses and victims. Despite the greatly increased efforts, it was soon obvious that it would not be possible to investigate all Nazi crimes, and initiate criminal proceedings against the suspects, by the end of 1969. The statute of limitations was then extended another ten years, to December 31, 1979.

Documentary evidence continued to accumulate in the 1970s, especially from Poland, albeit on a reduced scale. In 1978, concern about the statute of limitations was revived all over the world. Foreign countries and multinational organizations and institutions, including the European Parliament in Strasbourg, pressed for the total abolition of the statute of limitations as far as war crimes and crimes against humanity were concerned.

In early 1979, the American television series *Holocaust* was broadcast in the Federal Republic, reviving German interest, especially among young people, in the relentless prosecution of Nazi crimes. In July 1979, due to the impact of these developments, the Bundestag decided to abolish the statute of limitations for the

crime of murder in general, thus enabling Nazi killers to be brought to trial regardless of date.

From its inception in December 1958 until the summer of 1986, the Ludwigsburger Zentralstelle launched investigation of more than 5,000 cases, involving thousands of suspects. This led to a total of 4,853 official criminal trials covering the entire spectrum of Nazi violence.

Most proceedings ended without convictions, however. In many instances the participants in the crime could not be found or the evidence in hand was not enough to prove the guilt of the surviving suspects. Also of benefit to many suspects were legal principles developed by the German courts that protect individuals from being convicted of a crime on the basis of membership in a unit or organization that took part in a crime. For an individual to be convicted under those circumstances, his actual participation in the organization's criminal act had to be proven. This often proved to be an impossible task so many years after the crimes had been committed.

When it was determined that a party was guilty, but that the criminal act had occurred as a consequence of following the orders of one's superiors, the courts generally considered the accused to be an accessory to the crime and not the actual perpetrator. This finding allowed the convicted criminal to receive a prison term of limited duration rather than imposing the sentence of life imprisonment that was mandatory for murder. Considering the immense number of victims and the enormous cruelty of the murderous deeds, many—even the most unbiased of observers—believed that such leniency was uncalled for.

In the four decades following World War II, German courts in the Federal Republic tried 90,921 persons indicted for taking part in Nazi crimes; 6,479 persons were given substantial sentences, 12 being sentenced to death (as long as the death penalty was still in force) and 160 to life imprisonment. At least 1,500 additional suspects have been investigated since 1986. Since the collapse of the Soviet Union early in the 1990s, many more archives have become available to investigators in Germany and around the world, adding both to the workload and the conviction rate of those committed to establishing accountability. Prior to the reunification of Germany, officials of the German Democratic Republic (East Germany) acknowledged that while no systematic attempt was made to prosecute Nazi crimes, stiff sentences were imposed on those whose Nazi criminal actions came to public attention through other means. As of the end of 1976, roughly three decades after prosecutions began worldwide, a total of 12,861 convictions had been made in that country for "fascist war crimes and crimes against humanity."

Postwar Dispensation of Justice in Germany

In 1949, there was concern that Heinrich **HIMMLER**'s police and Nazi judges would be reinstated in the civil service. This in fact did take place. On the basis of the constitutional entitlement of former government officials to be maintained by the state (article 131 of the Constitution of the Federal Republic of Germany), nearly all the police, judges, and public prosecutors who had served under the Nazis were returned to their posts. Consequently, all attempts to convict Nazi judges of judicial murder failed. During the Hitler period, judges had obeyed Nazi laws and had been blind to the illegality of their actions; this blindness carried over into the new postwar period, and these judges were regularly acquitted of charges against them.

In 1955 the Federal Republic of Germany added to its criminal code a paragraph (220a) making a life sentence mandatory for anyone convicted of murder with the intention of destroying a national group. However, because genocide was

Due to contradictory testimonies given by different witnesses, and the diminished ability to remember events that had taken place so long before, it was often impossible to determine individual guilt, even when the crime itself was revealed down to the last detail. Furthermore, suspects whose crimes were committed in the course of following orders were often convicted of the lesser charge of accessory to the crime, thus receiving lighter punishments than they would have received as the perpetrators of the acts.

FINANCIAL REPERCUSSIONS A HALF-CENTURY LATER

In reunified Germany since the early 1990s, attention has focused on the economic crimes of the Nazis, as well as those related to mass murder. In particular, new evidence has been analyzed concerning the status of reparations to Holocaust victims for work done under slave labor conditions as well as the status of property and money confiscated by the Nazi regime. International investigators have examined the tangled trail of deposits, transfers, and outright confiscation created by the Nazis to channel the assets of European Jewry—including gold, artwork, religious artifacts, and whole libraries—into the Nazi treasury by way of Switzerland through diplomatic and banking avenues. A report released in June 1998 also traced the wartime and postwar conduct of Sweden, Spain, Portugal, Turkey, and Argentina, as well as allegations that gold of the wartime Axis government of Croatia had been transferred to the Vatican.

Reparation plans have been established, but in general terms, it has been difficult for victims to file claims and receive settlements. The U.S. Office of Special Investigations continues to work to locate, declassify, and disclose to the public classified documents pertaining to Nazi criminals and to transactions in plundered assets of Holocaust victims.

In 1997, the German Parliament voted to discontinue making disability payments to anyone linked to war crimes. At the time the legislation was enacted, there were at least 20 known criminals whose benefits were to stop immediately, and as many as 50,000 whose service records would be carefully examined for any evidence of participation in activities covered by war crimes statutes. No conviction would be required for benefits to be rescinded.

not identified specifically as a crime while the Nazis were in power, the Federal Republic did not apply this standard against Nazis found guilty of that crime. Murder, physical injury, and deprivation of liberty *were* illegal in the Third Reich. However, such criminal acts were not subject to prosecution in Nazi Germany when they were committed on official orders. After the war the courts claimed that at the time the criminal acts were committed, they had been under duress and unable to try the offenders. Doubt also remained as to whether the legal officers who had served under the Nazi regime were capable of dispensing justice.

This atmosphere of leniency did not change until the late 1950s, when a generation which had not witnessed or supported Nazi crimes, or taken part in them, began reaching adulthood and assuming positions of authority. Although most Germans still called for an end to the prosecution of Nazi crimes, a minority vehemently insisted that the crimes involving mass extermination be prosecuted.

In West German courts, the chain of command leading to the "Final Solution" was considered to have two main "links": There were the originators—Adolf Hitler,

Hermann Göring, and Reinhard **HEYDRICH**—at the top level and then there were the actual murder personnel—camp guards, camp commandants, Operational Squad members—at the lowest level. The responsibility of the intermediate level—the bureaucratic-military-industrial elites, which the Nuremberg Military Tribunals had exposed—was not recognized by the West German courts. The renewed interest in accountability during the late 1950s led to investigation of members of the lowest ranks in the chain of command, the subordinate echelons of the police and the SS who were charged with the physical destruction of the masses of victims delivered into their hands.

In general, the German courts decided that the crimes they were asked to judge did not meet the criteria of murder as required by law. If the defendants were shown to have killed, they were also generally shown to have acted as tools of the Nazi machine. At most, they were guilty of being accessories to murder, an offense punishable by terms in prison ranging from three years to life (or, as of 1975, from three to fifteen years). The accused also benefited from the fact that they were no longer considered to represent a threat to the community.

The full force of the law was applied only in the rather rare cases of excessively cruel and sadistic criminals. Inflicting more pain and physical or mental torture "than was necessary" was shown to be in violation of orders the defendants had received. Federal German criminal courts regarded such behavior as indication of murderous intent, and in these cases they could therefore pass sentences of life imprisonment.

In contrast to the Nuremberg judgments, the German population was more accepting of the German courts' dispensation of justice to Nazi criminals. The guilt of the concentration camp killers and SS firing squads was not in doubt. Yet they were given every consideration by the courts, which felt that although the accused had engaged in a mass murder operation, they were not "murderous types." In the view of the judges, the extermination personnel became the "murderous type" only if they exhibited and promoted Hitlerian racist hatred, or if they performed the killing in an excessively cruel manner.

Poland

In view of the enormous crimes committed by the Nazis in Poland, the capture and punishment of war criminals was considered an urgent priority by Polish authorities in the liberated territories. The Polish Committee of National Liberation, established in liberated **LUBLIN** on July 21, 1944, issued an order on August 31 of that year concerning the punishment of Nazi criminals and Polish traitors. This order established strict criminal responsibility for all kinds of war crimes and crimes against humanity. Special courts were established on September 12, 1944, for the trial of Nazi criminals. The proceedings were of a summary nature and there was no appeal.

On January 22, 1946, the Supreme National Court was created to deal with trials of special significance. In 1949 the special courts were abolished and subsequent trials of war crimes came before regular courts, with selected judges conducting the trials according to the general rules of procedure.

A mass of documentation accumulated in the trials of Nazi war criminals by Polish courts covered a variety of subjects, including: the almost total extermination of the Jewish population; the selective killing of other parts of the Polish population; terror actions and persecution on grounds of ethnic origin, religion, and race; the network of extermination camps, concentration camps, and labor camps; the

The conviction of Nazi criminals in West German courts in the 1950s was hindered by the time that had elapsed between the crimes and the trials. Facts were difficult to ascertain. As a rule, the courts accepted the perpetrators' own testimony of having acted in obedience to orders. Few witnesses had survived, and those who had survived often did not accurately remember particulars as dates, times of day, places, faces, and ranks. It was therefore rarely possible to achieve a finding of guilt.

A Victim, A Defendant

Many survivors of Nazi atrocities were called to testify at the various international trials. One such witness was a Dutch Jew by the name of Max Nabig, who fell victim to the experiments of Dr. Hans Eysele at Buchenwald. Nabig miraculously survived a stomach resection performed by Eysele without anesthesia. Although most who endured Eysele's experimentation were killed by lethal injection shortly after the procedures were complete, Nabig was protected by other prisoners and nurtured back to health. Nabig's testimony helped convict Eysele in his postwar trial.

And what happened to Dr. Hans Eysele after his conviction? Given the death penalty, Eysele served just five years of what had been commuted to an eight-year prison sentence. In 1952, he was released, and when he returned to his home province of Bavaria, he began practicing medicine again in Munich and was loaned the sum of 10,000 marks in "compensation" for losses incurred as a result of the war. In 1955, further evidence of his inhumane treatment of prisoners surfaced. To avoid being arrested once again, Eysele sought asylum in Egypt, where he was able to establish a comfortable medical practice.

actions designed to restrict the natural growth of the native populations of the occupied countries; the forced-labor organization that involved moving people, by force, out of the borders of their own country; the destruction and theft of art works and antiquities; the forced assimilation into the German nation of select groups of children and youngsters; the ruin of the economy of the occupied countries; the destruction and theft of private property; the destruction of **WARSAW** in 1944; and other war crimes and crimes against humanity.

SPECIAL COURTS The special courts established in September 1944 lost no time in tackling their task. The first trial of war criminals in Poland was held from November 27 to December 2, 1944, while fighting was still in full swing. The accused were staff members of the **MAJDANEK** camp who had fallen into Polish hands. The total number of Nazi war criminals tried after the war was 5,450—a tiny fraction of the total, since most of the criminals had fled with the retreating German forces. The attempts made after the war to extradite war criminals to Poland were only partially successful; the total number extradited was 1,803. In 1947 and 1948 difficulties were encountered in extraditing Nazi war criminals to Poland from the western zones of occupation in Germany, and from 1950 on, no more extraditions were granted. This meant that at least 5,600 Nazis listed as war criminals by the United Nations War Crimes Commission could not be prosecuted.

The trials before the Supreme National Court were of special importance. The first such trial (June 7 to 21, 1946) was that of Arthur Greiser, the *Gauleiter* (district leader) of the Warthegau. Next to be tried (August 27 to September 5, 1946) was Amon Goeth, who had been the commandant of the **PŁASZÓW** camp.

In the trial of Ludwig Fischer, who had been governor of the Warsaw district, and in that of Ludwig Leist, the former governor of Warsaw, and of two Higher SS and Police Leaders, Josef Meisinger and Max Daum (December 17, 1946, to late February 1947), all the accused were found guilty of crimes against the population of Warsaw and its vicinity, including the abominable treatment of the population after the suppression of the 1944 **WARSAW POLISH UPRISING**. Fischer was also convicted on the charge of setting up the Warsaw ghetto and the Treblinka extermination camp.

The trial of Rudolf **HÖSS**, the man who set up the Auschwitz-Birkenau extermination camp and was its commandant until October 1943, was held March 11 to 29, 1947. This trial reconstructed, with great precision, the teams that had established and operated Auschwitz. These were the men who were responsible for the fate of the 300,000 prisoners whose names were listed in the camp rolls and of more than one million other prisoners who were not even registered in the camp and, on their arrival in Auschwitz, were taken straight to the gas chambers.

The first Auschwitz trial was followed by the trial of Arthur **LIEBEHENSCHEL** (November 24 to December 16, 1947), who succeeded Höss as the commandant of Auschwitz, and 39 other defendants, many of whom had held responsible posts in the camp. In the trial held from April 5 to 27, 1948, the accused was Albert Forster, who had been district leader of Danzig and then of Danzig-East Prussia.

The last trial before the Supreme National Court (April 17 to June 5, 1948), was Josef Bühler, who had been deputy governor of the **GENERALGOUVERNEMENT** (that is, the deputy of Hans Frank, who was tried at the Nuremberg Trial). The Nazi criminals who were tried by the Supreme National Court were all sentenced to death and executed, with the exception of Leist and some of the Auschwitz camp staff.

The Polish courts regarded the administrative institutions of the concentration camps—the camp command, administrative officers, and personnel—as criminal organizations, under the definition of that term by the Nuremberg International Military Tribunal.

SEVEN SIGNIFICANT TRIALS IN POLAND Of the thousands of trials held before the special courts and, later, the regular courts in Poland, the most important were those of the following persons:

1. Erich Koch (1959), who had been governor of East Prussia, which had parts of northern Poland annexed to it.

2. Jürgen **STROOP** (1951), who in 1943 was in charge of suppressing the **WARSAW GHETTO UPRISING**.

3. Franz Konrad (1951), an SS officer charged with committing multiple murders in the Warsaw ghetto and assisting in the suppression of the ghetto uprising.

4. Herbert Buttcher (1949), SS and Police Leader in the Radom district, who was charged, in part, with the extermination of the Jews of Ostrowiec, Częstochowa, and Piotrków Trybunalski.

5. Hans **BIEBOW** (1947), chief of the **ŁÓDŹ** ghetto administration.

6. Jacob **SPORRENBERG** (1950), SS and Police Leader in the Lublin district, charged with, among other crimes, the mass murder of Jews, mainly in Aktion **ERNTEFEST** ("**HARVEST FESTIVAL**").

7. Paul Otto Geibel (1954), SS and Police Leader in Warsaw, charged with the role he played in the destruction of the Polish capital in 1944, among other crimes.

Also brought to trial were several dozen persons who had served on the staffs of the Auschwitz, Majdanek, and **STUTTHOF** camps.

The trials of Nazi criminals in Poland were conducted in accordance with established legal procedure, with the accused having the rights of defense. The accused were tried for acts and crimes in violation not only of state law, but also of international law, mainly the Fourth Hague Convention.

See also **BARBIE TRIAL; CRIMES AGAINST HUMANITY; OFFICE OF SPECIAL INVESTIGATIONS.**

SUGGESTED RESOURCES

Conot, Robert E. *Justice at Nuremberg.* New York: Harper & Row, 1983.

Garscha, Winfried R., and Claudia Kuretsidis-Haider. "War Crime Trials in Austria," in *Proceedings of the Conference of the German Studies Association* (1997). Reproduced at http://www.doew.at/warcrime.html#trials (accessed on September 1, 2000).

Harris, Whitney R. *Tyranny on Trial: The Evidence at Nuremberg.* New York: Barnes and Noble, 1995.

Sprecher, Drexel A. *Inside the Nuremberg Trial: A Prosecutor's Comprehensive Account.* Lanham, MD: University Press of America, 1999.

Taylor, Telford. *The Anatomy of the Nuremberg Trials: A Personal Memoir.* New York: Knopf, 1992.

Teicholz, Tom. *The Trial of Ivan the Terrible: State of Israel vs. John Demjanjuk.* New York: St. Martin's Press, 1988.

Trial of Adolf Eichmann and *Hitler and the Nuremberg Trials* [videorecording]. Columbia Tristar, 1996.

Ukraine

Jews have lived in Ukraine for a thousand years. Their population grew steadily over the centuries, despite the existence of **ANTISEMITISM** and occasional periods of violent persecution. Terrible massacres of Jews took place in the 1600s and 1700s, when tens of thousands of Jews were murdered and entire communities destroyed. During the civil war of 1918, some 100,000 Ukrainian Jews were murdered in **pogroms**. Jews were disabled for life, their property was pillaged and destroyed, and many of the towns and villages where they had lived were totally abandoned. Still, the Ukrainian Jews developed diverse and vibrant communities.

pogroms
Organized attacks against Jews and their property.

In September 1939, the western part of Ukraine was incorporated into the **SOVIET UNION**. Before long, its Jewish institutions and organizations were abolished. Thousands of Jewish leaders and activists were exiled, and the Jewish economy was completely "Sovietized." With its new borders, the Ukraine had a Jewish population of 2.4 million in early 1941.

On June 22, 1941, **GERMANY** attacked the Soviet Union. German forces advanced rapidly, and by that October Germany had conquered the entire Ukrainian republic, except for the Lugansk district. The German army was accompanied by Ukrainian nationalist military units. Important public figures in western Ukraine—including major religious leaders—welcomed the Germans as liberators, in the hope of being granted independence from the Soviet Union. The Germans were also received warmly in eastern Ukraine. Some of the Soviet **PRISONERS OF WAR** who were Ukrainians, as well as young Ukrainian civilians, volunteered for service in auxiliary units of the German army, police, and the **SS**. In late 1943, a Ukrainian SS division was formed, made up of volunteers.

OPERATIONAL SQUADS (*Einsatzgruppen*) C and D, marching in with the German army, quickly installed a regime of terror and mass murder in Ukraine. They killed hundreds of thousands of Jews, as well as tens of thousands of other citizens whom they suspected of being Communists or Soviet officials.

Ukraine.

The Ukrainian nationalists soon realized that Germany would not grant independence to Ukraine. The Germans turned the larger part of the region over to a civil administration (the *Reichskommissariat Ukraine*), and put the rest of eastern Ukraine under a military administration. The region known as Eastern Galicia was annexed as a district to the **GENERALGOUVERNEMENT**. Despite their earlier promises, the Germans did not abolish the collective farms established by the Soviets. Instead, they took huge quantities of grain, other foodstuffs, and raw materials from Ukraine. The local population was left to starve, especially in the cities. Millions of people were sent as **FORCED LABOR** to Nazi German territory.

In response, a large partisan resistance movement was formed under Communist leadership. These paramilitary **PARTISANS** operated mostly in the northern, heavily wooded part of Ukraine, where they took guerrilla action against German occupying forces.

In western Ukraine and in Bukovina, with the help of the **UKRAINIAN AUXILIARY POLICE** (*Ukrainische Hilfspolizei*), the local population staged violent pogroms in which thousands of Jews were murdered and their property pillaged and destroyed. In **LVOV**, 5,000 Jews were murdered in two of these pogroms. The operational squads also carried out mass violent "actions" (*Aktionen*), which were organized killing sprees, in such places as **LUTSK** (where they murdered 2,000 Jews), Ostrog (3,000), and **TERNOPOL** (5,000).

In much of the eastern side of the old Polish-Soviet border, the operational squads sought total liquidation of the Jews. (The exception was in **KAMENETS-PODOLSKI**.) The extermination proceeded at a rapid pace, following a regular pattern. Immediately after occupation, the German military administration issued a

series of decrees, ordering the Jews to wear distinctive badges (*see* **BADGE, JEWISH**) and to register with the authorities. The Jews were ordered to set up committees (a form of **JUDENRAT**), confined to specific streets, and put on forced labor.

After a few months, the Jews were rounded up and taken to ravines, abandoned quarries, or anti-tank ditches, where they were killed. The job of rounding up, guarding, and transporting the Jews was in the hands of German and Ukrainian police and, at times, also of rear-echelon German army units. The killing itself was carried out by the operational squads or the **SD** (*Sicherheitsdienst*; Security Service). Jews who tried to escape or who could not keep up with the rest were killed on the spot. Eight gas vans (*see* **GAS CHAMBERS/VANS**) were also used for the murders.

The Jews of Zhitomir were the first victims of the systematic murder process. By September 19, 1941, the entire Jewish population of the city, numbering 10,000, had been killed. On September 29 and 30, the Jews of Kiev were brought to the ravine of **BABI YAR** and murdered there. On October 13, some 15,000 Jews from Dnepropetrovsk were murdered. The Jews of **KHARKOV** were rounded up in December, held in the sheds of a tractor plant, and from there taken to the Drobitski Yar ravine in January 1942, where they were murdered there. In Transnistria, then under Romanian rule, some Jews escaped Operational Squad D and were able to survive, as were some of the Jews from Bessarabia and Bukovina. But the Jews of Odessa—80,000 of them—were all killed. Most of the Jews of Volhynia, Kamenets-Podolski, and Eastern Galicia were murdered during 1942 and 1943.

There were many instances of resistance (*see* **RESISTANCE, JEWISH**) during this liquidation process. Tens of thousands of Jews tried to escape. There were uprisings in ghettos and armed resistance based in fortified bunkers. Many of the young people who managed to escape established Jewish fighting units. Others joined the Soviet partisan movement and fought in the catacombs of Odessa, in the Dnepropetrovsk and Kiev areas, and in various partisan groups.

During the government-organized evacuation of Ukraine on the eve of the German occupation, 800,000 of eastern Ukraine's 1.5 million Jews (within the 1939 borders) were evacuated or escaped. In comparison, no more than 50,000 Jews from among the 900,000 living in western Ukraine and Bukovina survived. The Jews of Transcarpathian Ukraine, which during the war was under Hungarian rule, were deported to **AUSCHWITZ** in the summer of 1944. Most of them perished there.

The German defeat at Stalingrad in early 1943 marked the start of Ukraine's liberation, which was completed in late August 1944. Following the liberation, many Jews wanted to return to their homes in Ukraine, but they encountered fierce antisemitism. In Kiev, this assumed the dimensions of a pogrom. Many of the survivors therefore decided to settle elsewhere. The surviving remnants of the Jews of western Ukraine and Bukovina took advantage of their right to repatriate to **POLAND** or Romania, and soon joined the *Beriha*—the organized exodus to those countries. Many made their way to Israel between 1945 and 1948.

> The Jews were crowded into gas vans, which were hermetically sealed. Exhaust fumes were then piped into the vans, and the victims choked to death while the vans were on the road to the burial pits.

SUGGESTED RESOURCES

Fishman, Lala. *Lala's Story: A Memoir of the Holocaust.* Evanston, IL: Northwestern University Press, 1997.

Gitelman, Zvi, ed. *Bitter Legacy: Confronting the Holocaust in the USSR.* Bloomington: Indiana University Press, 1997.

Kahana, David. *Lvov Ghetto Diary.* Amherst: University of Massachusetts Press, 1990.

Sobel, Nathan, ed. *Luboml: The Memorial Book of a Vanished Shtetl.* Hoboken, NJ: Ktav, 1997.

Weiner, M. *Jewish Roots in Ukraine and Moldova: Pages from the Past and Archival Inventories.* Secaucus, NJ: Miriam Weiner Routes to Roots Foundation, 1999.

Zipperstein, Steven J. *Imagining Russian Jewry: Memory, History, Identity.* Seattle: University of Washington Press, 1999.

Ukrainian Military Police

Ukrainian Military Police units (Ukrainische Hilfspolizei) were established in the earliest days of the German invasion of the **SOVIET UNION** and the occupation of Ukrainian-inhabited areas. These units were organized, with the encouragement of the local military governors, by the Ukrainian nationalists who accompanied the German forces on their entry into **UKRAINE**.

As soon as the **SD** (Sicherheitsdienst, or Security Service) established its offices in an occupied area, it instituted a check on the political reliability of the Ukrainian militia personnel, especially the officers. On July 27, 1941, on Heinrich **HIMMLER**'s orders, the mobile Ukrainian Military Police was created, under the jurisdiction of the **SS** and German police commanders in the various subdivisions of the German civil administration. The battalions were housed in police barracks in key places, and were deployed in major police operations such as the drive against the **PARTISANS**. After the civil administration had been installed in August, 1941 in the Galicia district and, throughout September, in the other parts of the German-occupied Ukraine, the militia units were renamed the Ukrainian Auxiliary Police Constabulary (Ukrainische Hilfspolizei Schutzmannschaft), and an individual policeman was generally referred to as a *Schutzmann* (constable). The units were subordinate to the German police and gendarmerie.

The Ukrainian Military Police wore black uniforms and were equipped with captured Soviet light weapons. Collective fines were imposed upon the Jews to defray the costs of providing the police with uniforms and boots. The senior commanders of these units were Germans. In the first few days of the occupation, Ukrainian police, as an organized group and individually, participated in pogroms against the Jews, in **LVOV**, in the cities of Eastern Galicia, and in Volhynia. Later, when Ukrainian police escorted groups of Jews to places of work or were on guard duty in the ghettos, they extorted money from the Jews, harassed them, and frequently shot Jews merely for the sake of killing. When the ghettos were being liquidated, units of the Ukrainian Military Police took part in operations such as blockading the ghettos, searching for Jews who had gone into hiding, and hunting those who had escaped. They led Jews to their execution, which generally took place in a large pit, and served as the guards surrounding the murder sites, barring access to them. Known for their brutality, they killed many thousands of Jews who tried to escape or could not keep up on the way to the execution sites or.

In the spring of 1943, large numbers of Ukrainian police deserted with their weapons and joined the Ukrainian Insurgent Army (Ukrainska Povstanska Armiya). Others, especially those who served in the mobile battalions, retreated westward with the German forces, and in the final stage of the war were incorporated into the Eastbattalion or into divisions of the Ukrainian National Army.

SUGGESTED RESOURCES

Gitelman, Zvi, ed. *Bitter Legacy: Confronting the Holocaust in the USSR.* Bloomington: Indiana University Press, 1997.

Partisans of Vilna [sound recording]. Flying Fish, 1989.

Porter, Jack Nusan, ed. *Jewish Partisans: A Documentary of Jewish Resistance in the Soviet Union During World War II.* Washington, DC: University Press of America, 1982.

UNDERGROUND, JEWISH. SEE RESISTANCE, JEWISH.

UNITED KINGDOM. SEE GREAT BRITAIN.

United Partisan Organization

The United Partisan Organization (FPO; Fareynegte Partizaner Organizatsye) was a Jewish, anti-German underground organization in the **VILNA** ghetto. In July 1940, **LITHUANIA**—including Vilna—was occupied by the **SOVIET UNION**. At that time, the existing Zionist youth organizations had to go underground, continuing their activities in secret and in defiance of the Soviet forces. When the city was captured by the Germans on June 24, 1941, these organizations continued to exist. In the first few months of the German occupation, their efforts concentrated mainly on saving their members from the killing sprees that were being conducted in Vilna by Nazi **OPERATIONAL SQUADS** (*Einsatzgruppen*). The underground groups discussed where they should focus their efforts. Should they continue their underground activity in the Vilna ghetto, where most of the Jews had been murdered? Or should they move to ghettos in **BELORUSSIA** or the **GENERALGOUVERNEMENT**, where the Jews were still living in relative quiet? All the movements, except for He-Haluts ha-Tsa'ir-Dror, which was headed by Mordechai **TENENBAUM**, wanted to stay in Vilna.

Birth of a United Resistance Movement

On New Year's Eve, December 31, 1941, 150 members of the Pioneer (*Haluts*) Youth Movements in the ghetto attended a meeting. There, Abba Kovner's appeal "not to go like sheep to the slaughter" was read. Kovner announced that all the Jews who had been taken taken from Vilna were murdered at **PONARY**. He called upon the Jewish youth to organize for armed struggle against the Germans. On January 21, 1942, representatives of the Zionist **YOUTH MOVEMENTS**—among them Kovner of Ha-Shomer ha-Tsa'ir, Nissan Reznik of Ha-No'ar ha-Tsiyyoni, Josef **GLAZMAN** of Betar, and Yitzhak Wittenberg of the Communists—decided to establish a united resistance movement: the United Partisan Organization (FPO). Wittenberg was elected commander of the FPO. Kovner, Glazman, and Reznik served on his staff.

The organization's aim was to prepare for armed resistance in the face of **DEPORTATIONS** and Nazi violence toward Jews. Another goal was to spread the idea of resistance to other ghettos.

To accomplish its goals, the FPO divided itself into underground "cells," or small groups. The FPO headquarters included representatives of all the parties and youth movements that had united to join in underground activities.

Representatives were sent to the **GRODNO**, **BIAŁYSTOK**, and **WARSAW** ghettos in order to establish contact with them. They were to spread the idea of resistance and rebellion, and tell of the mass extermination of the Jews in Vilna and the rest of Lithuania. Attempts were also made to establish ties with the Polish underground

There were five people to a cell, based on their places of residence in the ghetto. Three cells made up a platoon, and six to eight platoons formed a battalion. The United Partisan Organization (FPO) had two battalions, each composed of 100 to 120 fighters.

Jewish partisans who left the Vilna ghetto and escaped to the Rudninkai Forest return to Vilna after the liberation in July 1944.

Home Army (*Armia Krajowa*) in Vilna, but these efforts failed. There was contact with a small, non-Jewish Communist group that was active in Vilna; the ghetto underground lent its support to this group. An attempt was also made to send women representatives through the front lines to the Soviet Union, to tell the world of the mass extermination of the Jews and to appeal for help. These emissaries were stopped by Germans near the front lines. They managed to escape, though, and made their way back to Vilna.

The FPO's most pressing problem was acquiring weapons. Few sources existed for the underground, although some guns could be purchased from the local population. Members of the underground working in a German captured-weapons depot were able to smuggle out some weapons and give them to the FPO. Primitive hand grenades and **Molotov cocktails** were made in the ghetto itself. The underground managed to acquire mostly pistols, plus a small number of rifles, hand grenades, and submachine guns. The weapons were kept in a cache in the ghetto. At its height, the FPO had some 300 organized members, and a weapon of some sort was available for each.

The FPO carried out acts of sabotage outside the ghetto. For example, FPO members mined the railway used by trains heading for the front lines, and they sabotaged equipment and arms in German factories where underground members were employed.

The chairman of the Vilna **JUDENRAT** (Jewish Council), Jacob **GENS**, knew of the underground's existence and maintained contact with its leaders. In the spring of 1943, the FPO smuggled more arms into the ghetto. It also contacted the **PARTISANS** who were active in the forests of western Belorussia. Several groups of young people who were not FPO members headed for the forests, and representatives of the partisans came to the ghetto. The Judenrat, warned of these activities by the German authorities, considered them dangerous to the continued existence of the ghetto. This led to friction between the Jewish Council and the FPO.

Acting on a tip, the Germans arrested the members of the Vilna Communist underground committee. They ordered Gens to hand Wittenberg over to them. Otherwise, the Vilna ghetto and its entire population would be liquidated. On July 15, 1943, Gens invited the FPO command to his house and arrested Wittenberg on the spot. As German security police were leading Wittenberg to the ghetto gate,

Molotov cocktails
A type of hand-made bomb.

On September 1, 1943, the FPO issued a call for revolt in the Vilna ghetto: "Jews, prepare for armed resistance …! Out into the streets …! Strike the murderers! In every street, in every yard, in every room, within the ghetto and outside the ghetto.… Jews, we have nothing to lose. We can save our lives only if we kill the murderers.… Long live armed resistance!"

they were attacked by FPO members, and Wittenberg was set free. The FPO then took up positions in several of the ghetto houses. On the following day, there was a confrontation between the FPO and the ghetto police. Many of the ghetto inhabitants sided with the police and demanded that Wittenberg be handed over, in order to save the ghetto from the Germans. To avoid a bloody battle among the Jews, Wittenberg gave himself up to the Germans. That same night, he committed suicide. Abba Kovner was elected to take his place as the FPO commander. For the FPO, these events served as a warning. A partisan base was subsequently established in the forest as a place of refuge for FPO members, should the need arise.

On July 24, 1943, a group of FPO men, headed by Josef **GLAZMAN**, left the ghetto for the Naroch Forest. On September 1, the Germans launched a deportation of Jews from Vilna to Estonia. This was an early step in the ghetto's total liquidation, so the FPO mobilized its members. They took up positions in one section of the ghetto and called for the Jews to rebel against deportation orders. The ghetto inhabitants did not respond to the call. They believed they really were being sent away for work elsewhere and were not destined for extermination. That evening, there was an armed clash between underground members and the German forces combing the ghetto. When darkness fell, the Germans left the ghetto and did not return to it for the duration of their operation, which lasted until September 4. Gens, the Judenrat chairman, had promised to provide the Germans with the required quota (number of Jews) to be sent to Estonia. The FPO gave up the idea of an uprising, since the ghetto inhabitants were not interested in participating. It began moving its members out, to the Naroch and Rudninkai Forests.

The Vilna ghetto was liquidated on September 23, 1943. Most of the inhabitants were sent to **CONCENTRATION CAMPS** and **EXTERMINATION CAMPS**. The last group of FPO members left the ghetto that day. Most of the 500 to 700 FPO members escaped to the forests and formed themselves into Jewish battalions as part of the Soviet partisan movement. Partisans from the Vilna ghetto fought in the forests until the Soviet army reached them. Then they took part in the liberation of Vilna, on July 13, 1944.

SEE ALSO **RESISTANCE, JEWISH.**

SUGGESTED RESOURCES

Partisans of Vilna [sound recording]. Flying Fish, 1989.

Porter, Jack Nusan, ed. *Jewish Partisans: A Documentary of Jewish Resistance in the Soviet Union During World War II.* Washington, DC: University Press of America, 1982.

United States Army and Survivors in Germany and Austria

At the end of World War II, the Allied powers were faced with seven million **DISPLACED PERSONS** (DPs) in **GERMANY** and **AUSTRIA**. In an extensive operation, the Allies succeeded in repatriating more than six million—that is, returned to the places where they had lived prior to Nazi aggression—but a million refused or were unable to return to their countries of origin. Included in this group were former citizens of the Baltic countries (**LATVIA**, **LITHUANIA**, and Estonia) that had been annexed by the **SOVIET UNION** in 1940, and Poles, Ukrainians, and Yugoslavs who resisted repatria-

tion either because of their opposition to the Communist regime or because they were afraid of being put on trial for collaborating with the Nazis. When old hostilities with the Soviet Union resurfaced and intensified, the **UNITED STATES** no longer tried to pressure the nationals of Communist countries to return to their former homes. This situation compelled the Allied forces to take care of masses of people representing 52 different nationalities who were housed in 900 DP assembly centers. The administration of these camps was to have been the responsibility of the United Nations Relief and Rehabilitation Administration (UNRRA), but for a variety of reasons—lack of trained personnel, absence of a clear policy, poor planning and management—the international agency was unable to fulfill its role properly. The private relief organizations that were gradually permitted to operate in the camps could provide only partial aid at best. Consequently, the U.S. Army, despite a shrinking budget and inexperienced personnel, assumed the major responsibility for the DPs.

The Jewish population in the American zone in Germany and Austria grew from 30,000 in 1945 to 250,000 in the summer of 1947, as Jews from eastern Europe moved in. Most of these Jews had no homes and no families to return to. The only solution for them was emigration, but the gates of all the countries in the world, including the United States and Palestine, were closed to them. As time went on, the number of Jewish DPs increased just as the military budget was being reduced. Opposition to the Jews became stronger, even among the senior American officers. Compounding the frustration for all concerned, the American policy of transferring authority over DPs to the Germans, both on a local and on a national level, conflicted with the DPs' refusal to accept and submit to German authority.

In June 1945, President Harry S. Truman sent Earl G. Harrison, dean of the law faculty at the University of Pennsylvania, on a mission to Europe to investigate the DPs' situation. Harrison recommended establishing separate camps for Jews and improving their treatment in terms of food, housing, and clothing. The sympathetic attitude of the American people toward survivors of **CONCENTRATION CAMPS**, together with Harrison's report, led to a decisive change for the better in the conditions of the **HOLOCAUST** survivors. Gen. Dwight D. Eisenhower, the commander in chief of the American forces in Europe, appointed to his staff an adviser on Jewish affairs, who made sure that problems affecting the Jews were dealt with speedily and efficiently at the highest level.

On two occasions in 1946 the administration in Washington decided to close the borders between the American zones and the east, but after Jewish lobbying in Washington they were soon reopened. In the final analysis, the infiltration of great numbers of Jews into the American zones in Germany and Austria would not have been possible without the humanitarian approach of American army personnel, who more often than not closed their eyes to the immigration.

With the establishment of the state of Israel in May 1948 and the passage of a DP bill by Congress in June of that year (the Wiley-Revercomb Displaced Persons' bill, which provided for the admission of 100,000 DPs to the United States in 1949 and 1950), the DP problem underwent a drastic transformation. Large-scale emigration to Israel and the United States now emptied the camps, diminished the black-market operations, and improved the army's attitude toward the remaining DPs.

Views differ concerning the overall relations between the American army and the Jewish DPs. All in all, despite occasional friction, especially between the DPs and American soldiers of lower echelons, the American army deserves credit for its massive help to the Jewish DPs.

SEE ALSO **DISPLACED PERSONS; RESCUE OF CHILDREN; UNITED STATES OF AMERICA.**

Addressing the diverse needs of the DPs was difficult. The American army's policy of evenhandedness toward all the DPs, instituted to avoid charges of discrimination, had an adverse effect on the Jewish DPs, who were housed in the same camps with DPs from Poland, Ukraine, and the Baltic countries who continued to display antisemitic behavior and attitudes toward the Jews.

SUGGESTED RESOURCES

Abzug, Robert H. *Inside the Vicious Heart: Americans and the Liberation of Nazi Concentration Camps.* New York: Oxford University Press, 1985.

Hyett, Barbara Helfgott. *In Evidence: Poems of the Liberation of Nazi Concentration Camps.* Pittsburgh: University of Pittsburgh Press, 1986.

Parshall, Gerald. "Freeing the Survivors." *U.S. News and World Report,* April 3, 1995.

Survivors of the Holocaust [videorecording]. Turner Home Entertainment, 1996.

Tito, E. Tina. *Liberation: Teens in the Concentration Camps and the Teen Soldiers Who Liberated Them.* New York: Rosen Pub. Group, 1999.

United States Department of State

The **UNITED STATES** Department of State was the North American governmental body most directly responsible for dealing with the fate of European Jewry during the years preceding World War II and, to a certain extent, during the **HOLOCAUST** years, through its powers to grant visas, formulate refugee policy, and deal with foreign governments and international agencies. It has come under criticism for its lack of response to the widespread massacre of Jews throughout Europe.

The State Department's career officers were traditionally part of an upper-class elite and were insensitive, and often antagonistic, to non–"Anglo-Saxon" immigrants. This helped shape their response to the events of the Holocaust, at a time when much of the department's policy formulation was in their hands.

After Adolf **HITLER** came to power in 1933 and the plight of Jews in **GERMANY** grew increasingly difficult, the already stringent United States visa regulations were often amended by American consuls, which decreased the likelihood that German Jews would obtain United States entry visas. In this, and in its opposition to increasing the number of refugees permitted to enter the United States, the State Department reflected the prevailing public view on immigration.

The State Department's attitude toward the plight of the refugees hardened when, in January 1940, Breckinridge Long, a political associate of President Franklin D. Roosevelt, was appointed assistant secretary of state. His power included authority over the Visa Division and responsibility for formulating U.S. refugee policy. Fearful of spies and saboteurs infiltrating the refugees, and hoping to keep the United States from being inundated by ethnic and political elements then perceived as undesirable, Long instituted policies that created even more obstacles for potential refugees from Europe.

In the summer of 1942, the State Department attempted to prevent news of the Holocaust, transmitted through its channels, from reaching American Jewish leadership (*see* **RIEGNER CABLE**). In February 1943, the State Department gave specific instructions to its representative in Switzerland not to transmit such information. When President Roosevelt agreed to the Jewish leadership's request to allow the transfer of funds to the Jews of Romania, the State Department delayed the transaction. Throughout the war it opposed any serious rescue or relief efforts for the Jews of Europe.

The apparent apathy of State Department officers toward the fate of the European Jews led top officials of the Treasury Department to accuse them, in a report to the president, of deliberate acquiescence in the murder of the Jews of Europe.

This report was the major factor in Roosevelt's action, in January 1944, to create the **War Refugee Board**, which subsequently made the main decisions regarding United States–initiated relief and rescue attempts.

SUGGESTED RESOURCES

America and the Holocaust: Deceit and Indifference [videorecording]. PBS Video, 1994.

Newton, Verne W., ed. *FDR and the Holocaust.* New York: St. Martin's Press, 1996.

Wyman, David S. *The Abandonment of the Jews: America and the Holocaust, 1941–1945.* New York: Pantheon Books, 1984.

Wyman, David S., ed. *Showdown in Washington: State, Treasury, and Congress.* New York: Garland, 1990.

United States Holocaust Memorial Museum. See

Museums and Memorial Institutes.

United States of America

The U.S. government's response to the anti-Jewish National Socialist regime in **Germany** is best viewed within the context of three factors that include (1) America's foreign policy of isolationism during the 1920s and 1930s; (2) the domestic impact of the Great Depression on the economy of the United States; and (3) deep-seated attitudes of **racism** and **antisemitism** at all levels of American society.

The Roots of U.S. Response to Nazism in Europe

Initially, the relationship of the United States to Germany reflected the U.S. policy of **isolationism**. In practice, this meant refusing to become involved in international conflicts where U.S. interests were not directly threatened, and protecting economic relationships that were beneficial to the United States. Public disillusionment with America's entry into World War I was a major reason for this policy. The Franklin D. Roosevelt administration's ability to intervene as the National Socialists (Nazis) rose to power was limited by strong isolationist sentiment among the American people. Isolationist legislation, such as the Hoover-Stimson Doctrine (1931), the Ludlow Amendment (1934–36), and the Neutrality Laws of 1936, 1937, and 1939, undoubtedly signaled to the aggressors in **Berlin** and Tokyo that, despite being a major world power, the United States would not likely intervene in their plans to expand their empires through invasion and brute force.

On the economic front, Americans were focused on their own needs during the years immediately following World War I, and were generally uninterested in assuming a role in the rebuilding of Europe after the war. When spending and financial speculation spiraled out of control by the end of the 1920s, the United States—and indeed all of its trading partners—were plunged into the economic crisis known as the Great Depression. During the next decade, as the refugee phase of the crisis in Europe began to reach its peak (1933–41), there was great reluctance to increase immigration to the United States, where joblessness was rampant and communities were already having difficulty providing for those most severely affected by the Depression.

isolationism
A policy of national isolation reflected in a country's choice not to enter into political and economic alliances with other countries.

Those who opposed a rescue policy for European Jews argued that the stream of refugees in the United States would increase unemployment.

More difficult to appraise is the role of antisemitism in the response of the United States to the crisis of European Jews. Whereas in Berlin the "Jewish question" was ideologically tied to all public policy, antisemitism was not officially part of public policy or government action in the United States. Overt antisemitic behavior in the United States was not sanctioned by the government, even if there were also no laws against it. Jews were leaders in business and government, particularly in the major northeastern population centers, and the Jewish community was considered to have close ties to the Roosevelt administration.

This, in fact, led to some of the conflict for President Roosevelt, especially in the foreign-policy area, where Jewish leaders had taken a strong interventionist position regarding world affairs and the responsibility of the United States to intervene on behalf of European Jews. As a result, they earned the staunch opposition of isolationist spokesmen like Charles Lindbergh, who, in a speech in Des Moines in September 1941, warned the nation that Anglophiles and Jews were trying to bring the United States into the war. More outspoken antisemites, such as National socialist Fritz Kuhn and American clergymen Charles E. Coughlin and Gerald L. K. Smith, and had long before forged a negative link between the movement to "stop Hitler" and the Jews, who were accused of placing Jewish interests before those of the United States as a whole.

During the 1930s, antisemitic sentiment stemmed primarily from the conservative right wing of the political spectrum. The political culture of American Jewry placed it at the opposite end of that spectrum, on the liberal left. Jews supported the resurgence of organized labor and the organization of the Congress of Industrial Organizations (CIO). Jews were the nation's staunchest supporters of the welfare-state program, which dovetailed with their own social democratic priorities. Consequently, some of the conservative critics of Roosevelt's "New Deal" programs complained about the increasing number of Jews in high positions in the administration, and began calling the New Deal the "Jew Deal." Roosevelt's administration was reluctant to fuel that sentiment. There was also a need to work productively across the political spectrum to solve America's social and economic problems; further alienating conservative congressmen by embracing "the Jewish agenda" would have been counterproductive.

Early Response

As the crisis in Europe unfolded, there was some response from the United States. In 1937 a "special care" instruction was issued to American consulates, alerting them to the need for special attention to this issue. Hugh R. Wilson, the U.S. ambassador to Germany, was "recalled for consultation" after the **KRISTALLNACHT** violence in November 1938. After the Anschluss (annexation of **AUSTRIA**) in March of that year, the German and Austrian U.S. immigration quotas were unified in order not to lose the opportunity to accept refugees from Austria. And in 1939, after the international **EVIAN CONFERENCE**, the United States agreed to fully utilize existing immigrant quotas for the first time. But a bill in Congress to admit 10,000 Jewish refugee children outside the quota (the Wagner-Rogers Bill), introduced in 1939 and again in 1940, did not emerge from committee. Throughout World War II, the "Jewish question" maintained the low priority it had had before the war.

The "great debate" over isolationism in American foreign policy was resolved by the Japanese attack on Pearl Harbor, but that hardly stilled the strident antisemitism that persisted in sectors of the American populace. Anti-refugee and anti-rescue sentiment was now reinforced by fears that Germany would infiltrate spies into the refugee stream. Roosevelt's awareness of these popular passions convinced him that the war must never be allowed to be depicted in terms of a war to save the Jews.

Indifference to the refugees extended to the question of rescuing those in camps. Even when it became clear that the Germans had actually embarked on the **"FINAL SOLUTION,"** the State Department tried for a time to suppress confirmation of the news, which had been transmitted from Leland Harrison, its own consul in Bern, Switzerland. Instead, a fruitless search was undertaken for areas where masses of Jews might be resettled. Jews were not willing to pioneer outside Palestine, and the administration had "frozen" the Palestine problem, which was considered a British affair, until after the war. Efforts to rescue Jews by means of refugee ships failed; in one example, the **ST. LOUIS**, destined in 1939 for Cuba with a cargo of hapless refugees, was rejected by Cuba and compelled to return to Europe, where death awaited many of the passengers. Only the Dominican Republic Settlement Association, a small-scale venture whose genesis can be traced to the Evian Conference, succeeded in providing a safe haven for Jewish refugees.

Most of the steps taken by the Roosevelt administration were intended more as gestures than as a consistent policy to ameliorate the plight of the victims. The Evian Conference, called at Roosevelt's behest in mid-1938 to bring order into the chaotic refugee situation, was doomed to fail. The American delegation was instructed beforehand that U.S. immigration laws could not be changed. With the United States unable to contribute any genuine solutions for the problem, nations such as Britain and **FRANCE** could hardly be expected to take the lead. Similarly, the concept of resettling Jews, on which so much was staked, turned into an appalling failure. Receiving nations wanted to rid themselves of Jews rather than offer haven to them.

Allied Responses, 1942–45

Between 1942 and the end of the war in Europe in 1945, the Allies gave no priority in their war aims to the rescue of Jews. They rejected repeated suggestions for retribution, negotiations, or ameliorating the situation, such as sending food packages to camps or changing the designation of their inmates to that of **PRISONERS OF WAR**, contending that such steps would interfere with the prosecution of the war. The systematic murder of the Jews was not mentioned at any of the Allied war conferences held at Tehran, Casablanca, and Yalta. As news continued to reach the West and the public at large between May and December 1942, the British government was under great pressure to do something to help the Jews. When told of the British desire to make some sort of gesture, the U.S. State Department opted to issue a declaration rather than take concrete action. A statement drafted by the British Foreign Office and edited by the U.S. State Department was issued on December 17, 1942, in the names of **BELGIUM**, Czechoslovakia, Greece, Luxembourg, **THE NETHERLANDS**, Norway, **POLAND**, the **SOVIET UNION**, **GREAT BRITAIN**, the United States, and the French National Committee. Clearly condemning the "bestial policy of cold-blooded extermination," the declaration noted that hundreds of thousands had been killed. In the British Parliament, Anthony Eden prefaced his reading of the declaration by saying that it was about the sad fate of the Jews. The declaration, however, did not appease all those who clamored for aid to the Jews.

Details of the fate of the Jews filtered out of Nazi-occupied Europe after October 1942. In London and Washington, government officials responded by convening a second refugee conference, in Bermuda, in April 1943. It soon became apparent that the purpose of this conference was to assuage public opinion without taking concrete rescue steps. Most recommendations for rescue were rejected. Negotiating with Berlin for the release of the Jews and a halt to the slaughter was also rejected. The delegates did make some tentative plans to establish a refugee camp in North Africa. However, so little was accomplished at the conference, it was decided not to

"Alone they faced mighty legions, the mightiest in Europe then. Alone. That is the key word, the haunting theme."

Elie Wiesel, on the situation of European Jews when it became clear that virtually no country in the world would open its doors to Jewish refugees.

publicize the results. Rescue advocates dubbed the conference a "cruel mockery." It was held at the same historical moment as the **WARSAW GHETTO UPRISING**, so that the connection between the martyrdom of the Jews and the indifference of the Allies was startlingly apparent.

By the fall of 1943, rescue advocates were pushing hard for the creation of a government agency specifically focused on the rescue of European Jewry. Congressional hearings were held in November 1943; it looked as if a rescue resolution would be formulated and announced sometime early in 1944.

Firm action on the rescue question finally came from the Treasury Department, however, which was headed by Henry **MORGENTHAU**, Jr., a Jewish American who had direct access to Roosevelt. An official in the Treasury Department had conclusive evidence that the State Department had tried to suppress news of the implementation of the "Final Solution" and had otherwise sought to undermine all rescue efforts. A secret report containing this information was delivered by Morgenthau to the president on January 16, 1944, along with a plan to create an interdepartmental rescue agency. Whether out of a desire to claim credit for taking action before Congress could act, or to avoid the embarrassment of letting it be known that the United States had deliberately suppressed news about the killing of European Jews—or both—Roosevelt created the **WAR REFUGEE BOARD** (WRB). Headed by Treasury official John Pehle, the WRB was to be staffed with personnel from Jewish agencies knowledgeable on rescue matters. Financing was to be provided by the American Jewish **JOINT DISTRIBUTION COMMITTEE**.

The War Refugee Board

Almost immediately, the WRB had to deal with a crisis in **HUNGARY**. Berlin was anxious to get rid of the Jews of Hungary before the demise of Germany itself. The WRB made a broadcast to the Hungarian people, urging them not to cooperate with the scheduled **DEPORTATIONS**. Appeals were sent to all nations that still had diplomatic contact with Hungary to increase the size of their diplomatic staff in Hungary so that the deportations could be monitored. Money was provided to underground Zionist youth groups to enable them to open up escape routes through Yugoslavia, **SLOVAKIA**, and Romania. A special executive order issued by Roosevelt in April 1944 ordered that a temporary haven for rescue be established by the Army Relocation Authority in Fort Ontario, near Oswego, New York. This effectively, though temporarily, circumvented immigration laws, which had been a major rescue roadblock. Various neutral countries, especially in Latin America, were pressured to accept refugees. Switzerland was also asked to help Hungarian Jews, as was the International Red Cross.

Yet despite the increase in activity by the Roosevelt administration, the rescue of the surviving Jews proved to be very difficult. The Allies still lacked control of the physical scene of the deportations. Bombing the camps and the railways leading to them, which had been suggested by rescue advocates as early as the spring of 1943, might have served as a substitute for such on-the-ground control. But in both Britain and the United States the military high command rejected the bombing idea as needlessly interfering with the major "win-the-war" priority, and it was viewed as being of "doubtful efficacy." The creation of the WRB came too late and was too weakly implemented to save the surviving Jews of Europe.

SEE ALSO **AMERICAN JEWRY AND THE HOLOCAUST; AMERICAN PRESS AND THE HOLOCAUST; RESCUE OF CHILDREN.**

M ost of the steps taken by the Allies concerning the rescue of European Jews were gestures rather than meaningful action on behalf of the victims. Not until hundreds of thousands of Jews had been murdered by the Nazis did the governments of the United States and Great Britain begin to pursue significant rescue policies.

SUGGESTED RESOURCES

Abzug, Robert H. *Inside the Vicious Heart: Americans and the Liberation of Nazi Concentration Camps.* New York: Oxford University Press, 1985.

America and the Holocaust: Deceit and Indifference [videorecording]. PBS Video, 1994.

Newton, Verne W., ed. *FDR and the Holocaust.* New York: St. Martin's Press, 1996.

Novick, Peter. *The Holocaust in American Life.* Boston: Houghton Mifflin, 1999.

Wyman, David S. *The Abandonment of the Jews: America and the Holocaust, 1941–1945.* New York: Pantheon Books, 1984.

USSR. See Soviet Union.

Vallat, Xavier

(1891–1972)

Xavier Vallat was the French coordinator of the Vichy government's anti-Jewish program in 1941 and 1942 (*see* **France**). Vallat's political career and perspective on society was militantly nationalist, Catholic, and authoritarian. Vallat fought and was badly wounded in 1918, during World War I. By 1940 he was a member of the parliament.

In March 1941, Marshal Philippe Pétain appointed Vallat head of the Office for Jewish Affairs, which was charged with administering anti-Jewish policy and legislation in France. Committed to the elimination of Jews from French public life and to reducing their role in French society, Vallat stood for what he called *antisémitisme d'état.* This meant that French antisemitic policy was to serve the interests of the state, and not to follow the dictates of the Nazis. Vallat operated in a highly legalistic manner, although in rare instances he made exceptions, permitting distinguished French-born Jews to remain in French public life. Anti-German as well as anti-Jewish, he resisted following an antisemitic policy that would materially aid the Reich. The Germans forced him out of office in May 1942, when their plans called for the **DEPORTATION** and killing of the Jews. In 1947 Vallat was sentenced to ten years in prison but was released two years later.

SUGGESTED RESOURCES

Josephs, Jeremy. *Swastika Over Paris.* New York: Arcade, 1989.

Weisberg, Richard H. *Vichy Law and the Holocaust in France.* New York: New York University Press, 1996.

VATICAN. See Christian Churches.

VERNICHTUNGSLAGER. See Extermination Camps.

VICTIMS, NON-JEWISH. See Gypsies; Homosexuality in the Third Reich.

Vienna

The Jews of Vienna tried desperately to escape from the nonstop regime of terror that prevailed in their city. At the end of May 1938, 2,000 Jews belonging to the intelligentsia were arrested and sent to the Dachau camp in four transports. The dark streets of a blackout exercise in September 1938 were used for concerted attacks on Jews; so many were injured that the Jewish hospital courtyards could not hold them all.

Until 1918, Vienna was the capital of the Habsburg Empire. A Jewish community was first established there in the twelfth century. In the nineteenth and twentieth centuries, Vienna was a center of Jewish learning and Hebrew literature. A variety of Jewish welfare institutions and sports organizations were founded there, and Jewish newspapers, including a daily, were published. Vienna was also the center of the Zionist movement at its inception and the seat of the Zionist Executive. A significant number of Austrian Jews were leaders of the Social Democratic party.

In 1923, Vienna's Jewish population reached 201,513, the third largest in European cities. By 1936 it had decreased to 176,034, 9.4 percent of the population, likely in response to increasing anti-Jewish activity in **AUSTRIA**. **GERMANY**'s annexation of Austria in March 1938 was enthusiastically welcomed by most of the Viennese, and the ensuing persecution of the Jews, in which a substantial part of the population participated, was even more brutal than in Germany.

Right after the German takeover, Jewish community and Zionist organization offices were closed and their board members were arrested and sent to the **DACHAU** concentration camp. Jewish public life, however, did not come to a complete standstill. Financial assistance to the needy continued on the basis of an improvised list of the needy. The list of financial contributors, however, was found, and in retribution the Nazis imposed a fine of 500,000 reichsmarks on the Jewish community of Austria. This was the first such fine imposed on a Jewish community by the Nazis.

On May 2, 1938, the community offices were reopened; emigration and social welfare were now their major concerns. Adolf **EICHMANN** had been sent to Vienna to enforce the emigration of Austria's Jews by threats of arrest, through the **CENTRAL OFFICE FOR JEWISH EMIGRATION** (Zentralstelle für Jüdische Auswanderung). Many Jews who wanted to emigrate, however, had neither a destination available nor the funds needed to leave. A special tax was levied on prospective emigrants by the Nazis; the Jewish community depended on donations from the American Jewish **JOINT DISTRIBUTION COMMITTEE** to cover all the costs associated with emigration.

In June 1938 the Jewish community leaders inaugurated vocational training and retraining courses to equip the Jews with professional skills pending their emigration. In the course of a single year, 24,025 men and women attended 1,601 courses. As late as May 1940, 1,151 courses were still in operation. These also played an important social role, by giving people something to do. Job skills training helped people learn to repair and renew clothing, shoes, furniture, and even medical instruments. Some courses trained nurses and social workers. By the time the courses were suspended, on February 3, 1941, 45,336 students had participated in the program. Language courses were kept up until July 1941.

Under pressure of international public opinion to find a solution to the refugee problem and to aid in the emigration of Jews from Germany and Austria, a conference on refugee problems was convened at Evian-les-Bains (*see* **EVIAN CONFERENCE**) on July 6, 1938, at which 31 nations were represented. The aim of the meetings was to secure aid for persecuted Jews and identify opportunities for emigration. While the conference did not secure even a fraction of the emigration options needed, the Jews of Austria were in line to receive a goodly share of the meager number of emigration slots open for 1938. There were internal conflicts within the Jewish community about who should receive certificates to emigrate to Palestine; this was caused primarily by the pitifully small number of immigration certificates made available by the British.

Jewish citizens of Vienna were forced to scrub away election slogans from the streets of Vienna following the Anschluss in 1938.

Increasing Persecution

The practice of attacking Jews on Jewish holidays was introduced in Vienna. On October 4, 1938, the eve of the Day of Atonement, the **NAZI PARTY** in Vienna decided to drive the Jews out of the city, with excited mobs demonstrating in the streets to express their support—a kind of grand rehearsal for the November 1938 pogrom. That evening, Nazi party members wearing plain clothes began taking Jews out of their apartments in well-to-do parts of the city, sealing the apartments, and leaving the Jews homeless, taunting them with the hope that boats would take them to Palestine. On October 6 the operation was extended to include the outskirts of Vienna. It became routine practice to close off streets in Jewish neighborhoods in the middle of the day and arrest the Jews. On *Kristallnacht*, 49 synagogues, as well as prayer houses and private sanctuaries, were destroyed in Vienna, and 3,600 Jews were deported to Dachau and **BUCHENWALD**, to be released only when their relatives were able to produce documentary proof that they were going to emigrate. The Nazi party membership in Vienna, led by Odilo **GLOBOCNIK**, played a significant part in the pogrom. In 1939 the expulsion of Jews from their apartments was accelerated, a result of a Nazi policy aimed at concentrating the Jews in "Jewish" quarters. In the period from March to September 1939, 13,600 Jewish families were forced to vacate their apartments, and in the first half of that year, 9,500 formerly Jewish-owned apartments were turned over to "Aryan" owners.

After the occupation of **POLAND**, the emphasis in the policy on Jews switched from emigration to deportation. Even young people with emigration papers in their possession were not released. In September 1939 the Jewish community was ordered to draw up an alphabetical list of all the Jews in the city. Two transports with a total of 1,584 Jewish professionals left Vienna for Nisko, on the San River, on October 20 and 26, 1939 (*see* **NISKO AND LUBLIN PLAN**). Of them, no more than 198 persons were assigned to the job of setting up a barracks camp, while the rest were forced across the river into Soviet territory, with gunfire at their backs. These activities suggest that Nazi anti-Jewish policy was in transition.

A primary advocate for Jewish young people was himself a young man. Aron Menczer had refused to join his parents and five brothers, all active Zionists, on their way to Palestine, choosing to stay behind and serve the children of Vienna as a surrogate parent and an educator. On Jewish holidays Menczer arranged for youth services to be held, and on Passover he organized the children's own Seder service.

The Nazis were disappointed to discover that only 976 Jewish apartments were vacated in 1942, despite the large number of Jews who had been deported (32,721) or moved from their apartments to the "Jewish" quarters of the city. This ratio illustrates what cramped conditions the Jews must have been living in—up to six families in a small three-room apartment—and how destitute they had become by that time.

Life Goes On

The deportation program was halted while the Germans prepared for the offensive in western Europe. It was reinstated in February 1941, and within three weeks more than 5,000 Viennese Jews, in five transports, left for the **KIELCE** region of Poland. Once again the program came to a halt, this time because of the preparations for the invasion of the **SOVIET UNION**.

The interludes between pogroms and **DEPORTATIONS** and between one wave of deportations and the next were used by the Jews of Vienna to try and find ways of emigrating from the country and, as best they could, to bring some order into their lives. Zionist youth operations were at their height in July 1939, when 779 Zionist pioneers and teenagers were undergoing training in sixteen agricultural training camps and workshops and in three tree nurseries (*see* **YOUTH MOVEMENTS**). Of the 2,340 abandoned children left in Vienna in early 1940, only 338 were in the care of community institutions; 1,839 children, ranging in age from ten to eighteen, were being cared for by families and other young people.

Religious life, which had been conducted as usual—albeit on a more modest scale—up to the November 1938 pogrom, was subsequently continued in secret, with people gathering in small groups for services in private apartments. Requests by the community to permit services to be held in parts of the synagogues that had been left standing were turned down. In January 1939, visits by clergy to Jewish prisoners was no longer permitted.

On February 5, 1941, the Zionist youth organizations were ordered closed. The two major agricultural training camps were turned into labor camps, in which all the youth instructors were concentrated. As of May 12, 1941, Jewish education programs were officially terminated and it was announced that young people interned in Dachau and Buchenwald would no longer be released for emigration, even with proof of emigration certificates.

Last Stage of Deportations

On July 31, 1941, Vienna still had 43,811 Jews "by religion" living in the city, as well as 8,728 persons defined as Jews by race under the **NUREMBERG LAWS** (two-thirds of the latter figure were converts from Judaism). Further emigration of Jews between the ages of 18 and 45 was prohibited on August 5, 1941, and the final, systematic deportation of the Jews of Vienna was launched on October 15 of that year. By October 5, 1942, 5,000 Jews had been deported to **ŁÓDŹ**, 5,200 to **RIGA**, 6,000 to Izbica, and 10,476 to **MINSK**.

In the period from June 20 to October 9, 1942, 13,776 Viennese Jews were deported to **THERESIENSTADT**. One of the transports, which left Vienna on September 23, was made up of prominent, so-called "privileged" Jews, including Jewish community leaders and Zionist youth instructors, headed by Aron Menczer.

On November 1, 1942, the Jewish community organization was disbanded and changed to the Council of Elders of the Jews of Vienna (Ältestenrat der Juden in Wien). The remaining assets of the community, amounting to 6.5 million reichsmarks, were transferred to Prague, ostensibly to be used for the financing of the Theresienstadt ghetto. The Central Office for Jewish Emigration was closed on March 31, 1943, and the responsibility for the deportations was transferred from one branch of the **SS** to another.

As of December 31, 1944, 5,799 Austrian Jews still lived in Vienna. Of this number 3,388 were partners in so-called privileged mixed marriages (*privilegierte*

Mischlingen), and 1,358, in regular mixed marriages. At the time of the liberation of Vienna, some 150 Jews remained in hiding, and a similar number survived who worked in the warehouses where confiscated Jewish possessions were stored, or as laborers in SS households. Also among the survivors were 35 Jewish community employees and 84 disabled war veterans, some of whom owed their lives to their Christian wives. A day before the liberation of Vienna by the Soviet army, on April 12, 1945, nine Jews who had been in hiding were shot to death by SS men about to make their escape from the city.

SUGGESTED RESOURCES

Bukey, Evan Burr. *Hitler's Austria: Popular Sentiment in the Nazi Era, 1938–1945.* Chapel Hill: University of North Carolina Press, 2000.

Clare, George. *Last Waltz in Vienna: The Rise and Destruction of a Family, 1842–1942.* New York: Holt, Rinehart, and Winston, 1982.

Kristallnacht: The Journey from 1938 to 1988 [videorecording]. PBS Video, 1988.

Newman, Richard. *Alma Rosé: Vienna to Auschwitz.* Portland, OR: Amadeus Press, 2000.

Vilna

Vilna, known in Lithuanian as Vilnius and in Polish as Wilno, was the capital of the Lithuanian SSR. From 1920 to 1939 Vilna was under Polish rule, and on the eve of World War II its population was about 200,000.

Jews lived in Vilna from the first half of the sixteenth century, and it became a center of Torah learning. In the nineteenth century Vilna was a hub of Jewish culture. With flourishing Jewish newspapers, publishing firms, and printing presses, Vilna was known as "the Jerusalem of **LITHUANIA**." By the end of that century the city was also a focus of Jewish political life. In the interwar period, under Polish rule, the economic situation of the Jews deteriorated and they also suffered from **ANTISEMITISM**. At the outbreak of World War II, Vilna's Jewish population was more than 55,000.

On September 19, 1939, the Red Army entered Vilna, but a few weeks later the city was handed over to the Lithuanians. Vilna's Jews welcomed both the Soviet rule and the subsequent Lithuanian regime, since this meant the city would not come under German occupation. Some 12,000 to 15,000 Jewish refugees from German-occupied **POLAND** made their way there. In July 1940, Lithuania (and with it Vilna) was incorporated into the **SOVIET UNION** and became a Soviet republic.

The Soviet regime outlawed the activities of Jewish organizations and political parties, and took over the Jewish schools and cultural institutions. Jewish studies—the Hebrew language as well as Jewish religion and history—were prohibited. Nationalization measures by the Soviets were a severe blow to the livelihood of the Jews; the refugees, in particular, made efforts to emigrate to the West. In the period from September 1939 to the German invasion of the Soviet Union, 6,500 Jewish refugees left Vilna for Palestine, the **UNITED STATES**, China, Japan, and other places. Some of them were granted Soviet transit visas. On June 24, 1941, two days after invading the Soviet Union, the Germans occupied Vilna. Three thousand Jews were able to flee into the Soviet interior before the Germans took the city, at which time the Jewish population stood at 57,000.

VILNA GHETTO DIARY

This is from a diary kept between June 1941 and April 1943 in the Vilna Ghetto. The writer went into hiding with his family early in April 1943; they were found nearly six months later and most family members, including Yitskhok, were killed. The diary was later found by a cousin, covered with dirt and mud, in the hiding place they had shared.

Wednesday the 10th of December [1941]. It dawned on me that today is my birthday. Today I became 15 years old. You hardly realize how time flies. It, the time, runs ahead unnoticed and presently we realize, as I did today, for example, and discover that days and months go by, that the ghetto is not a painful squirming moment of a dream which constantly disappears, but is a large swamp in which we lose our days and weeks. Today I became deeply absorbed in the thought. I decided not to trifle my time away in the ghetto on nothing and I feel somehow happy that I can study, read, develop myself, and see that time does not stand still as long as I progress normally with it. In my daily ghetto life it seems to me that I live normally but often I have deep qualms. Surely I could have lived better. Must I day in day out see the walled-up ghetto gate, must I in my best years see only the one little street, the few stuffy courtyards?

Still other thoughts buzzed around in my head but I felt two things most strongly: a regret, a sort of gnawing. I wish to shout to time to linger, not to run. I wish to recapture my past year and keep it for later, for the new life. My second feeling today is that of strength and hope. I do not feel the slightest despair. Today I became 15 years of age and I live confident in the future. I am not conflicted about it, and see before me sun and sun and sun....

—YITSKHOK RUDASHEVSKI

Children in the Holocaust and World War II: Their Secret Diaries, *Laurel Holliday, ed. (New York: Pocket Books/Simon & Schuster) 1995, pp. 172–73.*

German Occupation

A few days later, the German military authorities and the Lithuanian administration issued a series of anti-Jewish decrees. Jews were ordered to wear the yellow badge (*see* **BADGE, JEWISH**); they were not allowed to use the sidewalks or walk on certain streets. A night curfew was imposed. They could make their purchases only at certain times and in certain stores. On July 4 the Germans ordered the establishment of a **JUDENRAT** (Jewish Council). In July, Einsatzkommando 9, assisted by *ypatingi buriai* ("the special ones"; Lithuanian volunteers who collaborated with the Germans), rounded up 5,000 Jewish men from the streets and houses and took them to **PONARY**, 7.5 miles (12 km) from Vilna, to murder them. The Jews in Vilna knew nothing of the fate of these men; there were only rumors that they were working somewhere in the east. Between the end of July and early August, Lithuania was transferred from German military rule to German civil administration. District commissioner Hans Christian Hingst was appointed governor of Vilna. On August

A scene from David Pinski's "The Eternal Jew," produced in the Vilna ghetto, June 1943.

6, as its first step, the new administration imposed a levy of 5 million rubles (500,000 Reichsmarks) on the Jews.

Between August 31 and September 3, 1941, 8,000 more Jews were taken to Ponary and murdered, among them most of the members of the Judenrat. This episode became known among the Jews as "the great provocation," since it was preceded by the Germans' staging an attack on German soldiers, blaming the violence on the Jews, and presenting the killing spree that followed as a retaliatory move. In the following days, from September 3 to 5, the area from which the Jews had been evacuated was fenced in and two ghettos were established, Ghetto No. 1 and Ghetto No. 2, separated from each other by German (Deutsche) Street. On September 6 all the remaining Jews of Vilna were forced to move into the ghettos—approximately 30,000 into Ghetto No. 1, and between 9,000 and 11,000 into Ghetto No. 2. Another 6,000 were taken to Ponary and murdered. On the following day the Germans established two Jewish Councils (Judenräte), one for each of the ghettos. As the ghetto administration organizations, the Judenräte had departments for food, health, lodging, education, and employment, and a general department for organizational and other affairs. A Jewish police force was also established, with Jacob **GENS** as its commander.

The Yellow *Schein Aktionen*

In the period from September 15 to October 21, families in which neither parent was employed in a place that issued *Scheine* (work permits), were transferred into Ghetto No. 2. The other families—those in which at least one parent was in possession of a *Schein*—were put into Ghetto No. 1. It was during this period that the "Yom Kippur" Aktion (October 1, 1941) took place.

In three more *Aktionen*, on October 3–4, 15–16, and 21, Ghetto No. 2 was liquidated and its inhabitants taken to Ponary and murdered. The Germans distributed 3,000 "yellow *Scheine*" (so called by the Jews because of the color of the paper on which they were printed) among the Jews in Ghetto No. 1; distribution depended on the place where they worked and the priority each place had with the authorities. A "yellow *Schein*" enabled its bearer to register on it the other parent

Aktion
A planned "operation" of violence against the Jews which generally involved beatings, deportations, and murders.

103

and no more than two children. The Germans planned to permit a maximum of 12,000 Jews to remain in the Vilna ghetto, out of the total of 27,000 to 28,000 surviving in Ghetto No. 1 at the time. On October 24 and November 3–5 the "yellow *Schein Aktionen*" took place, followed in December by further *Aktionen* on a smaller scale, the last on December 22. By the end of 1941, the Germans had killed 33,500 of the 57,000 Jews who had been in Vilna when the occupation began. A total of 12,000 "legal" Jews (those in possession of *Scheine*) were left in the ghetto, plus nearly 8,000 "illegals" that had gone into hiding. Another 3,500 had either fled to cities and towns in **BELORUSSIA**, where the Jews were still living in relative safety, or had found a place to hide outside the ghetto.

Ghetto Life

For about a year, between the spring of 1942 and the spring of 1943, there were no mass *Aktionen*. This was referred to as "the period of relative quiet." The ghetto, under Judenrat direction, became productive, with most of its inhabitants employed in jobs outside the ghetto or in workshops established inside. The Judenrat's strategy was based on the assumption that if the ghetto were productive and served German interests, the Germans would keep Jews alive and in the ghetto. Toward the end of its existence, in the summer of 1943, the ghetto had 14,000 persons—over two-thirds of its population—employed in various jobs.

The dominant figure in the ghetto leadership was the Jewish police commander, Jacob Gens, who in July 1942 became Judenrat chairman. The ghetto had schools, a rich cultural life, including a theater, social-welfare institutions, soup kitchens, and a medical care system that sought to combat starvation and disease. The mortality rate was low, compared to other large ghettos. The police kept order, and there was a law court.

In the spring of 1943, the situation of the Jews in the Vilna area began to deteriorate. Four small ghettos—in Švenčionys, Mikališkes, Oshmiany, and Salos, with a total of 5,000 Jews—were liquidated. About a quarter of them reached Vilna; the rest were taken to Ponary and murdered. In June and July, labor camps in the Vilna area with Jews from the Vilna ghetto were liquidated. The liquidation of the small ghettos and the labor camps, and the murder of most of their inmates, caused great fear in the Vilna ghetto and undermined whatever faith the Jews still had in the ghetto's future.

At the beginning of 1942, the underground **UNITED PARTISAN ORGANIZATION** (Fareynegte Partizaner Organizatsye; FPO) was established in the ghetto. During "the period of relative quiet" there existed a somewhat peaceful coexistence between the Judenrat and the underground. This was broken in the spring of 1943, when the situation in the ghetto deteriorated amid increasing indications that the end was approaching. Gens's attitude toward the underground changed; in his eyes, smuggling weapons into the ghetto and maintaining contact with the **PARTISANS** in the forests were a threat to the ghetto's continued existence. The first open clash occurred when Gens tried to remove the leaders of the underground—particularly Josef **GLAZMAN**, his former deputy and now vice commander of the FPO—from the ghetto and send them to labor camps outside. Another serious confrontation took place in mid-July 1943, when FPO members while under arrest freed Yitzhak Wittenberg, the commander of the FPO. The Nazis demanded his return, threatening the ghetto population. After further threats by Gens, the FPO command agreed to surrender Wittenberg.

On June 21, 1943, Heinrich **HIMMLER** ordered the ghettos in the Reichskommissariat Ostland to be liquidated. Inmates who were fit for work were to be sent to **CONCENTRATION CAMPS**, and the rest killed. In two stages, between August 4 and

24 and between September 1 and 4, over 7,000 men and women capable of working were rounded up and sent to concentration camps in Estonia.

During the September *Aktionen* the FPO called on the ghetto population to disregard the order to report for deportation and to rise up in rebellion. In the late afternoon of September 1, a clash broke out between the underground and the German forces that were combing the ghetto. In the ensuing exchange of fire, the commander of a major FPO combat group" was killed. In order to forestall more violence between the underground and the German forces, Gens, who believed that this would lead to the total liquidation of the ghetto, offered to provide the German authorities with the required quota for deportation to Estonia, on the condition that they pull their forces out of the ghetto. The Germans agreed, and the ghetto fighting came to an end. Following the expulsions to Estonia, 12,000 people were left. On September 14, Gens was summoned by the **GESTAPO** and killed on the spot.

The final liquidation of the Vilna ghetto took place on September 23 and 24, 1943. Thirty-seven hundred men and women were sent to concentration camps in Estonia and **LATVIA**; over 4,000 children, women, and old men were sent to the **SOBIBÓR** extermination camp, where they were murdered. Several hundred old people and children were taken to Ponary to be killed. About 2,500 Jews were left in Vilna, in the Army Motor Vehicle Depot labor camps and in two other smaller camps that provided labor for the German military. Over 1,000 people had gone into hiding inside the ghetto, which was otherwise empty; in the ensuing months, most of them were caught. A few hundred members of the FPO succeeded in escaping from the ghetto during the September *Aktionen*, establishing themselves in two partisan groups in the Rudninkai and Naroch forests. Eighty Jewish prisoners were kept in Ponary to open up the mass graves and burn the bodies of the victims who had been buried there. On July 2 and 3, 1944, ten days before Vilna was liberated, the Jews in the local labor camps were taken to Ponary to be killed. Approximately 150 to 200 were able to flee before the final liquidation and save themselves.

On July 13, 1944, Vilna was liberated; afterward, several hundred survivors gathered in the city. Of the 57,000 Jews who had been in Vilna when the Nazis occupied it, less than 3,000 were left. About a third of them had taken refuge in the forests. The rest survived in concentration camps in Estonia and **GERMANY**, in hiding places, or by having had "Aryan" documents in their possession.

SUGGESTED RESOURCES

Dawidowicz, Lucy S. *From That Place and Time: A Memoir, 1938–1947*. New York: W. W. Norton, 1989.

Gitelman, Zvi, ed. *Bitter Legacy: Confronting the Holocaust in the USSR*. Bloomington: Indiana University Press, 1997.

Partisans of Vilna [sound recording]. Flying Fish, 1989.

Rabinovici, Schoschana. *Thanks to My Mother*. New York: Dial Books, 1998.

VILNIUS. SEE VILNA.

Vitebsk

Vitebsk is a city in the northeastern region of Belarus that dates from the eleventh century. Jews lived in Vitebsk from the late sixteenth century, and the city was a center of Hasidism. Before World War II there were about 50,000 Jews there.

In his diary, Yitskhok Rudashevski, who did survive this episode, described the terror of hiding from the ghetto fighting in September 1943: "We are like animals surrounded by the hunter. The hunter [is] on all sides: beneath us, above us, from the sides. Broken locks snap, doors creak.... They pound, tear, break. Soon the attack is heard from another side.... We are lost...."

On July 11, 1941, Vitebsk was occupied by the Germans and was partially destroyed and burned down in the battle. On July 24 many refugees, mostly Jews, were arrested and killed outside the city. Every day Jews were seized for **FORCED LABOR**. On one of those days 300 young Jews were singled out, accused of arson, and put to death. Later, 27 Jews were caught, accused of not presenting themselves for work, and shot to death in the center of the city.

In the early days of the occupation a governing body was appointed in Vitebsk, and a **JUDENRAT** (Jewish Council) was responsible for supplying Jews for forced labor. It had to organize the work gangs and equip them with work tools and food. The Judenrat was ordered to draw up a list of the Jewish population, including the children of mixed marriages (*see* **MISCHLINGE**). It was also responsible for concentrating the Jews in the ghetto, which was established in the area of the railway station, a locale where most of the houses had been destroyed and burned. The ghetto was surrounded by wire fences and about 16,000 people were crowded into it. The slaughter of Jews and of other groups continued.

Early in August 1941, 332 Jewish intellectuals were assembled and murdered. On September 4, 397 Jews imprisoned in the civilian prisoner camp were taken out, accused of organizing a revolt, and put to death. On October 1, 52 Jewish refugees from the town of Gorodok who were living in Vitebsk were killed. Jewish youngsters fled to the surrounding forests and joined units of the Soviet partisan movement. The liquidation of the Vitebsk ghetto began on October 8, on the pretext that it was a source of epidemics. The slaughter lasted three days. Jews were taken to the Vitba River and shot; their bodies were thrown into the river.

When Vitebsk was liberated by the Soviet army on June 26, 1944, there were no Jews in the city. About two years later, in 1946, some 500 Jews had returned to live there.

SUGGESTED RESOURCES

Chagall, Bella. *Burning Lights: Thirty-six Drawings by Marc Chagall.* New York: Schocken Books, 1946. Reprint, New York: Biblio Press, 1996.

Gitelman, Zvi, ed. *Bitter Legacy: Confronting the Holocaust in the USSR.* Bloomington: Indiana University Press, 1997.

Volksdeutsche

Volksdeutsche was the Nazi term for ethnic Germans living outside of **GERMANY** in countries of which they were nationals. They were not citizens of the Third Reich—Germany under **NAZI PARTY** leader Adolf **HITLER**. That is, they did not hold German or Austrian citizenship as defined by the Nazi term *Reichsdeutsche* (Reich Germans).

Nazi Germany made every effort to win the support of the *Volksdeutsche*. A few years before its rise to power in 1933, the Nazi Party established the Foreign Organization of the Nazi Party (*Auslandsorganisation Der NSDAP*). This organization's task was to spread Nazi propaganda among the ethnic German minorities living outside the borders of Germany. In 1936, the Ethnic Germans' Welfare Office (*Volksdeutsche Mittelstelle*; commonly known as VoMi), was set up under the jurisdiction of the **SS**. VoMi cooperated with Nazi-type organizations active in a number of places, including **SLOVAKIA**, Luxembourg, and **FRANCE**.

Nazi Germany tried to increase the number of *Volksdeutsche* in the territories it conquered through a policy of "Germanizing" certain classes of the conquered peoples, mainly among the Czechs, Poles, and Slovenes. The Nazis encouraged the children of Germans, or people who had family connections with Germans, to join the *Volksdeutsche*. However, they were allowed to do so only if they were not descended from Jews or **GYPSIES**. Those who did join the *Volksdeutsche* received a privileged status and special benefits.

In **BOHEMIA AND MORAVIA**, in addition to those who had considered themselves as belonging to the German people during the period of the Czechoslovak republic, three other groups were recognized as *Volksdeutsche:* people of German origin, returning ethnic Germans, and those affiliated with the German people.

In October 1939, after Germany's occupation of **POLAND**, a central bureau was established in that country for the registration of *Volksdeutsche*. A new Nazi term was created to designate the registry of those belonging to the *Volksdeutsche*—the German Folk List (*Deutsche Volksliste*; also known as the *Volksliste* or DVL).

At the beginning of 1940, people registered in the *Volksliste* were divided into four categories. The first group consisted of ethnic Germans active on behalf of the Third Reich; the second group included all other ethnic Germans. The third group was made up of Poles of German extraction (that is, direct descendants of Germans); the fourth consisted of Poles who were related to Germans.

The German occupying authorities encouraged Poles to register with the *Volksliste*. In many cases, Poles were even forced to do so, especially in the territories annexed to the Reich. Within these areas, a total of 959,000 people in the first and second categories, who had considered themselves as belonging to the German minority living in independent Poland, were registered with the *Volksliste*. In the third and fourth categories, 1,861,000 Poles were recognized as having joined the ethnic Germans and were new *Volksdeutsche*. The number of *Volksdeutsche* living in the **GENERALGOUVERNEMENT** was estimated at 100,000. In addition, 350,000 ethnic Germans had settled in the western territories of occupied Poland between the beginning of the war in 1939 and the spring of 1941. These *Volksdeutsche* had migrated from the Baltic countries and the Volhynia region, which had come under Russian rule.

The *Volksliste* was also introduced into Yugoslavia following the German occupation of that country. In the Soviet territories (especially **UKRAINE**), conquered after the German invasion of the **SOVIET UNION** in the summer of 1941, the *Volksliste* was introduced in the same format as in Poland. In those countries, decrees were issued granting the *Volksdeutsche* privileged status and material benefits.

Among its activities, VoMi organized large-scale looting of property. The *Volksdeutsche* were given apartments, workshops, and farms that had belonged to Jews and Poles who had been deported from the Polish territory annexed to the Reich, with all their furniture and contents. They were also given hundreds of thousands of items of clothing taken from Jews who had been put to death in the **EXTERMINATION CAMPS**. The *Volksdeutsche* of Romania were given the apartments of Jews who had lived in the Transnistria region, complete with all their furniture and contents.

Nazi Germany received far-reaching support from the *Volksdeutsche*. Hundreds of thousands of them joined the German forces. With the conquest of Poland in September 1939, armed units were organized from among the *Volksdeutsche*. Called Self-Defense (*Selbstschutz*), these units helped the **OPERATIONAL SQUADS** (Einsatzgruppen) to carry out terrorist activities against Polish intellectuals and Jews. At the beginning of 1940, Self-Defense was disbanded, and its members were transferred to various units of the **SS** and German police. In Yugoslavia, the "Prinz Eugen"

These words from a speech Heinrich Himmler made in 1943 reveal the racism of the Volksdeutsche policy and indeed of all Nazi policy toward non-Aryans: "What happens to the Russians, what happens to the Czechs, is a matter of utter indifference to me. Such good blood of our own kind as there may be among the nations we shall acquire for ourselves, if necessary by taking away the children and bringing them up among us. Whether the other peoples live in comfort or perish of hunger interests me only in so far as we need them as slaves for our Kultur."

107

Division of the Waffen-SS (the German armed forces) was formed from *Volksdeutsche* members. This division was prominent in operations against PARTISANS and in *Aktionen* (violent "operations") among the population. About 300,000 *Volksdeutsche* from the conquered lands and the satellite countries volunteered for or were recruited to the Waffen-SS. From HUNGARY alone, some 100,000 ethnic Germans volunteered for service in the Waffen-SS, which released them from serving in the Hungarian army. Among the populations in the German-occupied lands, *Volksdeutsche* became a term of dishonor and shame.

SUGGESTED RESOURCES

The SS. Alexandria, VA: Time-Life Books, 1989.

Williamson, Gordon. *The SS: Hitler's Instrument of Terror.* Osceola, WI: Motorbooks International, 1994.

VOLKSDEUTSCHE MITTELSTELLE. SEE VOLKSDEUTSCHE.

VOMI. SEE VOLKSDEUTSCHE.

Wallenberg, Raoul

(1912–?)

Raoul Wallenberg was a Swedish diplomat who saved the lives of tens of thousands of Jews in BUDAPEST, HUNGARY. Wallenberg was born into a distinguished family of bankers, diplomats, and officers. His father, who died before he was born, had been an officer in the Swedish navy. Wallenberg grew up in the house of his stepfather, Frederik von Dardell. He studied architecture in the UNITED STATES, but then took up banking and international trade, which brought him to Haifa in 1936 for six months. In July of 1944 the Swedish Foreign Ministry, on the recommendation of the Swedish branch of the WORLD JEWISH CONGRESS and with the support of the American WAR REFUGEE BOARD, sent Wallenberg to Budapest to help protect the remaining Jews (over 200,000) in the Hungarian capital after 437,000 Hungarian Jews had been deported to AUSCHWITZ.

The Swedish diplomatic personnel in Budapest initiated its operation on behalf of the persecuted Jews a short while after the German occupation of Hungary, on March 19, 1944. At that time, Adolf EICHMANN and the Hungarian authorities began organizing the deportation of the Jews to their death. The Swedish foreign minister, Ivar Danielsson, had proposed giving provisional Swedish passports to Hungarian Jews who had family ties or commercial connections with Swedish citizens. By the time Wallenberg arrived in Budapest, several hundred such "protective passports" had been issued. His arrival, on July 9, 1944, coincided with the stoppage of the DEPORTATIONS, a decision taken by the Hungarian government as a result of international pressure, including intervention by King Gustav V of Sweden.

The protective operation carried out by the Swedish diplomats, in conjunction with other missions, was nevertheless maintained, and Wallenberg was put in charge of part of the operation. He had special authority to handle the transmission of funds by means of the War Refugee Board (which in turn received the money from Jewish organizations in the United States).

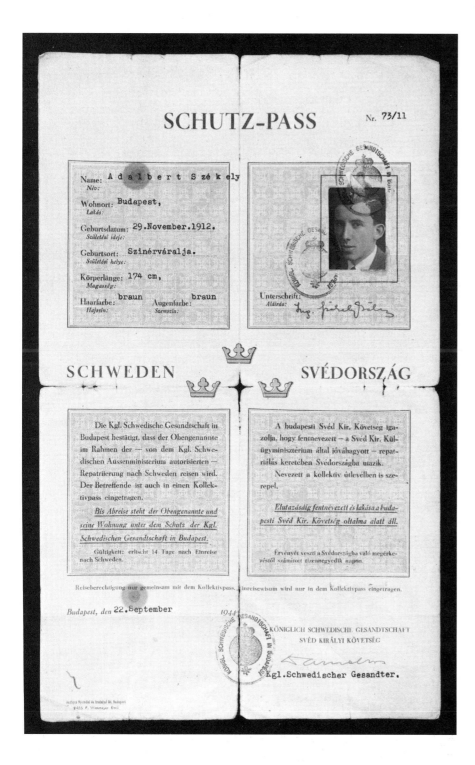

A Swedish Schutz-Pass, a protective passport issued by Swedish diplomats to protect Jews in Hungary. As a diplomat in Hungary, Raoul Wallenberg issued such passes that saved tens of thousands of Jewish lives.

The summer of 1944 was relatively quiet, but this quiet came to an end on October 15 when the antisemitic fascist **ARROW CROSS PARTY**, headed by Ferenc Szálasi, seized power in the country. The Jews of Budapest now faced mortal danger, both from the murderous actions of the Arrow Cross and from Eichmann's deportations. From that moment on, Wallenberg displayed his courage and heroism in the rescue actions he undertook. Over the course of three months he issued thousands of "protective passports." Most of the time, both the Hungarian authorities and the Germans honored the signature of the Swedish legation, and the protective documents afforded protection for many Jews.

Raoul Wallenberg, Swedish diplomat and Russian political prisoner during WWII.

When Eichmann organized the **DEATH MARCHES** of thousands of Jews to the Austrian border, Wallenberg pursued the convoy in his car and managed to secure the release of hundreds of bearers of such passports and take them back to Budapest. His impressive and self-assured manner enabled him even to remove persons from the trains in which they were about to be sent to Auschwitz, or to release them from the **HUNGARIAN LABOR SERVICE SYSTEM** (Munkaszolgálat) into which they had been drafted.

The Jews were also in danger of being killed by Arrow Cross men, and to prevent this, Wallenberg set up special hostels accommodating 15,000 persons. Other diplomatic missions were also involved in this and in issuing protective documents of their own. There were 31 protected houses, which together formed the "international ghetto," a separate entity, quite apart from Budapest's main ghetto. The management of these houses posed many complicated problems, since it involved the provision of food as well as sanitation and health services, all requiring large sums of money. As many as 600 Jewish employees were engaged in the administration and maintenance of the houses.

Both the "international ghetto" and the main ghetto were situated in Pest, which was the first part of Budapest to be occupied by the Soviets. Wallenberg made efforts to negotiate with the Soviets and to ensure proper care for the liberated Jews. The Soviets were highly suspicious of the Swedish mission and charged its staff with spying for the Germans. The large number of Swedish documents in circulation also raised doubt in their minds. When the Soviets requested him to report to their army headquarters in Debrecen, Wallenberg must have believed that he would be protected by his diplomatic immunity, especially since the Swedish legation had represented Soviet interests vis-à-vis the Germans, and he made his way to the Soviet headquarters. He returned to Budapest on January 17, 1945, escorted by two Soviet soldiers, and was overheard saying that he did not know whether he was a guest of the Soviets or their prisoner. Thereafter, all trace of him, and of his driver, Vilmos Langfelder, was lost. The other staff members of the Swedish diplomatic team were also held by the Soviets, but within a few months they all returned to Stockholm, via Bucharest and Moscow.

In the first few years following Wallenberg's disappearance, the Soviets claimed that they had no knowledge of a person named Wallenberg and were not aware that a person of that name was being held in any of their prisons. German **PRISONERS OF WAR**, however, coming back from Soviet imprisonment, testified that they had met Wallenberg in prisons and camps in various parts of the **SOVIET UNION**. In the mid-1950s, on the basis of these accounts, Sweden submitted a strong demand to the Soviets for information on Wallenberg, to which the Soviets replied, in 1956, that they had discovered a report of Wallenberg's death in 1947 in a Soviet prison. Wallenberg's family, and especially his mother, did not accept this claim, which conflicted with testimonies from other sources.

As the years went by, public opinion, in Sweden and all over the world, became increasingly critical of the manner in which the Swedish government had handled the issue. The subject of Wallenberg came up time and again, and with even greater force after the death of his mother in 1979. Books were published about Wallenberg and public committees were set up to deal with the case, especially in Britain, the United States, and Israel. Reports revealed that in the final days preceding Budapest's liberation, Wallenberg, with the help of Hungarians and the Zsidó Tanács (Jewish Council), was able to foil a joint **SS** and Arrow Cross plan to blow up the ghettos before the city's impending liberation. Through this act—the only one of its kind in the **HOLOCAUST**—some 100,000 Jews were saved in the two ghet-

tos. In recognition of this rescue action on Wallenberg's part, the U.S. Congress awarded Wallenberg honorary American citizenship. Memorial institutions were created in his honor, streets were named after him, and films were produced about his work in Budapest. Wallenberg's name and reputation as a "**RIGHTEOUS AMONG THE NATIONS**" have become legendary.

SUGGESTED RESOURCES

Anger, Per. *With Raoul Wallenberg in Budapest: Memories of the War Years in Hungary.* New York: Holocaust Library, 1981. Reprint, 1995.

Good Evening Mr. Wallenberg [videorecording]. Orion Home Video, 1994.

Lyman, Darryl. *Holocaust Rescuers: Ten Stories of Courage.* Springfield, NJ: Enslow, 1999.

Wallenberg, Raoul. *Letters and Dispatches, 1924–1944.* New York: Arcade, 1995.

Werbell, Frederick E., and Thurston Clarke. *Lost Hero: The Mystery of Raoul Wallenberg.* New York: McGraw-Hill, 1982.

Wannsee Conference

The Wannsee Conference was a meeting held at a villa in Wannsee, **BERLIN**, on January 20, 1942, to discuss and coordinate the implementation of the **"FINAL SOLUTION"**. Reinhard **HEYDRICH**, who was Heinrich **HIMMLER**'s deputy and head of the **REICH SECURITY MAIN OFFICE** (*Reichssicherheitshauptamt*; RSHA), invited the state secretaries of the most important German government ministries to attend the meeting. Heydrich was assisted by his Jewish expert, Adolf **EICHMANN**. The Wannsee Conference was noteworthy for two reasons. First, it was the only one to involve the broad participation of such prominent members of the ministerial bureaucracy. Second, it was the point at which Adolf **HITLER**'s decision to solve the so-called Jewish question through systematic mass murder was officially transmitted to this bureaucracy, whose participation was considered necessary.

On July 31, 1941, Heydrich met with Hermann Göring, who was still responsible for the coordination of Nazi Jewish policy. Heydrich was directed to submit the "overall plan" for the "final solution to the Jewish question." By the time of the meeting in January 1942, most of the invitees were clearly aware that the Nazi regime was engaged in the mass murder of Jews. Those in attendance included state secretary Dr. Wilhelm **STUCKART** of the Interior Ministry, Dr. Josef Bühler, state secretary of the **GENERALGOUVERNEMENT**, and under secretary Martin Luther of the German Foreign Office. Other participants were Alfred Meyer and Dr. Georg Leibbrandt, who were state secretary and chief of the political division, respectively, of the Reich Ministry for the Occupied Eastern Territories. Representing the Justice Ministry was state secretary Dr. Roland Freisler, the subsequent "hanging judge" of the notorious People's Court (*Volksgerichtshof*). Assistant Secretary Friedrich Wilhelm Kritzinger, reputedly one of the best-informed people in Nazi **GERMANY**, represented the Reich Chancellery. Dr. Erich Neumann was present as state secretary of Göring's Four-year Plan office.

Various **SS** leaders were also in attendance: Heinrich **MÜLLER** of the **GESTAPO**; Otto Hofmann of the **SS** Race and Resettlement Main Office (RuSHA); Dr. Karl Eberhard Schöongarth of the *SS und Polizei* (SS and Police) in **POLAND**; Dr. Rudolf Lange of Operational Squad A in the Baltic; and Gerhard Klopfer, state secretary of Martin **BORMANN**'s Party Chancellery. No fewer than eight of the fifteen partici-

Excerpts from the Wannsee Protocol

The following excerpts are from the recorded minutes of the Wannsee Conference, January 20, 1942. The English text is based on the official U.S. government translation which was prepared as evidence in the trials at Nuremberg.

"...in the course of the final solution the Jews are to be allocated for appropriate labor in the East. Able-bodied Jews, separated according to sex, will be taken in large work columns to these areas for work on roads, in the course of which action doubtless a large portion will be eliminated by natural causes.

"The possible final remnant will, since it will undoubtedly consist of the most resistant portion, have to be treated accordingly, because it is the product of natural selection and would, if released, act as the seed of a new Jewish revival.

"In the course of the practical execution of the final solution, Europe will be combed through from west to east....

"The evacuated Jews will first be sent, group by group, to so-called transit ghettos, from which they will be transported to the East."

John Mendelsohn, ed. The Holocaust: Selected Documents in Eighteen Volumes. *Vol. 11: The Wannsee Protocol and a 1944 Report on Auschwitz by the Office of Strategic Services (New York: Garland), 1982, pp. 18–32.*

pants held Ph.D. degrees. Most participants were well aware of or had participated in the extensive massacres of Jews that had already taken place.

The January 20 meeting was held at the villa Am Grossen Wannsee 56–58, a former Interpol property. Heydrich opened the conference with a long speech, in the first part of which he discussed the "Final Solution" to the Jewish question. He also reviewed the emigration policy that had led to 537,000 Jews leaving German-controlled lands.

In the second section of his speech, Heydrich announced that a total of 11 million European Jews, including even those from Ireland and England, would be evacuated. The evacuations, however, were to be regarded "solely as temporary measures." The Jews would be utilized for labor. Ultimately, though, the genocidal implications were totally and unmistakably clear. The "Final Solution" was meant to kill every last Jew in Europe, from Ireland to the Urals and from the Arctic to the Mediterranean.

In the third section of his speech, Heydrich discussed some of the specific problems that would have to be dealt with. He proposed an old people's ghetto to ward off anticipated interventions over individual cases, and the sending of Jewish advisers to certain satellite countries to make preparations. However, for Heydrich the most complex problem involved the fate of Jews in mixed marriages and their

part-Jewish offspring (*see* **MISCHLINGE**). A major portion of the conference was spent exploring this problem. The issues were not resolved, and were the subject of two further conferences in March and October 1942.

Thereafter, the discussion became quite freewheeling and unstructured. Neumann asked that Jews important to the war economy not be deported until they could be replaced, and Heydrich concurred. Bühler, on the other hand, urged that the "Final Solution" begin in the Generalgouvernement, because there was no transportation problem there and most of the Jews there were already incapable of work.

At this point the protocol notes cryptically: "Finally there was a discussion of the various types of possible solutions." On Heydrich's instructions, Eichmann did not include the details of this portion of the meeting in the protocol.

At that time, the Germans were still unsure about methods. The gas vans at the camp at **CHEŁMNO** had only been in operation for six weeks (*see* **GAS CHAMBERS/VANS**). The camp at **BEŁŻEC** was still under construction. In the main camp at **AUSCHWITZ**, experiments with **ZYKLON B** pellets in Bunker 11 and in the crematorium had been undertaken in the fall of 1941. But the first farmhouse converted into a gas chamber at Birkenau was just being prepared for use. Beyond the **EUTHANASIA PROGRAM** in Germany and the gas vans at Chełmno, therefore, the Nazis as yet had little experience in mass murder through gassing on the scale that would be required for the "Final Solution."

Heydrich closed the conference with a plea for the cooperation of all the participants. He was satisfied to find the state secretaries of the ministerial bureaucracy committed and enthusiastic about doing their part.

Following the conference, Eichmann prepared the protocol. Thirty copies were made, but only one, the sixteenth, was found after the war. It is presently kept in the archives of the German Foreign Office in Bonn.

SUGGESTED RESOURCES

Bachrach, Susan D. *Tell Them We Remember: The Story of the Holocaust.* Boston: Little, Brown, 1994.

Locke, Hubert G., and Marcia Sachs Littell, eds. *Remembrance and Recollection: Essays on the Centennial Year of Martin Niemöller and Reinhold Niebuhr, and the Fiftieth Year of the Wannsee Conference.* Lanham, MD: University Press of America, 1996.

Protocol of the Wannsee Conference. [Online] http://www.yad-vashem.org.il/holocaust/documents/117.html (accessed on September 5, 2000).

Wannsee Conference: 11 Million Sentenced to Death [videorecording]. Ergo Media, 1995.

War Refugee Board

The War Refugee Board (WRB) was the sole **UNITED STATES** government agency for rescuing and assisting World War II victims. In January 1944, Franklin D. Roosevelt issued an executive order to establish the War Refugee Board. This agency was to carry out the U.S. government's new policy of taking "all measures within its power to rescue the victims of enemy oppression who are in imminent danger of death." Unfortunately, Roosevelt did not take this action until 14 months after the **UNITED STATES DEPARTMENT OF STATE** confirmed the news of the systematic extermination of European Jews. Even then there was little support throughout the U.S. government to carry out the rescue of Jews.

On paper, the War Refugee Board had impressive powers. According to the executive order, all government agencies were to assist it, with special responsibility assigned to the State, Treasury, and War departments. In fact, only the Treasury Department, led by Morgenthau, fulfilled its mandate. The War Department was uncooperative, the State Department was frequently obstructive, and the other government agencies did almost nothing.

In November 1943, Congress began to debate the passage of a rescue resolution. At the same time, Henry **MORGENTHAU**, Jr., secretary of the Treasury, had received a report about the State Department's attempt to prevent rescue, entitled, "Report to the Secretary on the Acquiescence of This Government in the Murder of the Jews." Roosevelt quickly created the WRB to avoid the scandal that would result if Morgenthau's information became public, and to keep Congress from getting the credit for passing rescue resolutions.

The WRB was hurt by the president's lack of interest and support, as well as by a general disinterest on the part of the rest of the government. A major government commitment to rescue European Jews was never obtained. Most important, the board was handicapped from the start by inadequate funding. Roosevelt allotted $1 million to be used for administering the WRB. For the actual rescue programs, which were far more expensive, the board had to turn to private Jewish organizations, especially the American Jewish **JOINT DISTRIBUTION COMMITTEE**. American Jews, through voluntary contributions to their organizations, provided close to $17 million for the government program. Instead of becoming an effective advocate for the rescue of the remaining Jews of Europe, backed by the full force of the U.S. government, the WRB became a limited, albeit valuable, institution whose work was carried out through cooperation of the government and private Jewish agencies, with the latter carrying most of the load.

Despite the difficulties they faced, the WRB's executive director, John Pehle, and his staff of 30 forged a wide-ranging rescue program. Its main tasks included (1) evacuating Jews and other endangered people from occupied territory; (2) finding places to which they could be sent; (3) using psychological measures (especially threats of war crimes trials) to prevent further **DEPORTATIONS** and atrocities; and (4) sending relief supplies into **CONCENTRATION CAMPS**. Much of this work was made possible by a handful of WRB representatives stationed overseas.

During 1944, the WRB was deeply involved in efforts to save the Hungarian Jews. By focusing international attention on the Hungarian government the WRB helped stop deportations before they encompassed the 230,000 Jews of **BUDAPEST**. Ultimately, somewhat more than half of these Jews survived the reign of terror inflicted by a later government under the fascist **ARROW CROSS PARTY**. The toll would have been much higher had it not been for the action of Raoul **WALLENBERG** in protecting the Budapest Jews. The young Swedish diplomat had been sent to Budapest by the WRB; while there he managed to rescue Hungarian Jews who were already in the midst of forced **DEATH MARCHES** or on board trains on their way to **AUSCHWITZ**.

One of the most publicized WRB projects was the evacuation of 982 Jewish refugees from **ITALY** to a safe haven in an unused army camp at Oswego, New York (Fort Ontario), in August 1944. The WRB had hoped to set up many such safe havens in the United States and to use these actions as a lever to pressure other countries to open their doors as well. Roosevelt, however, agreed only to the Oswego project. This only reinforced other countries to maintain their closed-door policies, and one of the WRB's main rescue strategies was thus crushed.

By the end of the war, the WRB had played a crucial role in saving approximately 200,000 Jews. About 15,000 were evacuated from Nazi-controlled territory (as were more than 20,000 non-Jews). At least 10,000, and probably thousands more, were protected within those areas by WRB-financed underground activities. The WRB's diplomatic pressures, backed by its program of psychological warfare, were instrumental in having the 48,000 Jews in Transnistria moved to safe areas of Romania. Similar pressures helped end the Hungarian deportations; ultimately, 120,000 Jews survived in Budapest.

The results of other WRB programs, though they unquestionably contributed to the survival of thousands more, can never be quantified. On the other hand, numerous WRB plans that might have succeeded collapsed because the rest of the U.S. government would not cooperate.

SUGGESTED RESOURCES

Newton, Verne W., ed. *FDR and the Holocaust.* New York: St. Martin's Press, 1996.

Wyman, David S. *The Abandonment of the Jews: America and the Holocaust, 1941–1945.* New York: Pantheon Books, 1984.

Wyman, David S., ed. *America and the Holocaust.* New York: Garland, 1989.

Warsaw

General Survey

Warsaw was established as a city in the thirteenth century; it became the capital of **POLAND** in 1596. It flanks both banks of the Vistula River: two-thirds of the city's area is on the west bank and one-third is on the east bank. In 1935 the city limits covered an area of 54 square miles (140 sq km), with a population of 1,300,000.

In early September 1939, a few days after the German attack on Poland and the outbreak of World War II, German forces had reached the southern and western parts of Warsaw. Soon they surrounded the city. Air attacks and artillery shelling caused heavy damage to residential houses and ancient buildings and resulted in thousands of deaths and injuries.

Warsaw became the seat of the Wehrmacht headquarters and an **SS** and police headquarters. The number of military and police personnel varied from time to time, and generally was not more than 20,000, and the size of the city's German population, most of whom arrived after the war broke out, did not exceed 30,000.

The German authorities terrorized the population in various ways—by arrests, murder in the streets, public and secret executions, **DEPORTATIONS** to **CONCENTRATION CAMPS**, and random seizures of persons for deportation to **FORCED LABOR**. The headquarters of the terror operations was in the Security Police (Sicherheitspolizei) office, where persons were detained for questioning. The main terror center was the Pawiak Prison. There were several sites for public and secret executions in and around Warsaw, and they were put into use as early as the autumn of 1939. In the first stage the killings were carried out in areas near Warsaw, which were dubbed "Warsaw's circle of death"; one was the Palmiry Forest, where executions took place in the spring of 1940. These killings continued throughout the occupation of the city, reaching a climax in 1943. As of August 1, 1944, about 23,000 ethnic Poles had been deported to concentration camps and 86,000 deported for forced labor in the Reich.

Apart from the direct terror operations, the Nazi authorities also imposed severe economic repression on the population. Ration cards became compulsory, although the food they provided did not meet minimal needs. The inhabitants sought to combat hunger by taking on extra jobs, stealing from the German occupiers, engaging in black-market dealings, and, primarily, by smuggling in illegal food supplies. A large part of the population was employed in armaments factories and other German-controlled enterprises.

A total of 685,000 residents of Warsaw lost their lives during the Nazi occupation. The losses in life included 20,000 in September 1939, and 32,000 by executions and other methods. The murdered Jews numbered 370,000; 166,000 persons were killed in the 1944 uprising, and 97,000 perished in the concentration and forced-labor camps.

Resistance to German Oppression

The Warsaw inhabitants countered the German regime of terror with a broad resistance movement, consisting of a number of political and military organizations and a wide-ranging program of activities. Warsaw was the headquarters of the major Polish resistance organizations and an important scene for their undertakings. The resistance movement was launched as early as September 1939. On September 26, Service for Polish Victory was formed, which was later renamed the Union for Armed Struggle; in February 1942 it became the Polish Home Army.

propaganda
Ideas, information or allegations designed to gain support for a particular cause.

In the initial stage, the resistance movement spread **propaganda**, by means of some 1,000 underground newspapers, and acquired weapons through various means, including purchase from German soldiers. Later, the resistance manufactured its own arms and ammunition. In a few instances, arms were parachuted by Allied aircraft or stolen from Germans. Early on there was little armed action; what armed struggle there was consisted mostly of executing spies and traitors. In 1943 some military-like actions were launched. Several particularly dangerous German officials were assassinated. The Polish resistance movement also assisted in hiding Jews.

The resistance movement continued to expand, despite a heavy loss of life and property owing to Nazi acts of reprisal, and it began preparations for a large-scale armed uprising. When the **WARSAW POLISH UPRISING** erupted in August 1944, Hitler wanted to bomb from the air the part of the city that was in the rebels' hands, but he gave up the idea. A few days later, after consultations with Heinrich **HIMMLER**, he ordered the total destruction of Warsaw, with a fortress to be constructed on the site.

Once the uprising was suppressed, the Germans ordered the civilian population to evacuate the city, sending them to the Pruszków, Ursus, and Piastów transit camps. Some 550,000 Warsaw inhabitants passed through these camps. More than 60,000 were sent on to concentration camps, and over 100,000 to labor camps in the Reich. Special squads of Germans blew up the buildings and systematically destroyed the abandoned city.

In January 1945, Soviet and Polish forces attacked the city from the south and north, crossing the Vistula and liberating Warsaw on January 17. It is estimated that 80 percent of Warsaw's buildings were destroyed.

Jews in Warsaw

Jews have lived in Warsaw date from the fifteenth century. In the 1792 census, 6,750 Jews were found to be living there, about one-tenth of the city's total population. In the nineteenth century Warsaw's Jewish population grew rapidly; it became the largest Jewish community in Europe and, in the twentieth century, the second largest in the world, after New York City. On the eve of World War I, the Jews in Warsaw numbered 337,000.

The cultural drive emanating from Warsaw, with its literary and artistic creativity, its publishing houses, theaters, and societies, stood in stark contrast to the depressed status and abject poverty that constituted the fate of the masses of Warsaw's Jewish population.

Just before World War II broke out, Warsaw's Jewish population was 375,000 (29.1 percent of the total). Jews were to be found in every part of the city, but its northern part contained a section that was predominantly Jewish, with many apartment houses and certain blocks inhabited exclusively by Jews. The antisemitic policies pursued by the Polish government led to widespread poverty among the Jewish population and contributed to the generally poor state of the Polish economy at this time.

In the prewar years Warsaw was the capital of Polish Jewry and an important world Jewish center. The head offices of the political parties, of a great many welfare, educational, and religious institutions, and of the trade unions were located

there. Warsaw was where most of the Jewish newspapers and periodicals were published in different languages. It was also the central point of leadership for education. Jewish sports organizations and **YOUTH MOVEMENTS** also located their headquarters in Warsaw.

Warsaw under Siege

Although it had been expected, **GERMANY**'s aggression on September 1, 1939, found both Poles and Jews unprepared and helpless in the face of the Nazi war machine that was about to engulf them. By the end of the first week of war, the German forces had managed to destroy Poland's military power, and the German army stood at the gates of Warsaw. At first the Polish high command resolved to make Warsaw an armed fighting fortress, but it later abandoned the plan. The civilian population, including many Jews, had been digging anti-tank ditches at the approaches to Warsaw in the early days of the war, and roadblocks had been put up inside the city.

The approach of the German forces prompted an exodus from the city that included government employees and top officials, as well as the leaders of the political and public organizations. Also swept along were Jewish public figures, leaders, and activists of the different political movements, among them the appointed head of the Jewish Community Council. No meaningful preparations had been made for an evacuation, and no individuals or organizations were assigned to take the place of the persons who were abandoning the city in the emergency.

From the very first days of the war, Warsaw was subjected to air raids. By the end of the first week the antiaircraft defense had been put out of action, and the aircraft were able to drop bombs at will. On September 24, Jewish leader Adam **CZER-NIAKÓW** confided in his diary: "All night long the guns keep on firing. There is no gas, no water, no electricity, and no bread; what a terrible day!" In the last week of September the city lay in ruins, a scene of chaos and death.

On September 28, Warsaw surrendered; the next day German forces made their entry into the city. There is no evidence that the Germans deliberately aimed their fire at the Jewish streets and the sections that were densely populated with Jews. However, the Jews felt that they had been targeted. The hail of shells that landed on the High Holy Days (the New Year and the Day of Atonement) reinforced that impression.

Warsaw's Jews under Occupation

Many recalled the World War I German occupation, which was orderly and tolerant toward the Jews. From the very first days of this occupation, however, the Jews discovered that the German army that entered the city in 1939 was nothing like the troops that had been stationed there in World War I. The Jews were immediately subjected to attacks and discrimination. Jews were driven away from food lines and seized for forced labor; religious Jews who were wearing their traditional garb were assaulted; Jewish shops and personal property were plundered.

In November the first anti-Jewish decrees were issued, such as the introduction of a white armband with a blue Star of David (Mogen David) on it to be worn by all Jews, the requirement of signs identifying Jewish shops and enterprises, the order to hand in radios, and a ban on train travel.

Severe economic sanctions were placed on the Jews: in addition to blocking Jewish accounts and putting a stop to economic activity by Jews, the Germans also embarked upon the confiscation of Jewish enterprises. This led to the wholesale

Chaim Aaron Kaplan was a Jewish teacher in Warsaw. On September 14, 1939, he made the following diary entry: "Yesterday, between five and seven in the afternoon, as the Jewish New Year, 5700, was being ushered in, the northern section, populated mostly by Jews, suffered an air raid." Adam Czerniaków, chairman of the Judenrat in Warsaw, wrote on September 22: "Today is the Day of Atonement, truly the day of judgment. All night long the guns were shelling the city."

The indiscriminate seizure of Jews for forced labor, regardless of age or state of health, paralyzed Jewish life in Warsaw as Jews stayed indoors to avoid seizure.

confiscation of Jewish enterprises and personal and commercial property. From the early stage of the occupation, the assets they had accumulated in the past served the Jews as their main source of subsistence. Jews who had managed to conceal savings or goods began trading them for food—a practice that was to continue throughout the war.

It may be assumed that tens of thousands of Jews left Warsaw in the exodus that took place in the first few days of the war; on the other hand, an estimated 90,000 Jews were added to the population until the establishment of the ghetto in November 1940—either as refugees or through deportation to Warsaw by the Germans.

Judenrat Activities

In place of the many Jewish service institutions that had existed in pre-war Warsaw, only those allowed by the Germans continued to function. The creation of a **JUDENRAT**, which took the place of the traditional Jewish Community Council, was mandated by the Nazis to manage the day-to-day needs of the Jews in Warsaw. Later, when the ghetto came into being, the Judenrat would be burdened with increased responsibilities and its authority would be extended to all aspects of Jewish life. But even the first welfare challenges demonstrated the Jews' helplessness in face of the tragic dilemmas that confronted them, on issues such as forced labor, the collection of large "contributions," confiscations, and the indiscriminate arrests and executions of groups of Jews as retaliatory measures.

One of the first problems to be addressed was that of random seizures of Jews for forced labor. The Judenrat proposed to the Germans that it would provide a fixed quota of men for work, in place of the haphazard kidnappings that had brought Jewish life to a total standstill. According to this arrangement, every Jew was assigned a fixed number of days per month for forced labor. The pay, such as it was, had to be covered by the Judenrat. As a result, the Judenrat, which did not have the financial resources to cover the wages of the forced laborers, was in financial straits at all times.

Mutual Aid

Throughout the occupation and the existence of the ghetto, Jews were allowed to continue to maintain welfare and mutual help activities within the community. The financial base for such operations consisted of funds that had been accumulated by the American Jewish **JOINT DISTRIBUTION COMMITTEE** (known as the Joint); these amounted to substantial sums and were available for welfare purposes under the new conditions. The Joint associated itself with welfare operations in a number of ways, including the care of refugees and the wounded during the fighting.

Before long it became evident that the number of needy cases was growing and that an organization had to be created, and properly equipped, that would be able to meet the requirements of the entire Jewish population. The Joint-sponsored Jewish Mutual Aid Society lent assistance to 250,000 Jews during Passover of 1940. Its most important means of aiding masses of people were its soup kitchens, which doled out a bowl of soup and a piece of bread to all in need. When this operation was at its height, more than 100 soup kitchens were in existence in Jewish Warsaw.

Important instruments created by Jewish self-help, under the direction of Emanuel **RINGELBLUM**, were the House Committees (Komitety Domowe). Ringelblum and his colleagues sought to make the House Committees into a network based on social principles. The committees' first task was to take care of the penni-

less tenants in their buildings, but they also set up kindergartens and youth clubs and arranged cultural activities. When the situation did grow worse, however, and more and more people were in need, the activities of the House Committees went into a decline, and the Mutual Aid Society gained prominence.

From its inception, the work of the Mutual Aid Society (ŻTOS) was guided by social and political principles. Its public council was composed of representatives of the underground political bodies, and that council determined the aid policy and its goals. In this manner, the ŻTOS assumed a dual role: on the one hand it operated legally, with the knowledge and approval of the authorities, and on the other hand it maintained ties with the clandestine political organizations and lent its assistance to underground activities. Many people regarded the ŻTOS as an alternative to the Judenrat.

The Jewish and Polish populations of Warsaw had few contacts with each other on a public level. While it was not the capital of the **GENERALGOUVERNEMENT**, Warsaw was the capital of underground Poland. The Polish underground military organizations were formed there, the political parties were clandestinely active in the city, and the Delegatura, representing the Polish government-in-exile, had its main office in Warsaw. Warsaw Jews had ties with Poles on an individual basis and certain Jewish political groups were in contact with their Polish counterparts, but no links of any sort were created between the Polish underground forces, or the military and political branches of the Polish government-in-exile, and Jewish public bodies. No Jewish element became a recognized part of a Polish-sponsored underground framework, and no Jewish representative was ever invited to join a body established by official Polish underground organizations.

Ghetto Established

In mid-November 1940, the Jewish ghetto in Warsaw, surrounded by a high wall, was sealed off. It was situated in the heart of the Jewish quarter, in the northern section of the city, and encompassed the Jewish-inhabited streets. The first attempt to set up a ghetto had been made by the SS in November 1939, but at the time the military governor put a stop to the plan. In February 1940, however, Waldemar Schön, the official in charge of evacuation and relocation in the German district administration, was ordered to draw up plans for the establishment of a ghetto. On October 12, 1940, the Day of Atonement, the Jews were informed of the decree establishing a ghetto. A few days later a map was published indicating the streets assigned to the ghetto area.

Up to the very last day, the Jews did not know whether the ghetto would be open or sealed off from its surroundings. On November 16 the ghetto was in fact sealed off, and thousands of Jews who had left their remaining belongings on the other side of the wall no longer had access to them.

The Germans had planned for 113,000 Poles to be evacuated from their homes and resettled elsewhere, and for 138,000 Jews to take their place. As soon as the ghetto was set up, a flow of refugees converged upon it. Some 30 percent of the population of Warsaw was being packed into 2.4 percent of the city's area. According to German statistics, the density of population in the ghetto consisted of at least six to seven people to a room. Of Warsaw's 1,800 streets, no more than 73 were assigned to the ghetto. The ghetto wall was 11.5 feet (3.5 m) high and topped by barbed wire. The ghetto cut the Jews off from the rest of the world and put an end to any remaining business ties with Poles.

The number of persons employed by the Judenrat increased rapidly and a 1,000-man Jewish police force **JEWISH GHETTO POLICE** (Jüdischer Ordnungsdi-

"**H**astily they tried other streets, avenues, alleys, only to find in every case barbed wire or a solid brick wall well guarded. There was no way out any more."

—**Tosha Bialer, Holocaust survivor and Warsaw Ghetto prisoner.**

Nora Levin, The Holocaust Years: The Destruction of European Jewry, 1933–1945 *(New York: Thomas Y. Crowell), 1968, p. 208.*

Warsaw Ghetto wall, Warsaw, Poland, 1941.

enst) was formed, which eventually was increased to 2,000. At its maximum size, the Judenrat staff consisted of 6,000 persons, compared to the 530 employed by the Jewish Community Council before the war. Food supplies were inadequate, as were sanitary conditions and basic services of all kinds. In November 1940, the month the ghetto was sealed off, there were 445 deaths in the ghetto. The number of deaths thereafter rose rapidly: in January 1941, to 898; in April, to 2,061; in June, to 4,290; and in August, to 5,560. The monthly figure thereafter generally fluctuated between 4,000 and 5,000 for as long as the ghetto existed.

An economic structure was gradually created in the ghetto, sustaining a thin upper stratum made up of people who smuggled food into the ghetto and smuggled valuables out to the "Aryan" side, and of skilled craftsmen who made deals (legal or not legal) with German enterprises. Stefan Ernst, one of the diarists who recorded events in the Warsaw ghetto, made the following entry, shortly before the liquidation of the ghetto: "The ghetto contains 20,000, maybe 30,000, persons who have enough to eat, and these are the social elite; at the other end of the ladder are about a quarter of

a million people who are all beggars, completely bereft of everything, and who wage a daily struggle to postpone their death by starvation. In between these two extremes are about 200,000 people, the 'average,' who somehow manage, are still able to take care of themselves, look clean and dressed, and their bellies are not swollen from hunger."

The ghetto's ties with the outside world were handled by the Transfer Office (Transferstelle), a German authority that was in charge of the traffic of goods into and out of the ghetto. In practice, only some goods—the food shipments into the ghetto and the products manufactured by the ghetto for clients on the outside—passed through the Transferstelle. Most of the economic activities in the ghetto were illegal, and the ghetto economy was essentially an illegal operation, made up of two basic elements: the smuggling of food into the ghetto and the illegal export of products fabricated inside it.

German involvement in the ghetto took a number of forms. The German authorities' main interest was to plunder Jewish property and to make use of Jewish expertise in certain fields. From the earliest stage of the occupation, some Jews were employed in collecting scrap metal, feathers, and textiles. Later, growing numbers of Jews were sent to labor camps, where they were made to do backbreaking jobs and suffered from hunger, poor sanitary conditions, and wearisome and grueling discipline. German entrepreneurs and factory owners soon became interested in the ghetto and the availability of cheap Jewish manpower, and they quickly found ways to exploit the ghetto as a source of forced labor.

The daily food ration allocated to the Warsaw Jews consisted of 181 calories—about 25 percent of the Polish ration, and 8 percent of the nutritional value of the food that the Germans received for their official ration coupons.

Jewish Labor, Legal and Illegal

German manufacturers appeared in the ghetto in the summer of 1941, having organized and obtained authorization to operate in the Warsaw area. At first the German companies placed orders with existing Jewish workshops, but before long they put up their own workshops in the ghetto.

The Judenrat, seeking to play a role in these operations, encouraged the Jews to accept employment in the German manufacturing establishments, and formed a special department for this purpose. Its efforts were to no avail, however, and it was only the specter of possible deportations from the ghetto that eventually persuaded a growing number of Jews to accept such work. As a rule, the Jews preferred to work in places that manufactured goods for "illegal export," where they were treated better and where the pay was much higher than in the German-owned factories. Smuggling on a large scale also went on through the ghetto gates, with the various policemen and guards—Germans, Poles, and Jews—involved in the conspiracy and receiving monetary bribes for letting the smuggled goods pass.

Children and women who, risking their lives, crossed over to the Polish side in order to bring back some food for their families also engaged in smuggling on a small scale. The overall smuggling operation was a complex organization, maintaining ties with partners and accomplices on the Polish side. The records and diaries kept in the ghetto all show that the smugglers' operations played a vital role—the smuggling allowed the ghetto to hold out and survive even in the face of the cruel steps taken by the Germans against the population. The smuggling done by children and women was of a different type; they operated on an individual basis, responding to the misery around them and seeking to save themselves and their relatives. Children aged seven or eight frequently gathered in the vicinity of the ghetto gates in order to look for a smuggling opportunity.

Attempts by the Germans to bring the smuggling to a complete stop met with the desperate resistance of human beings fighting for their lives. The Germans,

The pay received for a day's work in the German workshops was not enough to buy half a loaf of bread.

who had no compunctions about the methods they were using, and for whom torture and murder were the accepted means of breaking resistance, could have stopped the smuggling by mass killings. The local administrative officials apparently decided that there was no point in trying to stamp out the smuggling entirely, and that sporadic raids, confiscations, and executions would keep it within acceptable bounds and under reasonable control.

Religion, Education, and Culture in the Ghetto

While regular schools were banned in the ghetto, the Judenrat was permitted to maintain the vocational training schools. Cultural life in the ghetto consisted of activities conducted by the underground organizations. The ghetto had clandestine libraries that circulated officially banned books. An 80-member symphony orchestra had a repertoire that included the works of the great German composers; at one point it was warned to restrict itself to Jewish composers. Well-known writers and poets continued to create in the ghetto. The audiences appreciated the entertainment that would help them forget the surrounding reality.

Underground Political Parties and Youth Movements

Underground activities by political circles and organizations had already begun around the time that the Germans entered Warsaw. Missing were the veteran and experienced Jewish leaders, who had left the city (and the country). Nevertheless, after Warsaw was occupied, members of youth movements and political parties joined together and began to prepare plans of action. At an early stage, the question arose as to whether political organizations could confine themselves to material aid and abandon political activity. The next step was to establish an underground press and to persist in efforts to communicate with political elements outside the country.

The Germans' lack of interest in the ghetto's underground activities and their silence on the subject enabled the underground, prior to the spring of 1942, to engage in a broad range of activities without the Germans taking drastic steps to suppress them or to punish the participants. The underground press led to two results: It provided the news-hungry ghetto population with reliable information on international political developments and on the war fronts; and it raised political and ideological issues that encouraged discussion. Although this would not be the case in all Jewish ghettos, the Judenrat agreed to cooperate with the underground in Warsaw.

The Jewish youth movements and their leaders played an important role in the underground, especially in the later stages: following the great deportation, during the months of preparation for the uprising, and during the **WARSAW GHETTO UPRISING** itself. During the war and in the ghetto, the activities of the youth movements underwent a gradual change, as did their relative importance. They manifested a greater aptitude than did other movements for adapting to the changing circumstances and for taking dynamic action when necessary. The youth leaders assembled in Warsaw because of their keen instincts and leadership qualities and became the acknowledged leaders of the underground.

Prior to the onset of the mass killings of Jews, no basic differences existed among the political parties and the youth movements in the underground. The youth movements were more active and more daring, and engaged in a wider variety of operations, but they did not offer themselves as an alternative to the underground's political leadership or even to the Judenrat. They accepted the authority of the political parties, acknowledging them as the senior element in the underground. There was a con-

sensus that agreed that every effort had to be made to ensure physical survival, and although the youth movements occasionally voiced some objections, they were part of this consensus. In addition to the struggle for survival, however, they made the moral and spiritual condition of the ghetto youth their special concern.

A drastic change in the relationship between the component parts of the underground and the general power structure in the ghetto took place, however, when the mass murders were launched and the first reports came in of the massacres at **PONARY** and elsewhere. At this point a new concept arose—that the Germans had embarked upon the total destruction of the Jews and that the Jews therefore had no choice but to stand up and fight, even if there was no prospect of survival.

Deportations

In the months preceding the mass deportation from the Warsaw ghetto, increasing nervousness was felt, as rumors spread of deportations from other ghettos and cities in occupied Poland. Unrest and panic were created and grave doubts were raised among the ghetto population by the night raids undertaken by the German police. These raids were carried out according to prepared lists; the persons on the list were seized in their homes, taken out, and shot at a nearby location. The first, and worst, such murderous raid took place on April 18, 1942. Fifty-two persons were killed that night, "the bloody night," as it came to be known in the ghetto.

Adam Czerniaków met with underground activists and tried to persuade them to stop publishing the underground newspapers, since the Germans had claimed that the existence of the underground press was the reason for the executions. The underground leaders, consulting on the subject, came to the conclusion that the Germans were lying, and decided that rather than stop publishing the underground press; they would intensify their efforts.

Reports on the deportations were found in the underground press and in diaries. Czerniaków repeatedly recorded such rumors and fears in his diary.

Several days prior to the beginning of the planned *Aktion*, an SS officer, Hans Höfle, commander of the **AKTION REINHARD** unit, arrived in Warsaw. With the **GESTAPO** section for Jewish affairs, Höfle drew up the plan for the deportation from the Warsaw ghetto. Several members of the Judenrat were arrested and held as hostages, and on the eve of the deportation, notices were posted listing the categories of Jews who were to be "evacuated." The *Aktion* began on July 22, 1942, and continued until September 12. On July 23, Adam Czerniaków, the Judenrat chairman who tried to protect his people, committed suicide. He had been ordered to provide a daily quota of 7,000 Jews for deportation, and to include children in this number. Czerniaków was not prepared to have anything to do with turning over Jews, and preferred to put an end to his life.

In the first few days of the deportation, the ghetto inhabitants streamed into the German factories ("shops") or into workshops that were under German protection; there, they thought, they would be safe from deportation. The Jews used whatever savings they had left to buy their way into employment in a "shop." In the first few days the permits exempting Jews from deportation were honored, and the Germans indiscriminately stamped the large number of work permits that were submitted to them.

In the first ten days of the deportation *Aktion*, 65,000 Jews were taken from the ghetto. This meant that the Germans had filled the quota they had announced. Even in this first phase, which lasted to the end of July, people were sometimes rounded up at random in the streets, or dragged out of their homes, by the SS, the

L eon Berensohn, a prominent Jewish lawyer who died in the Warsaw ghetto, said that after the war the liberated survivors would have to put up a monument in memory of the Unknown Child—the smuggler in the Warsaw ghetto.

German police, and their Ukrainian and Latvian helpers, because daily quotas had not been met. No permits or paperwork provided protection from these seizures.

In the second phase, from July 31 to August 14, the German forces and their helpers took direct charge of the roundups and deportation, with the Jewish police in a secondary role. The German police and the auxiliary police, made up of Ukrainians, Latvians, and Lithuanians—a force of some 200 armed men—saw the *Aktion* through, day after day.

Rumors, of unknown origin, were rife in the ghetto that the *Aktion* would be over in a day or two, but they were false. In the first week of August, 200 children were taken out of Janusz **Korczak**'s orphanage. Dr. Korczak and his team of assistants went to the railway cars with the children, the elderly educator refusing offers to help him save himself. Ringelblum recorded in his diary: "Korczak set the tone: everybody [all the instructors at the orphanage] was to go to the *Umschlag* together. Some of the boarding-school principals knew what was in store for them there, but they felt that they could not abandon the children in this dark hour and had to accompany them to their death."

The third phase of the deportation began on August 15 and ended on September 6. At this point the deportation took on the character of a total evacuation. The Germans and their helpers conducted a manhunt, combing the streets and the apartment houses, seizing every person they found at home. Jews who were employed in the "shops" sought refuge there with their families, but the Germans showed no mercy. It became increasingly difficult to round up people, and the Germans compelled every Jewish policeman to bring in a quota of five Jews per day; a policeman who failed to fill the quota had his mother, wife, and children taken away. From mid-August, individuals who had managed to escape from the **Treblinka** extermination camp succeeded in infiltrating back into the ghetto, and reported on the fate in store for the deportees when they reached their destination.

The final phase began on September 6. The "shops" and the Judenrat were allotted a number of permits; 35,000 such permits were issued, meaning that the Germans intended to leave in the ghetto 10 percent of its pre-deportation population. The bearers of the permits were assembled in a street bottleneck in the David Quarter, where they had to pass through a final inspection and selection. Their bundles too were inspected. In their memoirs, some of the victims recorded that from time to time, when the guards stuck their bayonets into bundles carried on the back of some of the people in the line, the sound of a baby's cry would ring out from the bundle.

In addition to the 35,000 who had permits, another 25,000—and perhaps more—managed to remain in the ghetto. The Jews who were left, mostly women and young men, the last remnants of their families, went through a great psychological change. As long as the deportations were going on, the Jews had been in a constant state of tension, concentrating all their strength on one goal: to survive where they were. When the deportations came to a halt, they had time to take stock of their situation. It was clear to all that their lives were in as much danger as before, and that they had only a short period of grace before another deportation would take place—the final one. An increasing number of them said that they would not surrender to the Germans without a fight.

The Underground and the Ghetto

On July 23, the day after the deportation was launched, a meeting was called of underground leaders and public figures who were close to the underground. The representatives of the youth movements and of some of the political factions

On July 20, 1942, Adam Czerniaków wrote: "At the Gestapo at 7:30 in the morning … I asked whether I could inform the population that there was no reason for fear. He said I could, that all the reports were nonsense and rubbish." The implication from the Nazi leadership was that no deportations were scheduled to take place from the Warsaw ghetto.

favored forming a defense organization that would resist the deportation by force. The leading public figures participating were reluctant to take such a step or opposed it outright. One representative argued that armed resistance would put the whole ghetto in jeopardy; this was not the first time in history that the Jewish people had been asked to sacrifice some of its sons in order to assure its continued existence as a people, and such a sacrifice would have to be made this time. On the seventh day of the deportation, July 28, representatives of the groups Ha-Shomer ha-Tsa'ir, Dror, and Akiva held a meeting at which they decided to form the **JEWISH FIGHTING ORGANIZATION** (Żydowska Organizacja Bojowa; ŻOB).

Although the organization was founded, it had no resources, financial or otherwise, and had as yet to adopt a clear policy on the way it would conduct its struggle. One of the ŻOB's first steps was to publish and distribute leaflets informing the public of the fate of the deportees and what Treblinka stood for. The ghetto population objected, fearing that the leaflets would be seen as a provocative act that would give the Germans a pretext for the total liquidation of the ghetto.

The ŻOB began its effort to acquire weapons and to draw up a plan of action. An attempt to establish ties with the **HOME ARMY** (Armia Krajowa)—the Polish military underground organization—did not succeed. The Communists were more willing to help, so with their assistance the ŻOB obtained its first arms shipment—five pistols and eight hand grenades.

On September 3, 1942, the ŻOB faced its first crisis. In a surprise raid by the Gestapo on a "shop" where the ŻOB had its principal base, Josef **KAPLAN**, one of the organization's leaders, was arrested. Another prominent member, Samuel Breslaw, who tried to set Kaplan free, was shot in the street. In another incident, a young woman member of the ŻOB, who was transferring the organization's weapons from Mila Street to another location, was caught by the Germans with the entire collection of the ŻOB's arms. A deep sense of frustration set in among the ŻOB members, and youngsters among them demanded that they all take to the streets, seize anything they could use as a weapon, and put an end to the ghetto's placid acceptance of the situation. This was opposed by several of the ŻOB leaders, who persuaded the younger members to drop the idea and utilize the expected lull for thorough preparations for the final struggle.

A profound change in public opinion had taken place in the ghetto, and as a result, underground groups of different political orientations were now willing to join the Jewish Fighting Organization. By October the ŻOB had been consolidated and enlarged, with the addition of youth movements and splinter groups of underground political parties from Zionists to Communists. A ŻOB command was formed, made up of representatives of the founding organizations and the fighting groups.

Deportation and Resistance in January 1943

The second wave of deportations was launched on January 18, 1943. This time, however, the Jews who were ordered to assemble in the courtyards of their apartment houses to have their papers examined refused to comply and went into hiding. The first column that the Germans managed to round up, in the first few hours, consisting of some 1,000 persons, offered a different kind of resistance. A group of fighters led by Mordecai **ANIELEWICZ** and armed with pistols deliberately infiltrated the column that was on its way to the **TRANSFER POINT** (Umschlagplatz). When the agreed-upon signal was given, the fighters stepped out of the column and engaged the German escorts in hand-to-hand fighting. The column dispersed, and news of the fight quickly spread.

On Saturday, August 1, 1942, Warsaw diarist Abraham Lewin wrote: "'Outside, the sword deals death, and inside, terror' (Lamentations 1:20). This is the eleventh day of the *Aktion,* which becomes more terrible and more cruel from one day to the next. The Germans are clearing whole buildings and entire sections of streets of their inhabitants … today's sufferings are worse than any that preceded them."

The resistance, especially the fight that had taken place in the street, left its imprint on the January deportations. These continued until January 22, by which time the Germans had rounded up 5,000 to 6,000 Jews from all parts of the ghetto; after the events of the first day, hardly any Jews responded to the German order to report.

The fact that the *Aktion* was halted after only a few days, and that the Germans had managed to seize no more than 10 percent of the ghetto population, was regarded, by Jews and Poles alike, as a German defeat. The Warsaw Jews who had lived through the first great wave of deportations had believed that the next deportation would be the last, and that the ghetto would be liquidated. The actual outcome was regarded as a German retreat, caused by the resistance they encountered from the fighters and from the general population of the ghetto. It is now known that the Germans had not intended to liquidate the entire ghetto during the January deportations. In fact, they were carrying out an order given by Heinrich Himmler, after a visit he made to Warsaw on January 9, to remove 8,000 Jews from the ghetto and reduce its population to the level the Germans had decided on after the great deportation in the summer and fall of 1942.

The deportations and other events that took place in January were to have a decisive influence on the last months of the ghetto's existence, up to April and May of 1943. The Judenrat and the Jewish police lost whatever control they still had over the ghetto. In the central part of the ghetto, the population obeyed directives from the fighting organizations. A new ghetto commissar was appointed by the Germans. His assignment was to transfer the machinery and workers of the major "shops" in the Warsaw ghetto to labor camps in the **LUBLIN** area. This transfer however, ran into opposition from the workers, who were taking their instructions from the ŻOB.

The Jewish resistance also impressed the Poles, and they now provided more aid to the Jewish fighters than in the past. The fighting organizations used the few months they had left before the final liquidation to consolidate, equip themselves, and prepare a plan for the defense of the ghetto. The ŻOB now had 22 fighting squads, of 15 fighters each; the Military Union had about half the number of fighters, but it operated in a similar manner.

The ghetto as a whole was engaged in feverish preparations for the expected deportation, which all believed would be the final one. The general population concentrated on preparing bunkers. Groups of Jews, made up mostly of tenants of the same building, went to work on the construction of subterranean bunkers; such shelters, below ground level or in the cellars, had proved very useful during the January deportation. The January experience gave new hope to the ghetto population, who felt that the Germans might perhaps want to hold back and avoid a military clash with the Jews of the ghetto in a large city that was the capital of Poland and contained the hard core of the Polish resistance movement. Many Jews were now ready to entertain the hope that the combination of resistance and hiding out might provide the route to rescue. The fighters and the general population now had a common interest, with each having its allotted task. The ŻOB was to be the armed force that would battle in the open, and the masses of the people were to hide out in the bunkers, in what would be another form of joint resistance.

The network of bunkers in the ghetto was being expanded, and a substantial part of the ghetto population was kept busy at night digging the hideouts and communication trenches under the ground. The preparation of bunkers became a mass movement in the central ghetto area, and as the final deportation drew near, every inhabitant of the ghetto had two addresses—one on the ghetto surface and a subterranean one in a bunker.

Backyards of the Warsaw ghetto in Poland.

Final Liquidation and Revolt

The final liquidation of the ghetto began on Monday, April 19, 1943, the eve of Passover. The Jews had been warned of what lay ahead and they were prepared. Although the Germans had a substantial military force on the alert for the deportation, they do not seem to have expected the direct confrontation of street battles. SS and Police General Jürgen **STROOP**, who had had experience in fighting the **PARTISANS**, was assigned to supervise the deportation and liquidation of the ghetto. Stroop's daily reports on the battle against the ghetto and his final summing-up when the revolt had come to an end constitute the basic historical documentation of the resistance offered by the Jews and the methods used by the Nazis to overcome it.

In his final report on the military campaign that he led against the ghetto revolt, Stroop provided the following data: "Of the total of 56,065 Jews who were seized, 7,000 were destroyed during the course of the *Grossaktion* inside the former Jewish quarter; in the deportation to T2 [the Treblinka extermination camp] 6,929 were exterminated,

The ghetto fighters were preparing for a final act of protest, a last sign of life that they would send to the Jews and all of humanity in the free world. For this reason they made no attempt to prepare retreat or escape routes that would be available when the fighting was over. Their choice was to fight until the last breath in their bodies.

127

DETERMINATION TO SURVIVE

Common to the Jews of Poland, no matter what their attitudes and political views, was the stubborn determination to survive (*iberlebn*), to see the war through. The term that has been handed down to describe this determination to survive physically is *Kiddush Ha-Hayyim* ("sanctifying life"). Few Jews thought that the Germans might win the war and that it was necessary to prepare for a situation in which the Nazis would dominate worldwide. Such a possibility did not enter most minds, since the Jews would not believe that extreme evil in its Nazi incarnation could last for long. Perhaps they also realized that they had no chance of surviving under a prolonged Nazi regime, and therefore tried to ignore it or repress the very thought.

which adds up to 13,929 Jews destroyed. In addition to the 56,065, another 5,000 to 6,000 lost their lives in explosions and fires." Stroop's figures are exaggerated. His report also mentions that the German losses were 16 killed and 85 wounded; these figures do not tally with the daily casualty reports that Stroop submitted during the fighting. Some sources believe that the German losses were much higher.

In the last few months of its existence, some 20,000 Jews left the ghetto to seek refuge on the Polish side. The underground Polish political parties, created a special organization, Zegota, to extend aid to Jews. Approximately 4,000 Jews benefited from Zegota's assistance at various times. In Poland it was more difficult to help Jews than in other occupied countries; offering shelter to a Jew was punishable by death. In addition to the **"RIGHTEOUS AMONG THE NATIONS"** who helped Jews out of humanitarian motives, quite a few Poles sheltered Jews for money. No data are available on the number of Jews who were saved by hiding or by posing as Poles. Many of these Jews fell in battle or were killed during the Warsaw Polish uprising.

Warsaw Jews who were forced out of the bunkers or otherwise fell into German hands during the uprising were not all murdered on the spot; neither were all the people transported from the *Umschlagplatz* in April and May 1943 taken straight to their death. Transports made up of Jews from the "shops area," where resistance had not been so fierce, were sent to **PONIATOWA** and **TRAWNIKI**. From the central ghetto, many transports had **MAJDANEK** and **BUDZYŃ** as their destination. Most of these Jews were killed in early November 1943, in the **ERNTEFEST** (**"HARVEST FESTIVAL"**) murder operation. Several thousand Jews who were taken to the Majdanek concentration camp were deported, after a short stay, to **AUSCHWITZ** and to labor camps in the western parts of occupied Poland. When all the transfers and evacuations were over, no more than 1,000 to 2,000 of these Jews had survived.

After the end of the war, some of the surviving Jews made their way back to the cities where they had lived before the war. Some 2,000 survivors gathered in Warsaw within a few months, and were given first aid by the Jewish Committee that began functioning in the city. Warsaw did not attract a large concentration of Jews; Lublin was preferred as the place where the Polish administration and a new life were gaining hold. It was only when the reconstruction of Warsaw had progressed and the Polish institutions were reestablished there that the central Jewish organizations followed suit and moved to Warsaw.

The Jewish Historical Institute (Żydowski Instytut Historyczny), which was set up in a wing of the building that housed the Institute of Jewish Studies, embarked upon what became a highly important effort of collecting documents and mementos of the Jews of Poland and the **HOLOCAUST** period. Warsaw became the seat of the Central Committee of the Jews of Poland, followed, in 1950, by the Cultural and Social Union of the Jews of Poland. Eventually, 20,000 to 30,000 Jews settled in Warsaw, most of whom had not lived there before the war. The great majority of these Jews left in the waves of Jewish emigration from Poland in the postwar period.

SUGGESTED RESOURCES

Roland, Charles G. *Courage Under Siege: Starvation, Disease, and Death in the Warsaw Ghetto.* New York: Oxford University Press, 1992.

Shoah [videorecording]. New Yorker Video, 1999.

Stewart, Gail. *Life in the Warsaw Ghetto.* San Diego: Lucent Books, 1995.

Szpilman, Wladyslaw. *The Pianist: The Extraordinary Story of One Man's Survival in Warsaw, 1939–45.* New York: Picador USA, 1999.

Warsaw Ghetto Uprising

The **WARSAW** ghetto uprising was the first instance of a rebellion by an urban population in German-occupied Europe. Among the Jewish uprisings, it was also the one that lasted the longest, from April 19 to May 16, 1943. It was unique as a general, ghetto-wide rebellion, in which armed fighters took the offensive while masses of Jews rebelled by hiding out in bunkers and other secret places. Their utter determination made the Warsaw ghetto a bastion of resistance and fighting.

First Steps to Resistance

In the spring of 1942, some members of the Jewish underground of the Warsaw ghetto decided that they must form a defense force. They had heard reports of a mass-murder campaign in the East, and they believed that a defense force must be prepared if the Nazis tried to deport the Jews from Warsaw. They were unable to convince others of the need, however. So, by the time the Nazis launched the mass **DEPORTATIONS** of Jews from the Warsaw ghetto on July 22, 1942, no unified Jewish and lasting resistance force had come into being.

When the deportations began, the underground tried again to establish a fighting organization. The ghetto leadership did not support the plan out of fear of Nazi reprisals that would result in the deaths of all Jews of the ghetto, even those who might yet be saved. Still, the **JEWISH FIGHTING ORGANIZATION** (Żydowska Organizacja Bojowa; ŻOB) was founded on July 28. A small group, its membership included only the three Zionist pioneering movements, Ha-Shomer ha-Tsa'ir, Dror, and Akiva. The new organization had little effect in the summer of 1942, and initial attempts to establish contact with the Polish military underground Home Army (*Armia Krajowa*) were also unsuccessful.

The first wave of deportations ended in mid-September. Some 300,000 Jews had been removed from the ghetto. Of those, 265,000 were deported to the **TRE-BLINKA** extermination camp. This left 55,000 to 60,000 Jews in the ghetto. The survivors felt isolated and bitter; most were young people who now blamed themselves

The revolt in the ghetto had reverberated among the remaining Jews of Poland, among the non-Jews in the country, and in all of Europe. Even while the war was still in progress, the story of the Warsaw ghetto uprising became a legend that was passed on, with awe and emotion, as an event of rare historical significance.

The Warsaw ghetto burns during the Jewish uprising in April 1943.

for not having offered armed resistance against the deportation of their families. They also knew that deportations would likely recur at any time.

This mood rejuvenated the ghetto underground. In October, more factions joined the ŻOB, which now represented all the active forces in the underground. The Jewish Military Union (*Żydowski Związek Wojskowy*; ŻZW) was also established, and the ŻOB finally made contact with the Home Army, which gave the ŻOB a few arms—ten pistols and some explosive charges. This was a far cry from what the ŻOB needed, but it was an important boost to morale. A headquarters was established for the ŻOB, under the command of Mordecai **ANIELEWICZ**. The organization now began training the fighters and making plans for resistance.

On Monday, January 18, 1943, before the ŻOB had completed its preparations, the Germans launched the second wave of deportations, the "January *Aktion*" ("operation"). This would be the ŻOB's first military test.

Even though the ŻOB had not had time to prepare a full-scale rebellion, the operation did not proceed as the Germans had expected. Resistance fighters armed with pistols deliberately broke into a long column of Jews who were being marched to the assembly point for the deportation. When the agreed-upon signal was given, they confronted the German escorts in a face-to-face battle—this was the first time Germans were attacked inside the ghetto. Most of the Jewish fighters died or were injured in the battle, though Anielewicz was able to overcome a German soldier and was saved. The column of Jews scattered in all directions. News of the battle soon

The deportations from the Warsaw ghetto came as a surprise, and the ŻOB leadership did not have time to plan a coordinated reaction.

reached the rest of the ghetto inmates. In one place—a building on Zamenhof Street—a squad of Dror men, commanded by Yitzhak **Zuckerman**, lay in waiting; when the Germans appeared on the scene, they were met by a hail of gunfire.

This German offensive lasted four days, during which there was a decisive change in the ghetto population's pattern of behavior. The Jews refused to respond to the shouts ordering them to get out of their houses and report to the assembly points. Most of the Jews found improvised hiding places. The Germans also acted in a different manner—moving quietly, and keeping away from places where Jews might be hiding, not making their usual ear-splitting cries. The operation ended on the fourth day, by which time 5,000 to 6,000 Jews had been caught. The Germans had planned to take 8,000 (the Jews, however, feared that all in the ghetto would be taken). Both the Jews and the Polish underground interpreted the early discontinuation of the operation as a sign of German weakness and a retreat from the resistance.

The events of four days in January 1943 had a decisive impact on preparations for the next Jewish uprising in the Warsaw Ghetto.

Waiting, Watching, Preparing

In the next three months, the ŻOB prepared feverishly for the next episode of rebellion. The ŻOB had learned from the January events that the ghetto might once again be taken by surprise with a Nazi operation; therefore, the fighters had to be on a permanent alert. A total of 22 fighting units were formed. Another "January lesson" was that the enemy had to be taken unaware by the attacks, and these had to be launched from positions in the maze of the ghetto buildings and roof attics. So, the ghetto was divided into fighting sectors with designated positions, with a fighting unit attached to each. Anielewicz was in overall command of the ŻOB and the ghetto.

Most of the fighters' weapons were pistols. Some of them had been obtained from Polish organizations, but for the most part they had had to be purchased. The ŻOB also had automatic weapons and rifles that its men had seized from the Germans, and the ŻZW had obtained weapons from Polish sources. In addition, hand grenades were manufactured in the ghetto; these were to play an important role during the uprising. In this waiting period between January and April, expansion of the ŻOB was limited only by the lack of weapons; the population was now interested in resisting. Shortly before the uprising was launched, the ŻOB's armed and organized force consisted of 22 fighting platoons, with a total of 500 fighters. The ŻZW had 200 to 250 fighters, and the total Jewish fighting forces in the ghetto numbered 700 to 750.

The civilian population of the ghetto now believed that resistance would force the Germans to stop the deportations. They thought that the Germans would also have to consider the possibility that the rebellion in the ghetto might spread to the Polish population and even affect all of occupied **POLAND**. The civilians equipped a network of underground refuges and hiding places, where they could hold out for a long period even if they were cut off from one another. Eventually every Jew in the ghetto had a spot in one of the shelters set up in the central part of the ghetto. Many of these civilian shelters also had defensive weapons. The ŻOB command did not share the hope that armed resistance would keep the Germans from carrying out their plans, but it encouraged the preparation of bunkers.

The Uprising Begins

The last *Aktion* and the resistance campaign that came to be known as the Warsaw Ghetto Uprising began on April 19, 1943, which was the eve of **Passover**. The ghetto fighters had been warned of the timing of what was to be the final deporta-

Passover
The eight day commemmoration of the exodus of the ancient Jews from Egypt during the reign of the Pharaoh Ramses II.

131

Tthe Jews of the Warsaw ghetto fiercely battled the forces of Nazi Germany and stood up against them longer than some independent countries in Europe had held out against German aggression.

tion. There is no doubt that the chief of the **SS** and police in the Warsaw district, Ferdinand von Sammern-Frankenegg, was aware of the existence of a Jewish defense formation. However, he apparently did not dare admit to his superiors that a significant Jewish fighting force had been established in the ghetto. On the eve of the final deportation, Heinrich **HIMMLER** replaced Sammern-Frankenegg with a man who had had experience in fighting **PARTISANS**, SS and police leader Jürgen **STROOP**.

In the 27 days that the uprising lasted, the Nazis deployed a considerable military force, including tanks. In the first days of the fighting, they used, on the average, 2,054 soldiers and policemen and 36 officers. Facing them were 700 to 750 young Jewish fighters who had had no military training or battle experience and who for all practical purposes were armed with no more than pistols.

On the morning of April 19, when the German forces entered the ghetto they did not find a living soul in the central part, except for a group of policemen. The entire Jewish population had taken to the hiding places and bunkers, and by refusing to follow the Germans' orders, they became part of the uprising. That day, following the first clash, the Germans were forced to withdraw from the ghetto. They lost a tank and an armored vehicle that had been hit by Molotov cocktails (bombs), and they were unable to capture the ŻOB and ŻZW position on Muranowska Square. Two flags were raised on top of a building there—the flag of Poland and a blue and white Jewish national flag.

The face-to-face fighting lasted for several days. The Germans were not able to capture or hit the Jewish fighters, who after every clash managed to get away and retreat by way of the roofs; nor could the Germans lay hands on the Jews hiding in the bunkers. The Germans therefore decided to burn the ghetto systematically, building by building; this forced the fighters to take to the bunkers themselves and to resort to partisan tactics by staging sporadic raids. The flames and the heat turned life in the bunkers into hell; the very air was afire. The food that had been stored up spoiled, and the water was no longer fit to drink. Despite all this, the bunker dwellers refused to leave their hideouts.

The bunker war turned out to be the Germans' most difficult and troublesome task. Time and again Stroop claimed in his detailed daily reports that he had overcome resistance and that the uprising was dying out—only to report the next day that there was no end to the attacks and the losses suffered by his troops. Gradually, however, the Jews' power of resistance declined.

On May 8, the headquarters bunker of the ŻOB fell, and with it also Mordecai Anielewicz and a large group of fighters and commanders. The ŻOB fighters had not made any plans for a retreat from the ghetto, as they had thought that the battle would go on inside the ghetto until the last fighter had fallen. Thanks to a rescue mission arranged by the ŻOB men on the Polish side, who made their way through the sewers of the city, several dozen fighters were saved.

The fighting in the ghetto lasted nearly a month. The Jews in the bunkers who were not discovered by the Germans' dogs and special search instruments kept up their resistance as long as they were alive. The Nazis also threw gas grenades into the bunkers, when the Jews inside refused to leave even after they had been forced open.

On May 16, Stroop announced that the fighting was over and that "we succeeded in capturing altogether 56,065 Jews, that is, definitely destroying them." He stated that he was going to blow up the Great Synagogue on Tłomacka Street (which was outside the ghetto and the scene of the fighting) as a symbol of victory and of the fact that "the Jewish quarter of Warsaw no longer exists."

Even after May 16 there were still hundreds of Jews in the subterranean bunkers of the ghetto, which was now a heap of ruins. They sneaked out of the bunkers during the night in search of food and water and kept in touch with one another. The last survivors among these fighters succeeded in establishing contact with the Poles and escaping to the "Aryan" side. Only a handful held out in the bunkers until the **WARSAW POLISH UPRISING** took place in August 1944.

SEE ALSO **RESISTANCE, JEWISH.**

Waffen-SS troops leading Jews from the burning ghetto during the Warsaw Ghetto Uprising.

SUGGESTED RESOURCES

Gutman, Israel. *Resistance: The Warsaw Ghetto Uprising.* Boston: Houghton Mifflin, 1994.

Landau, Elaine. *The Warsaw Ghetto Uprising.* New York: Macmillan, 1992.

Warsaw Ghetto Uprising: An Audio-visual Program from the Exhibition at Ghetto Fighter's House [videorecording]. Ergo Media, 1993.

Zuckerman, Yitzhak. *A Surplus of Memory: Chronicle of the Warsaw Ghetto Uprising.* Berkeley: University of California Press, 1993.

Warsaw Polish Uprising

In the summer of 1944, a major uprising took place in **WARSAW, POLAND,** against the Germans who had occupied the country for five years. This revolt was

started by the largest Polish resistance organization, the *Armia Krajowa*, which took its orders from the Polish government-in-exile in London. The aim of the uprising was to take control of Warsaw before the **SOVIET UNION**'s Red Army entered the city—a development that was expected to take place soon. The Polish rebel forces amounted to some 23,000 poorly equipped troops. They were facing tens of thousands of German troops and police, who were plentifully supplied with weapons and other equipment. The uprising did not come as a surprise to the Germans.

The rebellion broke out on August 1, 1944. In the first few days, it spread over large parts of central Warsaw, extending to the more distant parts of several suburbs and to a number of points on the right bank of the Vistula River. However, not a single bridge or enemy stronghold was captured by the attacking Polish forces. The Germans launched a harsh counterattack. Under the command of Erich von dem **BACH-ZELEWSKI**, their attack was accompanied by mass terror and inhumane methods of fighting.

The aid that came to the Poles from the Allies did not amount to more than a few arms drops. In the early stages of the revolt, the Soviets hindered the Allied aid. Only in the later stages, in mid-September, did the Soviets themselves drop some supplies for the Poles.

Most of the Polish fighters were young people. Several smaller resistance organizations, led by the *Armia Ludowa*, joined the uprising. The *Armia Ludowa* included a group of Jews, members of the **JEWISH FIGHTING ORGANIZATION** (Żydowska Organizacja Bojowa; ŻOB), who had succeeded in leaving the ghetto after a major Jewish revolt there had been quashed the previous year (*see* **WARSAW GHETTO UPRISING**). Other Jews also took part in the uprising. On August 4, the rebels liberated several hundred Jewish prisoners (from Greece and **HUNGARY**) from the concentration camp on Gesia Street. These freed prisoners joined in the revolt. Warsaw's civilian population also gave strong support to the uprising, by publishing newspapers, providing first aid, organizing supplies and postal services, and performing other such services.

On September 14, Polish army units that had parachuted into Warsaw early seized control of the right bank of the Vistula River. They managed to transfer several battalions to the left bank. The Poles suffered heavy losses in the process. They could not, however, bring relief to the rebels. The besieged city center fell to the German forces on October 2, and this marked the end of the uprising.

Polish losses came to between 16,000 and 20,000 fighters killed and missing, 7,000 wounded, and 150,000 civilians killed. That last figure included several thousand Jews who had been in hiding with the Polish population after the liquidation of the Warsaw ghetto. German losses were much lighter—6,000 dead or missing, and 9,000 wounded.

The Germans sent most of the surviving civilians to nearby camps; 65,000 of them were subsequently transferred to **CONCENTRATION CAMPS**. About 100,000 people were held for **FORCED LABOR** in **GERMANY**. Following the insurgents' surrender, the Germans burned and razed those parts of the city that were still intact, causing great losses to Poland's cultural and spiritual treasures.

SUGGESTED RESOURCES

"Armia Krakowa." *Simon Wiesenthal Center Museum of Tolerance Online.* [Online]
http://motlc.wiesenthal.org/pages/t002/t00215.html (accessed on September 7, 2000).

Westerbork

Westerbork was a camp situated near the town of that name in the northeastern **NETHERLANDS**. From 1942 to 1944, Westerbork was a transit camp for Jews who were being deported from the Netherlands to eastern Europe.

The camp had been established in October 1939 by the Dutch government to house Jewish refugees who had entered the country illegally. A Dutch official from the Ministry of Justice was put in charge of it. The costs of putting up the camp and maintaining it were charged to the Jewish Refugee Committee in the Netherlands (established in 1933). When **GERMANY** invaded the Netherlands on May 10, 1940, there were 750 refugees in the Westerbork camp. The refugees were moved to Leeuwarden, only to be taken back to Westerbork following the Dutch surrender. After the surrender, refugees from other camps were moved to Westerbork. In 1941, the camp had a population of 1,100, accommodated in 200 small wooden houses.

At the end of 1941, the German administration decided to use Westerbork as a transit camp for Jews who were being deported to the east. A barbed-wire fence was put up around the camp, and 24 large wooden barracks were built. In the first half of 1942, some 400 German Jews were transferred to Westerbork from various cities in the Netherlands.

On July 1, 1942, the German Security Police (Sicherheitspolizei) took control of the Westerbork camp. An **SS** company was sent in to reinforce the Dutch military police who were responsible for guarding the camp. Erich Deppner was appointed camp commandant. He handled the first transport from Westerbork to **AUSCHWITZ**. He caused a riot when, to fill the required quota of 1,000 deportees, he included children without their parents, as well as women who happened to be standing in line for admittance into the camp (their husbands had already been registered for the camp and were not included in the transport).

On September 1, 1942, Deppner was replaced by an SS officer, Josef Hugo Dischner. Dischner was unable to deal with the sudden influx of 13,000 prisoners—Jews who had been seized in a raid. On October 12, Albert Konrad Gemmeker took over Dischner's job. Gemmeker generally left the day-to-day operation of the camp in the hands of the German Jews, who had been in charge of it from the beginning. This did not change even when most of the camp inmates were Jews of Dutch nationality; German Jews kept all the responsible posts.

The systematic transfer to Westerbork of Jews from all parts of the Netherlands was launched on July 14, 1942. On the following day, their deportation to Auschwitz and other camps was set in motion. Almost 100,000 Jews were deported from Westerbork. Gemmeker had the Jewish camp leadership prepare the lists of those prisoners to be deported. The leadership, however, was not allowed to include certain camp residents who were exempted from being moved; these included Jews of foreign nationality and about 2,000 inmates who had been given special status in the two weeks before the **DEPORTATIONS** were launched. Beginning February 2, 1943, the deportation trains left Westerbork every Tuesday, turning the night before into a time of horror and panic in the camp.

The camp administration consisted of ten subdivisions. Outstanding among the subdivision heads was Kurt Schlesinger, a businessman in his earlier life, who became Gemmeker's right-hand man. On August 12, 1943, Schlesinger was appointed head of the principal subdivision, which was also in charge of the main card index—the key instrument for the preparation of the lists of persons to be deported. Another subdivision was the **JEWISH GHETTO POLICE** (Jüdischer Ord-

The Westerbork camp led a double life. There were the "permanent" prisoners, who remained in place for a considerable length of time, ran their own affairs, and, in a strange way, led a near-normal life. And there were the masses who were brought into the camp from time to time, stayed there for a week or two, and were then sent to the camps in the East.

Jews being deported from the Westerbork transit camp in the Netherlands, 1943.

nungsdienst). At its full strength, this police force consisted of 200 young men, divided evenly between Dutch and German Jews. They helped arrange transports, in addition to maintaining order inside the camp.

The camp inmates were supposed to work for the war effort, but the will to work was very low. In 1943, when the permanent population was at its peak, the camp inmates, both Jews and non-Jews, had jobs in metalworking, health services, and education, as well as in camp administration, kitchen work, camp maintenance and security, and other internal departments. Some worked outside the camp, as well.

The number of people working in health services was exceptionally large. Westerbork had a hospital with 1,800 beds, 120 doctors and another 1,000 workers, and laboratories, pharmacies, and other departments needing workers. The camp commandant also encouraged entertainment activities—concerts, operas, and cabaret performances—in which outstanding artists among the camp population took part. There were no shortages in the camp, since the Dutch administration provided it with a regular supply of food and other goods. The camp commandant also had at his disposal a fund for additional purchases. This fund had its source in Jewish property that had been confiscated.

On April 12, 1945, when Allied forces were approaching Westerbork, Gemmeker officially handed the camp over to Kurt Schlesinger. On that day, the camp had 876 inmates. Of them, 569 were Dutch nationals. The rest belonged to various other nationalities or were stateless (they did not hold citizenship from any country).

After the war, a Dutch court sentenced Gemmeker to ten years in prison. A memorial and a permanent exhibition have been set up on the site of the Westerbork camp.

SUGGESTED RESOURCES

Boas, Jacob. *Boulevard des Misères: The Story of Transit Camp Westerbork.* Hamden, CT: Archon Books, 1985.

Camp of Hope and Despair: Witnesses of Westerbork, 1939–1945 [videorecording]. Ergo Media, 1994.

Hillesum, Etty. *Letters from Westerbork*. New York: Pantheon Books, 1986.

Verdoner-Sluizer, Hilde. *Signs of Life: The Letters of Hilde Verdoner-Sluizer from Nazi Transit Camp Westerbork, 1942–1944*. Washington, DC: Acropolis Books, 1990.

Wiesel, Elie

(b. 1928)

Elie (Eliezer) Wiesel is a **HOLOCAUST** survivor, prolific writer, and winner of the 1986 Nobel Peace Prize. Raised in a devout Jewish home in Sighet Marmaţiei, Transylvania (present-day Romania), Wiesel tenuously held on to his faith in God after being deported to **AUSCHWITZ** with his family in 1944. Liberated from **BUCHENWALD**, he later studied at the Sorbonne in **PARIS** and became a foreign correspondent for the Israeli daily newspaper *Yediot Aharonot*.

Elie Wiesel.

Wiesel has written more than 40 fiction and nonfiction books, including novels that bring to life pictures drawn from traditional Jewish writings, transforming them into vibrant human experiences. In his extraordinary memoir *Un di Velt Hot Geshvigen* (1956), written in Yiddish and adapted and translated into many languages (the English title is *Night*), Wiesel personifies the experience of a concentration camp inmate. His unique writing style has provided a powerful means of discussing the Holocaust.

Wiesel's works often deal with oppression and the fragility of the human condition. The anguished memories of his ordeals in the **CONCENTRATION CAMPS**, woven into the text of his stories, express the collective loss of a seared generation. Always mindful of the suffering of the other victims of the Holocaust, Wiesel signifies the uniqueness of the Jewish experience in the statement: "While not all victims [of the Nazis] were Jews, all Jews were victims."

On accepting the Congressional Gold Medal of Achievement from President Ronald Reagan in 1985, Wiesel appealed to the president not to visit the cemetery in Bitburg, **GERMANY**, in which 47 **SS** men are buried. "Your place, Mr. President, is with the victims," he declared. This impulse to jolt the conscience of society earned Wiesel the Nobel Peace Prize (though it did not keep Reagan from going to the Bitburg cemetery). In his presentation address at the Nobel Prize ceremonies, the chairman of the Norwegian Nobel Committee, Egil Aarvik, summed up Wiesel's message to humanity: "Do not forget, do not sink into a new blind indifference, but involve yourselves in truth and justice, in human dignity, freedom, and atonement."

As chairman of the U.S. Holocaust Memorial Council from 1980 to 1986, Wiesel instituted national "Days of Remembrance" in the **UNITED STATES**. His leadership inspired the introduction of Holocaust curricula in numerous states, cities, and counties. In his words and deeds, Wiesel has helped to bring the Holocaust to the consciousness of the world. He has received dozens of honorary degrees and many awards, and with his wife, Marion, established The Elie Wiesel Foundation for Humanity. Today he lectures widely and is a professor in the humanities at Boston University.

SUGGESTED RESOURCES

The Elie Wiesel Foundation for Humanity. [Online] http://www.eliewieselfoundation.org/default.htm (accessed on September 7, 2000).

Facing Hate with Elie Wiesel and Bill Moyers [videorecording]. Mystic Fire Video, 1991.

From *Night*

Never shall I forget that night, the first night in camp,
which has turned my life into one long night,
seven times cursed and seven times sealed.
Never shall I forget that smoke.
Never shall I forget the little faces of the children
whose bodies I saw turned into wreaths of smoke beneath a silent blue sky.

Never shall I forget those flames which consumed by faith forever.

Never shall I forget that nocturnal silence which deprived me,
for all eternity, of the desire to live.
Never shall I forget those moments which murdered my God
And my soul and turned my dreams to dust.
Never shall I forget these things, even if I am condemned to live as long
    as God Himself.
Never.

—ELIE WIESEL

Night, translated by Stella Rodway (New York: Hill and Wang), 1960.

A Portrait of Elie Wiesel [videorecording]. PBS Video, 1988.

Rosenfeld, A. H., and I. Greenberg, eds.*Confronting the Holocaust: The Impact of Elie Wiesel.* Bloomington: Indiana University Press, 1978.

Wiesel, Elie. *All Rivers Run to the Sea: Memoirs.* Knopf, 1995.

Wiesel, Elie. *Night.* New York: Hill and Wang, 1960.

Wiesenthal, Simon

(b. 1908)

HOLOCAUST survivor, writer, and Nazi hunter Simon Wiesenthal was born in Buchach, Galicia (present-day UKRAINE). He studied architecture at the Prague Technical University and was living in LVOV, POLAND, when World War II began in 1939. He was arrested by Ukrainian police and spent most of the war in concentration and forced-labor camps, among them JANÓWSKA (Lvov), PŁASZÓW, GROSS-ROSEN, and BUCHENWALD. Barely alive and weighing less than one hundred pounds, Wiesenthal was liberated in MAUTHAUSEN on May 5, 1945, by the U.S. Army. Wiesenthal and his wife, Cyla Mueller, lost dozens of family members in the Holocaust.

After the war, Wiesenthal devoted himself to the investigation of Nazi war criminals. He worked first for the War Crimes section of the U.S. Army in AUSTRIA. In 1947, he established the Jewish Historical Documentation Center in Linz. Public interest in Nazi war criminals decreased, and Wiesenthal closed the Linz center in 1954. He resumed his work in VIENNA in 1961 in the wake of the trial of Adolf EICHMANN, which created renewed interest in the prosecution of Nazi war criminals.

Among the most prominent Nazis whom Wiesenthal helped find or bring to justice were Franz STANGL, commandant of the TREBLINKA and SOBIBÓR EXTERMINATION CAMPS; Gustav Wagner, deputy commandant of Sobibór; Franz Mürer, commandant of the VILNA ghetto; and Karl Silberbauer, the policeman who arrest-

ed Anne **FRANK**. Not everyone has appreciated Wiesenthal's activities: In 1982, a bomb exploded at the front door of his home in Vienna. Several neo-Nazis were arrested for the crime; one was sentenced to prison.

In 1977, the Simon Wiesenthal Center for Holocaust Studies was established at the Yeshiva University of Los Angeles in honor of Wiesenthal's life's work (*see* **MUSEUMS AND MEMORIAL INSTITUTES**.) Besides his efforts to prosecute Nazi war criminals, Wiesenthal has played an important role in commemorating the victims of the Holocaust. His works include *The Murderers among Us*; *The Sunflower*; *Max and Helen*; and *Every Day Remembrance Day: A Chronicle of Jewish Martyrdom*.

SUGGESTED RESOURCES

Levy, Alan. *The Wiesenthal File.* Grand Rapids, MI: Eerdmans, 1994.

Pick, Hella. *Simon Wiesenthal: A Life in Search of Justice.* Boston: Northeastern University Press, 1996.

Wiesenthal, Simon. *Justice Not Vengeance.* New York: Grove Weidenfeld, 1989.

Wiesenthal, Simon. *The Sunflower: On the Possibilities and Limits of Forgiveness.* Revised and expanded edition. Edited by Harry James Cargas and Bonnie V. Fetterman. New York: Schocken Books, 1997.

Simon Wiesenthal.

Wirth, Christian

(1885–1944)

An **SS** major and head of the concentration camp organization in **POLAND**, Christian Wirth was born in Württemberg, **GERMANY**. He trained as a carpenter and later served in World War I, receiving high decorations. After the war, Wirth entered the police force and became notorious for his interrogation methods. He became a member of the **NAZI PARTY** in 1931. By 1939, Wirth had become a *Kriminalkommissar* in the Stuttgart criminal police, a department of the **GESTAPO**.

At the end of 1939, Wirth began to specialize in the "treatment" of the insane by means of euthanasia (*see* **EUTHANASIA PROGRAM**). At this time, he performed the first known gassing experiments on Germans who were certified as incurably insane. Wirth became an inspector of euthanasia establishments in Greater Germany in 1940. His success led to an assignment in the Polish city of **LUBLIN** in 1941. Here, he set up a new euthanasia center, the first outside the Reich. He followed this with the establishment of five **EXTERMINATION CAMPS** in Poland; the first of these to become operational was at **CHEŁMNO**.

During the next year and a half, Wirth supervised the killing of more than 1.5 million Jews in the camps of **BEŁŻEC**, **SOBIBÓR**, and **TREBLINKA**. He received the cooperation of Odilo **GLOBOCNIK** and the SS police headquarters in Lublin. Wirth's assignment involved the introduction of new gassing techniques. When the camp at Bełżec was closed in the fall of 1943, Wirth was promoted to SS-*Sturmbannführer* (major) and sent to Trieste, where his task was to hasten the deportation of the Jews. He was killed by **PARTISANS** (resistance fighters) while on a journey to Fiume.

SUGGESTED RESOURCES

Arad, Yitzhak. *Belzec, Sobibor, Treblinka: The Operation Reinhard Death Camps.* Bloomington: Indiana University Press, 1987.

Burleigh, Michael. *Death and Deliverance: "Euthanasia" in Germany c. 1900–1945*. New York: Cambridge University Press, 1994.

Friedlander, Henry. *The Origins of Nazi Genocide: From Euthanasia to the Final Solution*. Chapel Hill: University of North Carolina Press, 1995.

Wise, Stephen Samuel

Rabbi Stephen Wise played a key role in establishing the American Zionist movement.

(1874–1949)

An American Jew, Stephen Wise was a religious leader, a founder of and activist in the Zionist movement in the **UNITED STATES**, and a spokesperson for the cause of civic betterment. Much of the criticism of the role of the American Jewish community during the **HOLOCAUST** focuses on his leadership.

After serving as a Reform rabbi in Portland, Oregon, Wise moved to the east. In 1907, he founded the Free Synagogue in New York, remaining its spiritual leader until his death. In 1922, Wise established the Jewish Institute of Religion (JIR), an academy for training Reform rabbis. He served as president of the JIR until it merged with the Hebrew Union College of Cincinnati, Ohio, in 1948. Wise was a crusader for social causes. His sermons and speeches focused on every civic cause of the 1920s and 1930s, including municipal corruption and the right of labor to organize. His campaign to force the resignation of the corrupt mayor of New York City, James Walker, brought Wise into conflict with Franklin D. Roosevelt, who was governor of New York from 1928 to 1932. This rupture lasted until the presidential election of 1936, when Wise became a staunch supporter of the administration.

In 1897, Wise helped to found the New York Federation of Zionists, which became the Federation of American Zionists a year later. In 1919, Wise was a spokesman for the Zionist cause at the **PARIS** Peace Conference (1919–20) and he assumed the presidency of the Zionist Organization of America that same year. He headed the Zionist Organization of America from 1918 to 1920 and again from 1936 to 1938. Wise was among the organizers of the American Jewish Congress, which was founded in 1920. In 1936, he established the **WORLD JEWISH CONGRESS**, of which he was president until his death.

After 1933, when the Nazis came to power in **GERMANY**, the leadership role that Wise sought to fill proved increasingly difficult. American Jewry of the time was weak and divided. In 1933, Wise enlisted the support of the American Jewish Congress in a boycott of German products, seeing this as the morally correct thing to do. At the same time, he wavered in his support for the Haavara Agreement between Germany and the *Yishuv* (the organized Jewish community in Palestine). The Haavara Agreement (1933) was a pact between Nazis and Zionists that approved the emigration of Jews to Palestine; it was the only contract that existed between the Zionists and the Third Reich.

Abba Hillel Silver, a fellow Reform rabbi and Zionist, was a Republican supporter who had been radicalized by the events in Europe. He had made an agreement with the more moderate Wise to avoid confronting the administration publicly. In 1943, Silver broke the agreement by arousing American public opinion on behalf of Zionism. At the same time, the aging Wise came into conflict with the Revisionist Zionists, whose cause had been considerably strengthened by a group of Palestinian Jews headed by Peter Bergson; Wise was convinced that Bergson was intending to take over the American Zionist movement. At the same time, Wise faced opposition from the newly organized anti-Zionist constituency within the Jewish community. Clearly, the American Jewish community had become more fragmented than ever in

Bishop William T. Manning (seated left), Rabbi Stephen Wise (seated right), and two unidentified men (standing), attend a rally to protest the anti-Jewish laws and terrorism promoted by the new Nazi regime in Germany; March 27, 1933, Madison Square Garden, New York.

the crucial year of 1943. Wise's attempt to play the role of peacemaker was unsuccessful: the divisions within the community were too great, as was the gap between what the Jewish rescue advocates sought and what the Roosevelt administration was willing to give during wartime. Because of his leadership position, Wise was ultimately compelled to bear much of the responsibility for this failure.

By 1943, some felt that Wise's leadership had become weak and inconsistent. Under pressure by U.S. government officials, and in order to avoid accusations that Jews were atrocity-mongers, Wise agreed to delay public release of the news of the "FINAL SOLUTION" (as contained in the RIEGNER CABLE) until the information could be independently verified. This delayed any U.S. government action by more than a year, during which hundreds of thousands more European Jews perished. By 1944, Wise had become deeply disillusioned. The establishment of the Jewish state a year before his death gave him considerable gratification, but as the radical losses suffered by European Jewry became known, his despair intensified. His autobiography, *The Challenging Years: The Autobiography of Stephen Wise*, was published in 1949.

SUGGESTED RESOURCES

American-Israeli Cooperative Enterprise. "Stephen S. Wise." *The Jewish Student Online Resource Center (JSOURCE)*. [Online] http://www.us-israel.org/jsource/biography/wise.html (accessed on September 7, 2000).

Peck, Abraham J., ed. *The Papers of the World Jewish Congress 1939–1945*. New York: Garland, 1991.

Peck, Abraham J., ed. *The Papers of the World Jewish Congress 1945–1950: Liberation and the Saving Remnant*. New York: Garland, 1991.

Urofsky, Melvin I. *A Voice That Spoke for Justice: The Life and Times of Stephen S. Wise*. Albany: State University of New York Press, 1982.

Wisliceny, Dieter

(1911–1948)

Dieter Wisliceny served as Adolf EICHMANN's deputy in the Jewish Section (Section IV B 4) of the REICH SECURITY MAIN OFFICE (RSHA; Reichssicherheit-

shauptamt) in **SLOVAKIA**, Greece, and **HUNGARY** and was the organizer of the mass deportation of Jews from these countries between 1942 and 1944. Wisliceny joined the **SS** in 1934 and entered the **SD** (Security Service) the same year. Beginning in September 1940 he acted as "adviser on Jewish affairs" to the Slovak government and soon became known for his intelligence and opportunism.

During the **DEPORTATIONS** from Slovakia in the summer of 1942, Wisliceny was bribed by the Bratislava-based underground *Pracovná Skupina* (Working Group) to delay the deportation of Slovak Jews. He entered into negotiations on the so-called Europa Plan, initiated by Rabbi Michael Dov Weissmandel, to save the remaining Jews in Europe in return for a ransom of $2 million to $3 million, to be made available by Jewish organizations abroad. Wisliceny accepted a sum between $40,000 and $50,000 (the exact amount is not known) as a first installment and transmitted it to higher SS authorities.

In 1943 and 1944, Wisliceny headed the **SPECIAL COMMANDO** for Jewish Affairs in Salonika and was instrumental in the liquidation of Greek Jewry. In March 1944 he joined Eichmann's Special Commando in **BUDAPEST** to organize the deportations of Hungarian Jews and became involved as liaison in the "Blood for Goods" negotiations with the Relief and Rescue Committee of Budapest.

After the war, Wisliceny served as a witness for the prosecution at the Nuremberg Trial and was extradited to Czechoslovakia. While awaiting his trial in the Bratislava prison, he wrote several important affidavits on the **"FINAL SOLUTION"**; on Eichmann's role; on the mufti of Jerusalem, Hajj Amin al-Husseini; and on the negotiations over the Europa Plan and the "Blood for Goods" proposal. Wisliceny's testimony was used by the prosecution at the Eichmann trial in Jerusalem in 1961. Condemned to death, he was hanged in Bratislava in February 1948.

SUGGESTED RESOURCES

"Affidavit of Dieter Wisliceny," in *Nazi Conspiracy and Aggression.* Vol. VIII. USGPO, 1946. Reproduced at http://www.ess.uwe.ac.uk/genocide/Wisliceny.htm (accessed on September 7, 2000).

Wolff, Karl

(1900–1984)

A senior **SS** and police officer, Karl Wolff was born in Darmstadt, **GERMANY**, the son of a district court judge. In World War I, Wolff served as a lieutenant and earned an Iron Cross, First Class. After the war, he fought in the ranks of the paramilitary fighting units known as *Freikorps* in the state of Hesse. He held various business posts from 1920 to 1933 and then set up his own public relations firm in Munich.

In 1931, Wolff joined the **NAZI PARTY** and the SS, and in July, 1933, he was appointed Heinrich **HIMMLER**'s assistant to the commanding officer. In 1936, he was elected as a Parliamentary member of the Reichstag from Hesse. Wolff advanced rapidly up the SS ladder, being appointed *Standartenführer* (colonel) in January 1934, *Gruppenführer* (lieutenant general) in the Waffen-SS in May 1940, and SS-*Obergruppenführer* (general) and *General-oberst* (senior general) in 1942. He was awarded the Nazi party's gold medal on January 30, 1939.

Wolff was responsible for obtaining the necessary deportation trains from the German Railways administration for transporting thousands of Jews to the **TRE-**

BLINKA extermination camp. In September 1943, Wolff became military governor of northern ITALY and plenipotentiary of the Reich to Benito Mussolini's Fascist government. In February 1945, Wolff contacted UNITED STATES intelligence agent Allen Dulles in Zurich and arranged for the surrender of the German forces in northern Italy.

After the war, Wolff appeared as a witness for the prosecution in trials of Nazi criminals. He was tried by a German court and sentenced to four years of imprisonment with hard labor in 1946, but was released a week later. Wolff then became a highly successful public relations agent. At the time of the Adolf EICHMANN trial in 1961, he drew attention to himself with an interview that he gave to a German magazine in May.

No longer anonymous, Wolff was put under arrest in January 1962, charged with the murder of Jews and with direct responsibility for the deportation of 300,000 Jews to Treblinka. On September 30, 1964, Wolff was sentenced to fifteen years in prison and loss of civil rights for ten years; he was released in 1972 for good behavior.

SUGGESTED RESOURCES

The SS. Alexandria, VA: Time-Life Books, 1989.

Williamson, Gordon. *The SS: Hitler's Instrument of Terror.* Osceolo, WI: Motorbooks International, 1994.

Zuccotti, Susan. *The Italians and the Holocaust: Persecution, Rescue, and Survival.* New York: Basic Books, 1987. Reprint, Lincoln: University of Nebraska Press, 1996.

plenipotentiary
A diplomatic agent who has the power to conduct business.

World Jewish Congress

The World Jewish Congress (WJC), international Jewish organization, was founded in 1932 but it was in actual existence only from 1936. The WJC was a successor to the Comité des Délégations Juives (Committee of Jewish Delegations), an organization that had been established to represent Jewish claims at the PARIS Peace Conference after World War I.

Among the affiliates of the WJC was the American Jewish Congress (AJC), which had been formed on a temporary basis during World War I and reorganized on a permanent basis in 1922. The AJC opposed what it saw as a German Jewish leadership in the UNITED STATES in which the wealthy had become the controlling class; the AJC attempted to replace this leadership with a mass following of American Jewry that was organized on a democratic basis.

Based on the concept of the Jews as a nation, the WJC was organized as an attempt to create a worldwide defense of Jewry against Nazism and ANTISEMITISM. Under the leadership of American rabbi Stephen S. WISE, the AJC and the WJC were among the first and most active groups to fight Nazism. As early as March 1933, the AJC organized a mass rally in Madison Square Garden in New York against Nazi terrorization of Jews; in May of that year, it sponsored a parade protesting the burning of books in GERMANY. The AJC joined the boycott of German goods and became the mainstay of the boycott movement. It attempted to influence the government administration to relax immigration restrictions in order to allow in a greater number of Jewish refugees. However, along with other Jewish organizations, it hesitated to press for legislation that would permit larger quotas for fear that such an act would lead only to further restrictions.

After the outbreak of World War II in Europe, the executive of the WJC was relocated from Europe to the United States. The WJC carried on its work from there, using the officers of the AJC to gain access to government officials. Relief efforts of the WJC were hampered not only by the refusal of the U.S. government to allow food to be sent through the blockade of Europe and to permit money to be transferred to occupied countries, but also by the limited funds available to the WJC. Nevertheless, both the WJC and the AJC maintained constant pressure on the U.S. government and the embassies of the Allies, through lobbying efforts and mass demonstrations, to take action on behalf of European Jewry. In July 1942 and March 1943, the AJC organized mass rallies in Madison Square Garden in New York and in other cities around the United States to publicize the plight of European Jews. In August 1942, a cable was sent by Dr. Gerhart Riegner, the WJC representative in Geneva, that outlined the German plans for the **"FINAL SOLUTION."** Before this, Americans were not truly aware of what was happening to the Jews of Europe (*see* **RIEGNER CABLE**). As in this case, the representatives of the WJC in Europe were the main source of information regarding the fate of European Jewry throughout the war.

Rabbi Wise, who was president of both the WJC and the AJC, was the leading Jewish activist with connections in U.S. government circles, though his access to and influence upon President Franklin D. Roosevelt was very limited. However, he and Dr. Goldmann did obtain Roosevelt's consent, in July 1943, to send funds to Romania for the relief and rescue of Jews. Wise was also largely responsible for informing the secretary of the Treasury, Henry **MORGENTHAU**, Jr., of the tragedy overwhelming European Jewry and for gaining his sympathy for rescue attempts. These two factors were influential in leading to the creation of the **WAR REFUGEE BOARD**. The Board was established in 1944 to expedite the transfer of rescue funds.

SUGGESTED RESOURCES

Peck, Abraham J., ed. *The Papers of the World Jewish Congress 1939–1945.* New York: Garland, 1991.

Peck, Abraham J., ed. *The Papers of the World Jewish Congress 1945–1950: Liberation and the Saving Remnant.* New York: Garland, 1991.

Urofsky, Melvin I. *A Voice That Spoke for Justice: The Life and Times of Stephen S. Wise.* Albany: State University of New York Press, 1982.

Yelin, Haim

(1913–1944)

A writer and anti-Nazi fighter, Haim Yelin was born in the town of Vilkija, **LITHUANIA**. At the end of World War I, his family settled in **KOVNO** and earned its livelihood by importing Yiddish books and managing the *Libhober fun Vissen* (Pursuers of Wisdom) library. In 1932, Yelin graduated from the Hebrew *Realgymnasium* in Kovno. He was found physically unfit for military service. For a short while he was active in the Zionist Pioneering Youth, but he left the organization when he became attracted to the Communist party, which was illegal, during his studies in economics at Kovno University (1934–38). He was a regular contributor to Communist daily and monthly newspapers.

After the incorporation of Lithuania into the **SOVIET UNION** in July 1940, Yelin was appointed to a senior post in the government printing office. During the first few days of the German invasion, in June of 1941, he and his family tried to

escape into the Soviet interior, but they failed. Upon their return they were put into the Kovno ghetto. For a time Yelin lived under an assumed name in the ghetto, and he also changed his appearance, out of fear that if recognized he would be charged with the Communist activities he had engaged in under the Soviet regime.

At the end of 1941, along with some of his friends who were also veteran Communist sympathizers, Yelin established a group that called itself the Antifascist Struggle Organization; he was elected its commander. His duties included managing the group's internal affairs, and staying in touch with elements outside the ghetto. Disguised as a peasant or a railway worker, he would leave the ghetto, seeking to establish contact with remnants of the Communist party, as well as with the Soviet **PARTISANS** who were becoming active in the area.

It was not until the summer of 1943 that Yelin succeeded in establishing permanent contact with the partisans. He became a member of the Communist party and was permitted to enter the partisans' base in the Rudninkai Forest, 90 miles (145 km) east of Kovno. As a result of his efforts, all the underground groups in the ghetto, including the Zionists, were united in the effort to help Jewish youths join the partisan units in the forests. Yelin himself accompanied the first few groups who left the ghetto for this purpose. The operation, which enabled 350 young Jews to join the partisans, made Yelin a leading figure in the Kovno underground. On April 6, 1944, while on a mission outside the ghetto, he was ambushed by **GESTAPO** agents, and later executed.

SUGGESTED RESOURCES

Klein, Dennis B., ed. *Hidden History of the Kovno Ghetto.* Boston: Little, Brown, 1997.

Kovno Ghetto: A Buried History [videorecording]. History Channel, 1997.

YELLOW BADGE. SEE BADGE, JEWISH.

Youth Movements

The first Jewish youth movements came into being in **GERMANY** and in **POLAND**. Shaped by political developments, particularly the rise in **ANTISEMITISM** in their countries, the groups fostered their own cultural and ideological patterns of activities, based on Jewish motifs and traditions, as well as hopes for the future.

Germany and Austria

In 1931 and 1932 the *Ha-Shomer ha-Tsa'ir* and *Betar* Zionist movements were established in Germany. By the time the Nazis came to power, at the end of January 1933, the Jewish youth movements in Germany had crystallized their respective ideologies and organizational patterns and institutions. Ideologically, the Jewish youth movements consisted of two branches: the Zionist pioneering movements and the non-Zionist movements.

All the Jewish youth movements were compelled by the authorities to belong to the Reich Committee of Jewish Youth Organizations, which was a loose and voluntary umbrella organization of Jewish youth movements and youth organizations in Germany. It became the sole representative of all Jewish youth organizations, the channel

Group portrait of Zionist pioneering youth members of the Kibbutz Buchenwald.

of communication for all orders from the government, and the body responsible for the implementation of orders designed to carry out Nazi policy on Jewish youth affairs.

The development of Jewish youth movements in Germany and their activities in the Nazi period stemmed from their ideological attitude toward the traumatic changes that had taken place in the situation of German Jewry. The non-Zionist movements broke up or were disbanded by the authorities. The Zionist youth movements, on the other hand, experienced a tremendous growth in their membership after 1933. They showed the Jews a way out of their predicament through a solution based on national pride: emigration to the Jewish homeland. The Zionist pioneering youth movements in Germany maintained their way of life and their social, ideological, and cultural activities as best they could, despite deteriorating conditions and the restrictions imposed on the Jews.

The Jewish youth movements in **AUSTRIA** went through a social, ideological, and educational development very similar to that of their German counterparts. After 1938, only the Zionist *He-Haluts* youth movements continued to exist in **VIENNA**, fulfilling the same role as their German counterparts.

Eastern Europe

Jewish youth movements played a particularly important role in eastern Europe as Jews sought to cope with the challenges and trials of the early Nazi and World War II years. The groups influenced the attitudes and behavior of their own members, but they also had an impact on the Jewish public as a whole. The Zionist youth movements in Poland rejected the existing state of affairs and refused to accept, as their own way of life, the passivity of the adult Jewish society. They longed for change, for new energy in Jewish life, for both practical and cultural expressions of their Jewishness. In the Zionist youth movements, this longing took the form of working toward the creation of a Jewish homeland in Palestine through education in Hebrew and the establishment of agricultural training centers. Generally speaking, the youth movements did not follow any established political program and they should not be seen as political bodies.

Ha-Shomer ha-Tsa'ir was the first Jewish youth movement to develop in Poland. *Dror* was a movement whose outlook was similar to that of the *Ha-Shomer ha-Tsa'ir*. *Gordonia* adopted a moderate Zionist Socialist program, whereas the *Ha-No'ar ha-Tsiyyoni* and *Akiva* movements focused on Zionism and Hebrew culture. *Betar*, which became a mass youth movement, identified with and was loyal to a political movement called Zionist Revisionism.

In the period between the two world wars a very large number of young people joined the Jewish youth movements in Poland. While they never included the majority of Jewish youth there, they numbered about 60,000. On the eve of World War II, when the youth movements were at their numerical height, they are estimated to have had a combined membership of 100,000.

Under the Nazi occupation regime, the Jewish youth movements played a significant role in Jewish community life, eventually becoming major players in the Jewish resistance movement. In the first few months after the war broke out and the German occupation regime was installed, the youth movements in Poland were in disarray. The leaders of the youth movements left **WARSAW** and other large cities in central and western Poland and made their way to the eastern provinces. However, the youth movement leadership decided to send some of their senior members back to the German-occupied areas, to revive the movements there and reorganize them to exist as secret, underground organizations, since they were illegal under the Nazi regime.

YOUTH MOVEMENTS UNDERGROUND Because they were originally based on small and intimate "cells," the youth movements were able to preserve their distinctive character under the political circumstances. When they began operating clandestinely, they embarked on a remarkably intensive range of activities. They were responsible for most of the underground press published in Warsaw, both before and after the ghetto was set up, they conducted courses of study as a substitute for the regular schools, and they organized seminars, ideological symposiums, and other activities. The youth movements operated a network of couriers, most of them girls, who made illegal trips to the closed-off and isolated ghettos. These attempts at communication gave their branches, spread all over the occupied country, the sense that they were part of a centralized movement.

Many of the youth movements participated in the activities of the ghetto underground. This does not mean, however, that their leaders aspired to leadership of the community. The youth movements had no intention of taking the place of the Judenräte (Jewish councils; *see* **JUDENRAT**). In fact, they were opposed to the methods of the Judenräte, which tended to victimize the poorest sectors of the population and submit blindly to the Germans. Apart from the general goal of survival, the youth movements strove to prepare Jewish youth for the challenges in store for them once the war, the humiliation, and the persecution came to an end. Up to the time that the **"FINAL SOLUTION"** was launched by the Nazis, the youth movements had no intention of trying to take the place of the existing organizational pattern in the ghettos, either overtly or covertly.

Until the Germans invaded the **SOVIET UNION** on June 22, 1941, and embarked upon a mass murder campaign that spread to the occupied Polish areas, the youth movements did not focus on fighting back as a primary objective. This changed soon thereafter.

FIGHTING ORGANIZATIONS OF JEWISH YOUTH The Jews of **VILNA** suffered heavy losses at the very beginning of the murder campaign. The youth movement leaders of Vilna were the first to recognize that a new goal of the youth movements

In the face of an atmosphere of helplessness and disintegration, the Jewish youth organizations insisted on retaining their traditional principles and moral strength.

Under the Nazi occupation regime, the Jewish youth movements played a significant role in Jewish community life, eventually becoming major players in the Jewish resistance movement.

should be to fight back. As a result, the first **Jewish Fighting Organization**, made up of members of various youth movements, came into being. At a meeting of Zionist pioneering youth movements held on the night of December 31, 1941, this proclamation was presented: "All those who have been removed from the ghetto were taken to their death.… Hitler plans to annihilate all the Jews of Europe.… The Jews of Vilna have been selected to be the first in line.… The only way to respond to the enemy is to resist … we must resist up to our dying breath." These bold and far-reaching assertions were not based on proven information but on intuition and a penetrating insight into the course of events. The call for armed resistance was presented as an action that had to be taken. It was clear that there was no chance of survival and that resistance, by a national Jewish fighting unit that had faith in freedom and in the future of the Jewish people, was the only plausible response.

Most youth movement leaders were convinced that the Germans' murder campaign was ideologically motivated and based on a clear-cut, central, and high-level decision. They were resolved to prepare for resistance to the **deportations**, which they correctly believed would inevitably affect every ghetto.

In the early phases of the implementation of the "Final Solution," the leadership of the underground political parties opposed the youth movements' positions. This forced the youth group leaders to operate on their own to gain support for their course of action. In the final phase this turned the youth movements into a kind of alternative ghetto leadership; in the Warsaw ghetto, the youth fighting organization replaced the existing leadership, guiding and directing the course of activities in the ghetto's last days. The youth movements spread the idea of resistance to the different ghettos, sending emissaries from Warsaw to **Białystok**, **Kraków**, Częstochowa, and Zagłębie to help organize resistance and take part in the struggle.

The "pioneering" Zionist youth movements *Ha-Shomer ha-Tsa'ir*, *Dror*, and *Akiva* were very active in the fighting organizations. They helped initiate and plan resistance in all the ghettos that had a fighting body. Members of these movements headed the fighting organizations in the main ghettos. *Betar* participated in the **United Partisan Organization** (*Fareynegte Partizaner Organizatsye*) in Vilna. A group of its members also took part in the resistance in Białystok, and in Warsaw, *Betar* had its own fighting body. *Akiva* joined the ŻOB in Warsaw, and was the major element of the **Fighting Organization of Pioneer Jewish Youth** (*He-Haluts Ha-Lohem*)in Kraków. *Ha-Noar ha-Tsiyyoni* and *Gordonia* also took part in the fighting organizations in most of the ghettos.

The goal of the Jewish youth fighting organizations in Poland was to offer armed resistance or to rise in revolt in the ghettos, in face of the impending final deportation of the Jews to the **extermination camps**. Armed resistance and uprising were both fully put into effect in the **Warsaw Ghetto Uprising** of April 1943. In other ghettos, the plan was that when the ghetto was confronted with the final deportation, an armed struggle would be launched. It was also agreed that some of the fighters would try to make their way to the forests to join the **partisans**—also underground resistance fighters—to continue the struggle even after the ghettos had been liquidated.

In areas outside Poland, as in **Kovno**, **Lithuania**, the youth movements prepared for escaping into the forests and joining the partisan movement. They did not have a consistent policy of staging a revolt in the ghetto. However, youth movement members and former members played a significant role among the activists behind the spontaneous uprisings in and escapes from the small towns of **Belorussia** and **Ukraine**.

Retrospectively, it is evident that neither the Judenräte nor the youth fighting organizations could have saved masses of Jews. The eastern European youth movements had no illusions of paving the way for mass rescue. They regarded their struggle as one last, brave, defiant act by a community that had been condemned to total extermination. Throughout the **HOLOCAUST** years, the youth movements maintained an organized and disciplined structure, and their actions were guided by criteria based on social and national Jewish considerations.

Bohemia-Moravia

The German occupation of Czechoslovakia and its subsequent division into the Protectorate of **BOHEMIA AND MORAVIA** and the independent Slovak state caused a radical change among the Jews of the Protectorate. Torn from their sources of livelihood and their familiar social structures, the Jewish community found itself defined more by shared experiences more than by differences among themselves.

The youth movements, which showed greater enterprise than other groups in coping with the new challenges, played a leading role in the reorganization of Protectorate Jewry. The reorganization was not confined to the youth and came to affect the entire Jewish population.

The youth movements that were active in Bohemia-Moravia varied in character and in the pattern of their programs, but to a great extent all the youth movements cooperated with one another. Their ways parted only shortly before the first groups were about to be taken to **THERESIENSTADT**. The *Ha-Shomer ha-Tsa'ir* (The Young Pioneers) council advised its members to go underground or escape to **SLOVAKIA** or **HUNGARY**, while the other youth movements decided not to abandon their junior members, their families, and the community as a whole. Retrospectively, it would appear that the activist line adopted by *Ha-Shomer ha-Tsa'ir*, despite the painful separation from loved ones that it called for, was based on a more realistic analysis of the future.

In the fall of 1941 the Germans decided to move all of the Protectorate's Jews to Theresienstadt. They also continued sending frequent transports of Jews from Theresienstadt to camps in the east. Jews living in terrible conditions and the constant dread of being included in one of the transports had difficulty focusing on educational work. The youth movements nevertheless did all they could to focus on learning for the future in a valiant attempt to counter the fear and suffering that prevailed in Theresienstadt.

On November 10, 1942, a conference of *He-Haluts* leaders was held in Theresienstadt. The groups decided to join together as *He-Haluts he-Ahid* (Unified He-Haluts). In August, 1944, another *He-Haluts* conference was held. This conference confirmed the Zionist pioneering movement's aim in the ghetto, which was to train the children and young people for cooperative living, universal and national Jewish values, and socialist Zionism.

In September the Germans launched the evacuation of the Theresienstadt ghetto. Hardly any of the young pioneers remained or survived.

France

On the eve of World War II the *Haluts* (Pioneer) Youth movements and the Federation of Religious Youth had small branches active in **FRANCE**. The oldest Jewish youth movement was the *Eclaireurs Israélites de France* (French Jewish Scouts), founded in 1923, which introduced a pluralistic admissions policy and

About 2,000 members of the Jewish youth movements were active in the fighting organizations of the main ghettos in occupied Poland.

TO CAESAREA

A poem written by a young Hungarian Zionist expressing her joy at finally being in Palestine, where the Zionists hoped to establish a Jewish homeland.

Hush, cease all sound.
Across the sea is the sand,
The shore known and near,
The shore golden, dear,
Home, the Homeland.

With step twisting and light
Among strangers we move,
Word and song hushed,
Towards the future-past
Caesarea …

But reaching the city of ruins
Soft a few words we intone.
We return. We are here.
Soft answers the silence of stone,
We awaited you two thousands years.

—HANNAH SZENES, SDOT-YAM, CAESAREA 1941

Hannah Senesh: Her Life and Diary, *translated by Marta Cohn (London: Vallentine, Mitchell and Co. Ltd), 1971.*

accepted both religious and secular youth, Zionists and anti-Zionists. The Orthodox Jewish community had a small youth organization of its own, named *Yeshurun.*

After the fall of France in June 1940, all youth movements in the German-occupied northern part of the country were abolished by German decree. The scouts and the Zionist movement *Ha-Shomer ha-Tsa'ir,* however, resumed their activities under the guise of community clubs. In the Vichy-controlled south, the youth movements continued to operate openly for another two years. During the summer of 1942, with the mass arrests and deportations of the Jews of France, the Jewish youth movements went underground.

In May 1942, the leaders of the various Zionist youth movements agreed to give up their separate political identities to establish a unified Zionist youth movement. This organization became an active element in the community. Immediately after the war, however, the unified movement disbanded and each of its component parts reverted to its original identity.

Three out of four Jews who were in France in the summer of 1940 were saved. Tens of thousands of them were rescued because of the Jewish youth movements. Among the recorded significant achievements was the care taken of over 7,000 children whose parents had been deported. Every child had an underground member assigned to him or her, and this person made regular visits, was responsible for the child's physical and moral welfare, and made sure that the child remained aware of his or her Jewish heritage. Dozens of the young men and women who made up the Jewish underground teams were caught and murdered, but not a single child for whom they were responsible came to harm.

The events of September 1943 in Nice were a severe test for the Jewish youth movements. While the Italians were in occupation of the zone, they protected the Jews from the French officials. When the Italians signed a cease-fire agreement with the Allied forces on September 8, 1943, however, they abandoned the military positions they had held in France. These were taken over by German military forces and police. Consequently, the Jews in Nice and its surrounding areas were caught in a trap.

The *Armée Juive* (the Jewish resistance movement) was organized by Zionist activists. They recruited fighters among the members of the youth movements and trained them in the use of arms and in guerrilla warfare. The organization of partisan units sponsored by the *Armée Juive* began in the winter of 1943–44. *Armée Juive* units took part in the liberation of **PARIS** and other major French cities.

Three out of four Jews who were in France in the summer of 1940 were saved, many of them through the efforts of the Jewish youth movements.

SUGGESTED RESOURCES

Berson, Robin Kadison, ed. "Helmuth Hubener," in *Young Heroes in World History.* Westport, CT: Greenwood Press, 1999.

Dvorson, Alexa. *The Hitler Youth: Marching Toward Madness.* New York: Rosen Pub. Group, 1999.

Heil Hitler! Confessions of a Hitler Youth [videorecording]. Ambrose Video Publishing, 1991.

Keeley, Jennifer. *Life in the Hitler Youth.* San Diego: Lucent Books, 2000.

Schnibbe, Karl-Heinz. *When Truth Was Treason; German Youth Against Hitler.* Urbana: University of Illinois Press, 1995.

Zamość

A province in eastern **POLAND**, situated between the Bug and Vistula rivers, Zamość (in Russian, Zamoste) formed the southern part of the **LUBLIN** district prior to World War II. Its major city, also called Zamość, was founded at the end of the sixteenth century. The 2,317 square mile (6,000 sq km) area was predominantly agricultural, with a large part of the land belonging to feudal landlords; a considerable portion was forest land (such as Puscza Solska and Lasy Roztecza). Before World War II, the area was divided among four districts—Zamość, Tomaszów Lubelski, Hrubieszów, and Biłgoraj—that contained more than 1,660 population centers and about 510,000 inhabitants: 340,000 Poles, 110,000 Ukrainians, and 60,000 Jews. For the most part, the Ukrainians lived in the rural areas of Tomaszów Lubelski and Hrubieszów while the Jews were concentrated in the towns. Jews formed 51 percent of the urban population; in some towns, they accounted for over two-thirds of the population. Jews constituted the majority in a number of the cities, including Zamość, Tomaszów Lubelski, Tarnogród, Tyszowce, Krasnobród, Józefów, and Uchanie.

Under the German occupation, the Zamość population underwent exceptionally harsh treatment. More than 2,000 Poles were murdered upon the German invasion in 1939. Jews were forced into ghettos where many died and from which many others were deported to the **BEŁŻEC** extermination camp (by order of Odilo **GLOBOCNIK**). Periodic massacres occurred throughout the district.

On November 12, 1942, the Zamość area was declared the **GENERALGOUVERNEMENT**'s "First Resettlement Area" (*Erster Siedlungsbereich,*), which resulted in the evacuation of 110,000 Polish peasant families from some 300 villages. Ten thousand people perished in the course of the evacuation. The survivors were taken to

transit camps in Zamość and Zwierzyniec, to the **AUSCHWITZ** and **MAJDANEK EXTERMINATION CAMPS**, to the Reich for **FORCED LABOR**, or to villages in the Lublin and **WARSAW** districts. More than 30,000 Polish children were taken away from their parents and handed over to strangers. Some of them died in Auschwitz or in the course of the deportation, and some were designated for *"Germanization"* in the Reich.

These operations led to the strengthening of the resistance and partisan movement (**PARTISANS** were underground guerrilla fighters who harassed the enemy in the Zamość area). Partisan units engaged the Germans in battles in Wojda, Zaboreczno, and Osuchy. The Germans wanted to suppress resistance and continue the expulsion of the Polish population, who were to be replaced with German settlers. In order to do these things, the Nazis resorted to collective punishment. They made an example of selected areas, in which numerous villages were completely wiped out, including Sochy, Szarajowka, and Kitow. Large police and military forces took part in these operations. The Nazis also hunted down people who had gone into hiding in the forests, some of whom were Jews.

In the spring of 1944, the southeastern part of the Zamość area was the scene of heavy fighting between the Ukrainska Povstanska Armyia (Ukrainian Insurgent Army) and units of the Polish resistance. Both sides incurred heavy losses in the fighting, and the districts of Hrubieszów and Tomaszów Lubelski were emptied of their inhabitants.

The Zamość area was liberated by the **SOVIET UNION**'s Red Army in July 1944.

SUGGESTED RESOURCES

Klukowski, Zygmunt. *Diary from the Years of Occupation, 1939–44.* Urbana: University of Illinois Press, 1993.

ZENTRALSTELLE FÜR JÜDISCHE AUSWANDERUNG. SEE CENTRAL OFFICE FOR JEWISH EMIGRATION.

Ziman, Henrik

(1910–1987)

A Lithuanian Jewish scientist, journalist, Communist leader, and commander of anti-Nazi **PARTISANS**, Henrik Ziman (Genrikas Zimanas, known as "Hanak") came from a family of Jewish landowners in southern **LITHUANIA**. He taught Lithuanian at Jewish secondary schools in Ukmergė and, at the same time, majored in biology at the University of **KOVNO**. Ziman became a Communist activist in 1932 and was put in charge of the party's secret publications, which were written in several languages, in 1934. Following the annexation of Lithuania by the **SOVIET UNION** in the summer of 1940, Ziman directed the transformation of the country's culture from a Lithuanian to a Soviet orientation. He also played an important role in eradicating Zionist and Hebrew-language institutions.

When the Nazis invaded Lithuania in June, 1941, Ziman fled to the Soviet interior. In Moscow, he conducted anti-Nazi propaganda on behalf of the Soviet Lithuanian government. Ziman was appointed deputy chief of staff of the Lithuan-

"Germanization"
The Nazis' plan to eradicate all aspects of foreign cultures and force certain populations to accept German culture.

ian partisan movement in November 1942. Six months later, by which time he had been given the pseudonym "Jurgis" for war purposes, he parachuted into an area of **BELORUSSIA** controlled by the partisans that was close to the Lithuanian border. In October 1943, Ziman arrived at the Rudninkai Forest in southern Lithuania, where he assumed command of a partisan brigade that also included units made up of fighters from the **VILNA** and **KOVNO** ghettos. As a rule, Ziman did not favor the existence of separate Jewish partisan units, which was in line with the policy of the Soviet partisan movement.

After the war, Ziman resumed his activities in the Communist party and in the government institutions of Soviet Lithuania. He held a number of senior posts in the Central Committee of the Lithuanian Communist party and in the Supreme Soviet. From 1945 to 1970, Ziman was editor-in-chief of *Tiesa*, a daily newspaper published by the party; later he also edited the party's ideological organ, *Komunistas*. Ziman published hundreds of articles on cultural and political subjects. In some of them, he harshly criticized the Zionist movement and its policy during and after the **HOLOCAUST** period.

SUGGESTED RESOURCES

Porter, Jack Nusan, ed. *Jewish Partisans: A Documentary of Jewish Resistance in the Soviet Union During World War II.* Washington, DC: University Press of America, 1982.

Z IONISM. SEE ALIYA BET; WISE, STEPHEN SAMUEL; YOUTH

MOVEMENTS.

Zuckerman, Yitzhak

(1915–1981)

A founder and leader of the **JEWISH FIGHTING ORGANIZATION** (Żydowska Organizacja Bojowa; ŻOB) in **WARSAW**, Yitzhak (Antek) Zuckerman was born in **VILNA**. He came from a family that practiced Jewish culture and law. After graduating from the Hebrew high school in Vilna, he joined the Zionist **YOUTH MOVEMENTS** He-Haluts and He-Haluts ha-Tsa'ir. Zuckerman was invited to join the He-Haluts head office in Warsaw in 1936. When the united youth movement Dror-He-Haluts was formed in 1938, Zuckerman became one of its two secretaries-general. In the spirit of pioneering Zionism and socialism, he took an interest in education and in Yiddish and Hebrew literature. Zuckerman toured Jewish communities in towns and cities, especially in eastern **POLAND**, organizing branches of the movement and youth groups and offering them guidance in their activities.

World War II broke out in September 1939. With other activists in He-Haluts and the youth movements, Zuckerman left Warsaw for the east, the parts of Poland that had been occupied by the **SOVIET UNION**. There, he organized underground branches of the movement. He crossed back into German-occupied territory in April 1940, in order to promote underground activities there. Zuckerman became one of the outstanding underground leaders in Warsaw and, indeed, in all of Poland. He helped to found and edit the underground press, organized secret seminars and conferences, and set up the Dror high school. In addition, Zuckerman established the pattern of his movement's activities in underground conditions and

ghettos
Parts of cities where Jews were required to live.

made secret visits to **ghettos** in German-occupied territory. He took part in organizing and guiding the branches and cells of the movement in the provincial towns and in setting up hidden *hakhsharot*—the agricultural training farms that were part of the Zionist preparation for relocating to a Jewish homeland in Palestine. In addition, Zuckerman helped to coordinate activities with other youth movements that were operating illegally, especially the Zionist-Marxist Ha-Shomer ha-Tsa'ir. During this period, Zuckerman became close to Zivia Lubetkin, another underground leader; the two eventually married and became partners in various undertakings.

In 1941, mass murders were being carried out by the **OPERATIONAL SQUADS** (Einsatzgruppen) in the areas that the Germans had taken from the Soviets. Reports of the murders reached Warsaw in the fall of that year. In his memoirs, *Chapters from the Legacy*, Zuckerman records that when these reports were received, the reaction was that underground educational activities no longer seemed to be worthwhile or important. He wrote, "There was no point to them ... unless such activities went hand in hand with an armed Jewish resistance force." Zuckerman helped arrange a meeting of the leaders of various Jewish underground factions in Warsaw in early 1942. Discussions about the creation of a unified military resistance movement failed at this time. Instead, desiring some unified effort at resistance, Zuckerman joined the Antifascist Bloc, which was established in the spring of 1942. The organization did not last long and had no achievements to record.

When the mass deportation of Jews from Warsaw was launched on July 22, 1942, a group of public figures in the ghetto held an emergency meeting. On behalf of He-Haluts, Zuckerman demanded that the seizure of the Jews be resisted by force. His proposal was turned down and no agreement was reached on any other issue. On July 28, Zuckerman took part in a meeting attended exclusively by the leaders of the three pioneering movements, Ha-Shomer ha-Tsa'ir, Dror, and Akiva. At this meeting, the decision was made to set up the Jewish Fighting Organization (ŻOB) and Zuckerman became a member of its staff headquarters. Although the new organization was not able to carry out large-scale resistance operations in the ghetto while the **DEPORTATIONS** were taking place, it kept together a nucleus of determined activists and spread the ideas of armed resistance to other ghettos besides Warsaw. In December, 1942, the ŻOB sent Zuckerman on a mission to **KRAKÓW** to discuss possible avenues for its operations with the resistance movement there. Zuckerman was wounded in the leg on the night of December 22, following a military action by the Kraków organization. With great difficulty, he managed to make his way back to Warsaw.

The second phase of deportations from the ghetto was launched on January 18, 1943. With Zuckerman in the lead, a group of resistance fighters barricaded themselves in a building in the ghetto and opened fire on the Germans. Zuckerman participated in the intensive preparations for a revolt that continued from the end of January to April 1943. He was appointed commanding officer of one of the three main fighting sectors into which the ghetto was divided. As the time for the revolt drew near, Zuckerman was ordered to cross over to the Polish side of Warsaw as the authorized representative of the ŻOB. At the time that the **WARSAW GHETTO UPRISING** was in full swing, Zuckerman made efforts to supply arms to the fighters. In the final days of the revolt, he and other members of the organization formed a rescue team that made its way through the sewers into the ghetto, which was now going up in flames.

After the revolt, Zuckerman, with some other survivors, was active in the Żydowski Komitet Narodowy (Jewish National Committee). This group gave aid to Jews in hiding and maintained contact with Jews in some of the forced-labor

camps and with Jewish underground partisan fighting units that were based in the forests in central Poland. In March 1944, Zuckerman drew up a report on the establishment of the ŻOB and its record of activity; that May, the report was transmitted to London through the channels of the Polish underground. Zuckerman and other Jewish leaders who were in hiding with the Poles signed appeals for help. In the last two years of the war, these documents were forwarded to London and to authoritative Jewish organizations by way of the Polish underground. During the **WARSAW POLISH UPRISING** in August 1944, Zuckerman was in command of a group of Jewish fighters, remnants of the underground and the ŻOB.

In January 1945, Zuckerman and his wife Zivia were liberated by the Soviet forces. At once, he began to do relief work among the surviving remnants of Polish Jewry. Zuckerman took part in the restoration of the He-Haluts movement and in the mass exodus of Jews from Poland in 1946 and 1947.

Zuckerman left for Palestine in early 1947. He was one of the founders of Kibbutz Lohamei ha-Getta'ot (the Ghetto Fighters' Kibbutz) in western Galilee and one of the sponsors of the Ghetto Fighters' Museum that was established to perpetuate the memory of the fighters and the study of the **HOLOCAUST**. For the rest of his life, Zuckerman kept a loving eye on the development of the latter project. Appearing as a witness in the Adolf **EICHMANN** trial in 1961, Zuckerman read to the court the last letter that he had received from Mordecai **ANIELEWICZ**, the commander of the Warsaw ghetto revolt. The letter was dated April 23, 1943, when the fighting was at its height.

SUGGESTED RESOURCES

Gutman, Israel. *Resistance: The Warsaw Ghetto Uprising.* Boston: Houghton Mifflin, 1994.

Landau, Elaine. *The Warsaw Ghetto Uprising.* New York: Macmillan, 1992.

Zuckerman, Yitzhak. *A Surplus of Memory: Chronicle of the Warsaw Ghetto Uprising.* Berkeley: University of California Press, 1993.

ŻYDOWSKA ORGANIZACJA BOJOWA; ŻOB. SEE JEWISH FIGHTING ORGANIZATION.

Zyklon B

Zyklon B is the commercial name of hydrogen cyanide (HCN), a highly poisonous cyanic gas. It was used in the **EUTHANASIA PROGRAM** in which the Nazis killed people they considered "unfit to live," often because they had physical or mental disabilities. It was also used later in the Nazi **EXTERMINATION CAMPS**, especially at **AUSCHWITZ**. The gas was delivered to the camps in crystalline, pellet form, hermetically sealed in tin canisters. As soon as the crystals were exposed to air, they turned into lethal gas. An **SS** man wearing a gas mask emptied the crystals through a small opening (provided with a cover) into the hermetically sealed gas chamber in which the victims had been packed (*see* **GAS CHAMBERS/VANS**). Those inside the chamber were asphyxiated within minutes.

Ordinarily, Zyklon B was used as an insecticide. In the report he wrote in prison after the war, Rudolf **HÖSS**, the Auschwitz camp commandant, relates how

From Mordecai Anielewicz's last letter, read by Zuckerman at the Adolf Eichmann trial: "One thing is clear, what happened exceeded our boldest dreams. The Germans ran twice from the ghetto. One of our companies held out for 40 minutes and another for more than 6 hours.... It is impossible to describe the conditions under which the Jews of the ghetto are now living. Only a few will be able to hold out. The remainder will die sooner or later. Their fate is decided."

Cylindrical containers of Zyklon B gas and a gas mask were found on a wooden shelf at the Majdanek camp after liberation, 1944.

in the summer of 1941 he was ordered to prepare for the mass killing of Jews in the camp within the framework of the **"FINAL SOLUTION"**. He and Adolf **EICHMANN** looked for a lethal gas that would be suitable for this purpose. The method of gassing victims with carbon monoxide fumes funneled through an exhaust pipe into a hermetically sealed trailer truck, which was already in use at **CHEŁMNO** and the three camps serving **AKTION (OPERATION) REINHARD—BEŁŻEC, SOBIBÓR**, and **TREBLINKA**)—was not suitable for killing on the scale that was planned for Auschwitz. On September 3, 1941, an experiment was carried out at the Birkenau site in Auschwitz on a group of Russian **PRISONERS OF WAR** to determine whether Zyklon B, which the camp storehouses used for fumigation, could be an effective tool for mass killing of humans. The experiment proved this to be so. From then on Zyklon B was used in Birkenau (Auschwitz II) for the gassing of the Jews who were brought there from all over occupied Europe.

Zyklon B was manufactured and supplied to the camps by DEGESCH (Deutsche Gesellschaft für Schädlingsbekämpfung mbH, or German Vermin-Com-

bating Corporation) in Frankfurt. This firm was controlled by **I. G. FARBEN**, and by the Tesch and Stabenow Company in Hamburg. Because of the large demand for Zyklon B, I. G. Farben's dividends on the DEGESCH investment for the years from 1942 to 1944 were double those of 1940 and 1941. The management of DEGESCH must have been aware that Zyklon B was being used for something other than its intended purpose. German law required that an odor be added to Zyklon B as a warning to alert humans to the lethal presence of the gas. The SS ordered that the odor be removed from its massive orders of the chemical. This unusual request would seem to have offered a clear indication of the purpose it was to serve.

SEE ALSO **TRIALS OF THE WAR CRIMINALS.**

SUGGESTED RESOURCES

Müller, Filip. *Eyewitness Auschwitz: Three Years in the Gas Chambers.* New York: Stein and Day, 1979. Reprint, Chicago: Ivan R. Dee, 1999.

United Nations War Crimes Commission. "The Zyklon B Case; Trial of Bruno Tesch and Two Others," in *Law-Reports of Trials of War Criminals.* HMSO, 1947. Reproduced at http://www.ess.uwe.ac.uk/WCC/zyklonb.htm (accessed on September 5, 2000).

"Zyklon Introduction Columns." *Holocaust History Project.* [Online] http://www.holocaust-history.org/auschwitz/intro-columns/ (accessed on September 5, 2000).

Glossary

Abwehr the intelligence service of the German armed forces

aktion (plural, *aktionen*) *see* "operation"

Aktion (Operation) 1005 the code name for the Nazi plan to erase evidence of the murder of 125 million human beings in occupied Europe

Aktion (Operation) Reinhard the code name for the plan to murder the millions of Jews in the General Government (Generalgouvernement), within the framework of the "Final Solution." It began in October 1941, with the deportation of Jews from ghettos to extermination camps. The three extermination camps established under Operation Reinhard were Bełżec, Sobibór, and Treblinka

Aliya Bet organized but "illegal" immigration to Palestine

Allied powers, or Allies during World War II, the group of nations including the United States, Great Britain, the Soviet Union, and the Free French, who fought together against Germany and the other Axis countries

Anschluss the invasion and annexation of Austria by Nazi Germany on March 12–13, 1938

antisemites people who hate or discriminate against Jews or Jewish culture

antisemitism hatred of or discrimination against Jews

appeasement a policy of making certain concessions to an enemy or aggressor in the hope of conciliation and peace

Arisierung *see* "Aryanization"

Armée Juive the Jewish Army in France; unified fighting forces

Arrow Cross Party a Fascist political party in Hungary

Aryans according to Nazi doctrine, people of pure German "blood," members of what they called the "master race"

Aryanization in German, *Arisierung*; the forced transfer of Jewish-owned businesses and property to non-Jewish owners by the Nazi German authorities

assembly camp or center a place where people were gathered to be sent on to Nazi camps

assimilation the process of becoming incorporated into a country's mainstream society and culture

Auschwitz a huge complex consisting of Nazi concentration, extermination, and labor camps in Poland. Also called Auschwitz-Birkenau.

Auschwitz Protocols detailed reports by four Jewish escapees from Auschwitz who reached Slovakia in the spring of 1944

Axis powers Germany, Italy, and Japan, the countries that signed a pact on September 27, 1940, to divide the world into their spheres of political interest; they were later joined by Bulgaria, Croatia, Hungary, Romania, and Slovakia

Axis criminals those who were associated with the Axis powers in World War II, including Germany, Italy, and Japan and their satellite nations

Babi Yar a ravine near Kiev where tens of thousands of Ukrainian Jews were systematically massacred

badge, Jewish an emblem—usually a Star of David—that the Nazis ordered Jews to wear, to identify them as Jews and distinguish them from the rest of the population

Barbarossa *see* "Operation Barbarossa"

Barbie, Klaus the head of the SS and SD in France

Baum Gruppe (Group) an anti-Nazi organization in Berlin, Germany

Beer Hall Putsch the term for Adolf Hitler's failed attempt, on November 8, 1923, to take over the German government in Munich, at a meeting of Bavarian officials in a beer hall

Bełżec a Nazi extermination camp in eastern Poland

Bergen-Belsen a Nazi concentration camp in northwestern Germany

blitzkrieg meaning "lightning war," Hitler's offensive war tactic of using a combination of armored attacks and air assaults

blood libels false allegations that Jews were killing Christian children to use their blood in religious rituals

Bolsheviks Soviet communists

Bormann, Martin a Nazi Party official and deputy to Hitler who was active in such activities such as the Euthanasia Program, the pillage of art objects in occupied countries, and the expansion of forced-labor programs throughout Europe

Boycott, Anti-Jewish the boycott of Jewish businesses on April 1, 1933—the first national action against the German Jews after the Nazi seizure of power earlier that year

British White Paper of 1939 in Great Britain, a policy document that severely restricted immigration of Jews to Palestine

Buchenwald a concentration camp in north-central Germany

Bund the Jewish Socialist Party, founded in 1897, dedicated to gaining equal rights for Jews; Bundists joined in underground resistance against the Nazis

bystanders people who witness but do not participate in an event, either to stop it or to further it

chancellor the prime minister of Germany

Chełmno a Nazi extermination camp in western Poland; it was the first of the death camps

Churchill, Winston the British prime minister from 1940 to 1945, and again from 1951 to 1955

collaboration the cooperation of citizens of a country to further the aims of its occupiers, such as the Nazis

collaborators people who help enemy authorities, such as the Nazis, to achieve their aims

commissars Soviet Communist officials assigned to military units; their function was to reinforce Communist Party principles and ensure loyalty among members of the Soviet army who fell into German hands

collectivization the transformation of an agricultural system (or other economic enterprise) from privately owned farms to a government-supervised enterprise of production and distribution, generally in a communist system

columns rows of prisoners of the Nazis sent on forced marches

communism a political, social, and economic system that aims for a society free of division by class, in which resources and the means of production are controlled by the government, rather than by private enterprise

Communists people who work toward the goals of communism; Communists were the first opponents of the Nazis

concentration camps work camps—essentially prisons—set up by the Nazis to house and exploit the labor of people whom they considered to be "undesirable"; living conditions varied from camp to camp, but death, disease, starvation, crowded and unsanitary conditions, and torture were common

conceptual Jew a Jewish "type" or stereotype; a set of characteristics that, lumped together, was called "Jewishness"

coup d'état a takeover of a government

crematorium (plural, crematoria) a huge oven in a Nazi camp where the bodies of murdered prisoners were burned

Dachau a Nazi concentration camp in southern Germany; it was the first Nazi concentration camp, established in 1933

death camps *see* "extermination camps."

death marches forced marches of the prisoners of the Nazis, over long distances and under intolerable conditions, while being transferred between ghettos and/or camps

de Gaulle, Charles a general who was interim president of France from 1945 to 1946, and president from 1959 to 1969

dehumanization the Nazi policy of denying Jews and other groups basic civil rights

denazification the procedure used by the victorious Allied powers to rid Germany of nazism and to punish Nazi war criminals

deportation the evacuation of large numbers of victims to Nazi camps, usually by train in cattle cars

diaspora the "dispersal" of a people from a land or country, such as the ancient Jews from Egypt; also used in reference to Jews worldwide who live outside the homeland of Israel

Displaced Persons (DPs) people who were displaced—involuntarily driven out of their homes or countries—during World War II

Displaced Persons camps camps where millions of Displaced Persons were temporarily housed in Europe after World War II ended, while they awaited opportunities to emigrate or return to their homelands

displacement the process of people being involuntarily ousted from their homes because of war, government policies, or other societal actions, requiring them to find new places and ways to live

Eichmann, Adolf an SS lieutenant colonel who headed the Department of Jewish Affairs; he played a key role in the murder of European Jews, especially those in the camps

Einsatzgruppe (plural, *Einsatzgruppen*) *see* "operational squads"

emancipation the granting of full civil rights to a people

Enlightenment a period during the 1700s when philosophers, writers, and other intellectuals questioned all aspects of knowledge and social discourse, seeking to understand the world through reason and scientific observation

Erntefest ("Harvest Festival") the code name for an SS operation to exterminate the last surviving Jews of the Trawniki, Poniatowa, and Majdanek camps, which occurred in November 1943

Euthanasia Program the Nazis' deliberate killings of institutionalized people with physical, mental, or emotional handicaps; the Nazi euthanasia program began in 1939, with German non-Jews as the first victims; the program was later extended to Jews

Evian Conference an international gathering that was convened to address the problem of Jewish refugees; it was held in Evian, France, in July 1938

extermination camps camps built by the Nazis for the sole purpose of killing "enemies" of the Third Reich, especially Jews; the six extermination camps were Auschwitz-Birkenau, Bełżec, Chełmno, Majdanek, Sobibór, and Treblinka—all in occupied Poland; also called death camps or killing centers

fascism a social and political ideology with the primary guiding principle that the state or nation is the highest priority, rather than personal or individual freedoms

"Final Solution" "the final solution to the Jewish question in Europe": a Nazi euphemism for the plan to exterminate all the Jews of Europe

forced labor groups of people who were forced to build and operate the Nazi camps, usually with little or no pay, and to maintain a steady flow of workers for factories and other industries that supported the German war effort

Frank, Hans a Nazi official who was named the governor-general of Poland and was responsible for the extermination of Polish Jewry

French Resistance a well-organized network of people in occupied and Vichy France who worked secretly against the German occupation forces

Free French the non-Vichy French government headed by General Charles de Gaulle

Freemasons members of a fraternal order dating back to the 1700s that was committed to the ideas of religious tolerance and the equality of all people; Hitler banned this group in Germany

Freikorps a paramilitary group formed after Germany's defeat in World War I

führer a German word meaning "leader"; this became Hitler's title in Nazi Germany

gas chambers large, sealed rooms in Nazi camps in which groups of people were murdered by poison gas

gas vans vehicles that the Nazis equipped with poison gas, for use as mobile killing units

gendarmerie regional or rural police

Generalgouvernement (General Government) an administrative unit established by the Germans in October 1939, comprised of those parts of occupied Poland that had not been incorporated into the Third Reich

Generalplan Ost (General Plan East) the Nazis' long-range plan for expelling millions of people—Jews and non-Jews alike—from the central area of eastern Europe and settling it with Germans

genocide the deliberate and systematic murder of a religious, racial, political, or cultural group

Germanization the Nazi plan to "convert" some populations to German culture by erasing all aspects of the original culture and placing them under German rule

German Workers' Party the precursor to the Nazi Party; the party espoused nationalism, militarism, and a racially "pure" Germany

Gentiles non-Jewish people

Gestapo the German Secret State Police, which used brutal methods to investigate and suppress resistance to Nazi rule within Germany and in German-occupied Europe

ghettos in areas under German occupation, restricted and sometimes sealed sections of cities where Jews were forced to live, usually in extreme overcrowding and deprivation; ghettos were established mostly in eastern Europe

ghettoize a term meaning to isolate and disenfranchise a people from mainstream society as the Nazis did to the Jews

Goebbels, Josef the Nazi minister of Public Enlightenment and Propaganda, and the organizer of the Kristallnacht pogrom

Göring, Hermann a top Nazi official who was responsible for the Aryanization Program and the implementation of the "Final Solution"

Great Depression a deep, worldwide, economic downturn that began in 1929

guerrilla warfare fighting in which small independent bands of soldiers harass an enemy through surprise raids, attacks on communications sytems, targeted assassinations, and other tactics

Gypsies a collective term for Romani and Sinti, a people who were considered enemies of the state by the Nazis and persecuted relentlessly

Haganah an underground organization from Palestine that worked to aid and rescue Jews in occupied Europe

Hess, Rudolf Hitler's deputy in the Nazi Party

Heydrich, Reinhard the Nazi official who was responsible for implementing the "Final Solution"

Himmler, Heinrich as head of the SS and the Gestapo, Himmler controlled the vast network of Nazi camps and the operational squads

Hitler, Adolf the Nazi Party leader, and the German chancellor from 1933 to 1945; he was called Führer, or "Leader," by the Nazis

Hitler Youth in German Hitlerjugend, a Nazi youth group established in 1926; it expanded during the Third Reich, and membership was required after 1939

Holocaust a term used to refer to the systematic, state-sponsored extermination of about six million European Jews and millions of others by the Nazis between 1933 and 1945

Holocaust Denial efforts to deny or misrepresent the events that came to be known as the Holocaust

homophobia fear of and prejudice against homosexuals

homosexuals one of the groups of people targeted for persecution by the Nazis; they were identified in the Nazi camps by wearing a pink triangle sewn on their uniforms

"Horst Wessel" a Nazi song whose lyrics glorified the killing of Jews

Höss, Rudolf a high Nazi official who was the commandant of the Auschwitz-Birkenau complex

Hungarian Labor Service System an organization in which Hungarian Jews of military age were drafted into forced labor to support the Axis war effort

immigration quota the limit on the number of people allowed to enter a country as immigrants from any other country

International Military Tribunal court chartered by the United States, Great Britain, France, and the Soviet Union to prosecute Nazi war criminals

interwar period the years between the end of World War I (1918) and the beginning of World War II (1939)

Iron Guard the Romanian Fascist movement

isolationism a policy of national isolation, reflected in a country's choice not to enter into political and economic alliances with other countries

Israel the Jewish state that came into being in 1948 in the geographic region known as Palestine, previously under British control

Jehovah's Witnesses members of a religious group whose pacifist religious beliefs did not allow them to swear allegiance to any worldly power, making them

"enemies" of the Nazi state; the Nazis required Jehovah's Witnesses to identify themselves by wearing brown triangles sewn on their clothing

Jewish Brigade Group a group of the British army made up of Jewish volunteers from Palestine; formed in September 1944, the Jewish Brigade Group fought on behalf of the Allied forces in Italy from March to May 1945

Jewish Council *see* "Judenrat"

Jewish Fighting Organization (Żydowska Organizacja Bojowa; ŻOB) a Jewish group, established in Warsaw in July 1942, that allowed some Jews to offer armed resistance to the Nazis

Jewish Ghetto Police police units organized in Jewish communities, by order of the Nazi occupying forces throughout eastern Europe

Jewish Law (Statut des Juifs) anti-Jewish legislation passed by the Vichy government of France in 1940 and 1941

Jews people who belong to the religion of Judaism; Jews were defined in racial, rather than religious or cultural, terms by Nazi policies

Judaism the monotheistic religion of the Jews, based on the writings and teachings of the Old Testament

Judenfrei a Nazi term meaning "free of Jews," a reference to the absence of Jews in a given area, as a result of deportation and extermination operations

Judenrat (plural, Judenräte) a "Jewish Council," an administrative committee set up in a Jewish ghetto or other community under German occupation; the Judenräte were established on Nazi orders

Judenrein a Nazi term meaning "cleansed of Jews," a reference to the absence of Jews in a given area, as a result of deportation and extermination operations.

Kapo a concentration camp inmate appointed by the SS to be in charge of a work gang

killing centers *see* "extermination camps"

Kriminalpolizei German criminal police, also referred to as Kripo, which had four main divisions

Knesset Israel's Parliament

Kristallnacht "Night of the Broken Glass" or "Crystal Night;" a massive, organized pogrom against Jews throughout Germany and Austria in November 1938

League of German Girls the counterpart, for girls, of the Hitler Youth

Lebensraum a term meaning "living space," indicating the Nazis' desire for more land and access to resources for Germans; this basic principle of Nazi ideology and foreign policy was expressed in the drive for the conquest of territories, mainly in the East

Lend-Lease an American program to supply military goods to the Allies during World War II

liquidation the emptying of a Jewish ghetto through deportations and violence

Luftwaffe the German air force

Madagascar Plan a Nazi plan to expel European Jews to the island of Madagascar, off the coast of Africa; it was eventually abandoned as being impractical

Majdanek a Nazi extermination camp in eastern Poland

Marranos Jews who professed to accept Christianity in order to escape persecution during the Spanish Inquisition

Mein Kampf meaning "My Struggle," Hitler's book relating his radical political and social ideology; it formed the basis for the Nazi Party's racist beliefs and murderous practices

Mengele, Joseph the senior SS physician at Auschwitz-Birkenau from 1943 to 1944; known as the "Angel of Death"

Mischlinge meaning "mongrels," a Nazi term for people who had one or two Jewish grandparents; may also be translated as "part-jews"

Molotov cocktail a type of hand-made bomb

Munich Agreement a pact of appeasement that Great Britain and France signed with Germany and Italy in September 1938, allowing Germany to occupy and annex Sudetenland (a part of Czechoslovakia); also called the Munich Pact

Muselmann a term widely used by concentration camp prisoners to refer to inmates who were on the verge of death from starvation, exhaustion, and despair

Nazi Party the National Socialist German Workers' Party, or NSDAP, founded in Germany in 1919; led by Hitler, the Nazi Party was characterized by a centralist and authoritarian structure, and its platform was based on militaristic, racist, antisemitic, and nationalistic policies

Night of the Long Knives the name for the night on June 30–July 1, 1934, when Hitler murderously purged the ranks of the SA, eliminating officers who posed a challenge to any part of his plan for Nazi domination of Europe

non-Aryans a Nazi term used to designate Jews, part-Jews, and others the Nazis considered "inferior" racial stock

Nuremberg Laws laws announced by Hitler at the annual Nazi Party rally in Nuremberg on September 15, 1935, instituting official, systematic discrimination against the Jews, which led to the exclusion of Jews from German life and citizenship and made the persecution of Jews an official policy of the state

Nuremberg Trial the trial of twenty-two major Nazi figures in Nuremberg, Germany, in 1945 and 1946 before the International Military Tribunal

Operation a planned Nazi raid or attack *(aktion)* against Jews, usually to gather victims for extermination

Operation Barbarossa the code name for the German invasion of the Soviet Union, which began on June 22, 1941

operational squads (*Einsatzgruppen*; singular *Einsatzgruppe*) mobile units of the SS or local auxiliary police groups that followed the German armies to Poland in 1939 and to the Soviet Union in 1941; their charge was to kill all Jews as well as other groups considered "undesirable" by the Nazis

Organization Schmelt a system of forced labor for the Jewish population of Eastern Upper Silesia, a region of Poland under German occupation

Ostland the eastern European territories occupied by the Germans, consisting of the Baltic states (Estonia, Latvia, and Lithuania) and the western half of Belorussia

Pale of Settlement an area in the western part of the Russian Empire where Russian Jews were required to live from 1835 to 1917

Palestine ancient, Biblical land and former country in the Middle East (controlled by Great Britain from 1923–1948) which is now divided between Israel and Jordan

partisan company a group of resistance fighters who used guerrilla tactics against the Nazis and operated in enemy-occupied territory

partisans resistance groups that operated secretly, using guerrilla tactics to help Jews and others persecuted by the Nazis

perpetrators those who do something that is morally wrong or criminal

pogrom an organized and often officially encouraged attack on or massacre of a group of people, especially Jews

Potsdam Conference a meeting held by Winston Churchill, Joseph Stalin, and Harry Truman in the summer of 1945 to discuss the political and economic problems that arose after Germany's surrender

prejudice a preconceived judgment or opinion, often founded on suspicion, intolerance, and the irrational hatred of people of other races, religions, creeds, or nationalities

prisoners of war soldiers captured in war and held by the enemy

propaganda ideas, rumors, images or information—often false or misleading—that are spread to help or hurt a cause, a person or group, or an organization

protocols written records, such as interview transcripts or minutes of meetings of interrogations and investigations

rabbi the leader of a Jewish congregation, similar to the role of a priest or minister

Ravensbrück a concentration camp for women, north of Berlin, Germany

Red Army the name often applied to the Soviet army until June 1945

regent the head of state of Hungary

Reich the German word for "empire;" *see also* "Third Reich"

Reichstag the German Parliament

repatriate to return or be sent back to one's country of origin or citizenship

resettlement a Nazi euphemism for the deportation of prisoners to extermination camps in Poland

Revisionists people who deny that the Holocaust ever happened or who misrepresent portions of historical records about and from the Holocaust

Rhineland a demilitarized region between Germany and France; Hitler broke the Treaty of Versailles when he ordered German troops to invade this area in March 1936

Ribbentrop, Joachim von Nazi Germany's foreign minister

Righteous Among the Nations a title given by Yad Vashem, Israel's official institution of Holocaust remembrance, to non-Jews who risked their lives to save Jews in areas under Nazi German occupation in Europe

righteous gentiles non-Jews who risked their lives to save Jews from Nazi persecution

Roosevelt, Franklin D. the U.S. president from 1933 to 1945

SA (*Sturmabteilung,* or Storm Troopers) also known as Brown Shirts, they were the Nazi Party's main instrument for undermining democracy and facilitating Hitler's rise to power; they were of less political significance after 1934

scapegoat a person or group of people unfairly blamed for something that goes wrong; Jews were often made the scapegoats during times of economic hardship in Europe, unfairly blamed for high unemployment rates and other negative economic indicators

SD (*Sicherheitsdienst,* or Security Service) the SS security and intelligence service

selektion; plural, *selektionen* the recurring selection of prisoners, from among those arriving at a Nazi camp, to be used for forced labor, or to be killed immediately; also, the choosing of Jews in ghettos to be deported to the camps

Shoa or Shoah the Hebrew term for the Holocaust

shtetl general term for a small Jewish town or village in eastern Europe

Sobibór a Nazi extermination camp located in eastern Poland

Social Darwinism a sociological concept based on Darwin's concept of physical evolution—the "survival of the fittest"; based on Social Darwinism, Nazis created a pseudo-scientific brand of racism that was most rabid when directed against the Jews, although other cultural and/or ethnic groups were not exempt

socialism a theory or system of social organization that advocates the ownership and control of land, capital, industry, and so on, by the community as a whole; in Marxist theory, it represents the stage following capitalism in a state transforming to communism

special commando (*Sonderkommando*) a special unit of the SS; also the name of the slave labor units in extermination camps that removed the bodies of those gassed for cremation or burial

SS (*Schutzstaffel,* or Protection Squad) armed troops, originally organized in 1925 as Hitler's personal guard, that developed into the most powerful affiliated organization of the Nazi Party; the SS established control of the police and security systems, forming the basis of the Nazi police state and the major instrument of racial terror in occupied Europe

Star of David a six-pointed star that is a symbol of Judaism

stereotype a biased generalization about a group of people, based on hearsay and distorted, preconceived ideas

Stalin, Joseph the Soviet Communist leader from 1927 to 1953

swastika an ancient symbol that gained notoriety as the unmistakable emblem of Nazism and the Nazi Party

synagogue in Judaism, the house of worship, as well as a center of community life

thanatology the science of producing death, invented by the Nazis

Third Reich meaning "third regime or empire," the Nazi designation of Germany and its regime from 1933 to 1945

Treaty of Versailles a peace treaty signed by Germany and the Allies in 1919, after the end of World War I

Treblinka a Nazi extermination camp in the General Government (Generalgouvernement)

Truman, Harry S the U.S. president from 1945 to 1953, after the death of Franklin D. Roosevelt

Umschlagplatz "Transfer point"; the place in Warsaw, Poland, where freight trains were loaded and unloaded; it was used as an assembly point where Jews were loaded onto cattle cars to be taken to Treblinka

underground organized groups and individuals acting in secrecy to oppose a government, or, during war, to resist occupying enemy forces

Vichy France the region of France not immediately occupied by Nazi Germany, which was governed from the spa town of Vichy; the Vichy government collaborated with the Nazis

Volk the concept of the German "people" as a nation or race, which was an underlying idea in German history from the early 1800s; inherent in the name was a feeling of superiority of German culture and the idea of a universal mission for the German people

Volksliste a "racial list" of groups of people who were to be accepted into the Third Reich as Germans and accepted as "ethnic Germans," or *Volksdeutsche*

Waffen-SS militarized units of the SS

Wannsee Conference a Nazi conference held on January 20, 1942, at which SS official Reinhard Heydrich helped present and coordinate the "Final Solution"

Wehrmacht the collective name for all three branches of the German armed forces from 1935 to 1945

Weimar Republic the German republic, an experiment in democracy, from 1919 to 1933

Werwolf bands paramilitary guerrilla forces made up of uniformed Germans who operated as resistance fighters in Allied-controlled territories as Germany neared defeat in World War II

Yiddish a language that combines elements of German and Hebrew

Zionism a political and cultural movement calling for the return of the Jewish people to their biblical home in the region known as Palestine prior to 1948 and the establishment of the State of Israel

Zionists members of a social and political movement promoting the creation of a homeland for Jews in Palestine

Zyklon B hydrogen cyanide, a pesticide used by the Nazis in their Euthanasia Program and later in some of the gas chambers at the extermination camps

Primary Source Documents

NAZI PARTY DOCUMENTS

■ THE PROGRAM OF THE NATIONAL-SOCIALIST (NAZI) GERMAN WORKERS' PARTY

The Program of the German Workers' Party is a program for our time. The leadership rejects the establishment of new aims after those set out in the Program have been achieved, for the sole purpose of making it possible for the Party to continue to exist as the result of the artificially stimulated dissatisfaction of the masses.

1. We demand the uniting of all Germans within one Greater Germany, on the basis of the right to self-determination of nations.

2. We demand equal rights for the German people (*Volk*) with respect to other nations, and the annulment of the peace treaty of Versailles and St. Germain.

3. We demand land and soil (Colonies) to feed our People and settle our excess population.

4. Only Nationals (*Volksgenossen*) can be Citizens of the State. Only persons of German blood can be Nationals, regardless of religious affiliation. No Jew can therefore be a German National.

5. Any person who is not a Citizen will he able to live in Germany only as a guest and must be subject to legislation for Aliens.

6. Only a Citizen is entitled to decide the leadership and laws of the State. We therefore demand that only Citizens may hold public office, regardless of whether it is a national, state or local office.

   We oppose the corrupting parliamentary custom of making party considerations, and not character and ability, the criterion for appointments to official positions.

7. We demand that the State make it its duty to provide opportunities of employment first of all for its own Citizens. If it is not possible to maintain the entire population of the State, then foreign nationals (non-Citizens) are to be expelled from the Reich.

8. Any further immigration of non-Germans is to be prevented. We demand that all non-Germans who entered Germany after August 2, 1914, be forced to leave the Reich without delay.

9. All German Citizens must have equal rights and duties.

10. It must be the first duty of every Citizen to carry out intellectual or physical work. Individual activity must not be harmful to the public interest and must be pursued within the framework of the community and for the general good.

We therefore demand:

11. The abolition of all income obtained without labor or effort.

Breaking the Servitude of Interest.

12. In view of the tremendous sacrifices in property and blood demanded of the Nation by every war, personal gain from the war must be termed a crime against the Nation. We therefore demand the total confiscation of all war profits.

13. We demand the nationalization of all enterprises (already) converted into corporations (trusts).

14. We demand profit-sharing in large enterprises.

15. We demand the large-scale development of old-age pension schemes.

16. We demand the creation and maintenance of a sound middle class; the immediate communalization of the large department stores, which are to be leased at low rates to small tradesmen. We demand the most careful consideration for the owners of small businesses in orders placed by national, state, or community authorities.

17. We demand land reform in accordance with our national needs and a law for expropriation without compensation of land for public purposes. Abolition of ground rent and prevention all speculation in land.

18. We demand ruthless battle against those who harm the common good by their activities. Persons committing base crimes against the People, usurers, profiteers, etc., are to be punished by death without regard to religion or race.

19. We demand the replacement of Roman Law, which serves a materialistic World Order, by German Law.

20. In order to make higher education—and thereby entry into leading positions—available to every able and industrious German, the State must provide a thorough restructuring of our entire public educational system. The courses of study at all educational institutions are to be adjusted to meet the requirements of practical life. Understanding of the concept of the State must be achieved through the schools (teaching of civics) at the earliest age at which it can be grasped. We demand the education at the public expense of specially gifted children of poor parents, without regard to the latters' position or occupation.

21. The State must raise the level of national health by means of mother-and-child care, the banning of juvenile labor, achievement of physical fitness through legislation for compulsory gymnastics and sports, and maximum support for all organizations providing physical training for young people.

22. We demand the abolition of hireling troops and the creation of a national army.

23. We demand laws to fight against *deliberate* political lies and their dissemination by the press. In order to make it possible to create a German press, we demand:

    a) all editors and editorial employees of newspapers appearing in the German language must be German by race;

    b) non-German newspapers require express permission from the State for their publication. They may not be printed in the German language;

c) any financial participation in a German newspaper or influence on such a paper is to be forbidden by law to non-Germans and the penalty for any breach of this law will be the closing of the newspaper in question, as well as the immediate expulsion from the Reich of the non-Germans involved.

Newspapers which violate the public interest are to be banned. We demand laws against trends in art and literature which have a destructive effect on our national life, and the suppression of performances that offend against the above requirements.

24. We demand freedom for all religious denominations, provided that they do not endanger the existence of the State or offend the concepts of decency and morality of the Germanic race. The Party as such stands for positive Christianity, without associating itself with any particular denomination. It fights against the Jewish-materialistic spirit *within* and *around* us, and is convinced that a permanent revival of our Nation can be achieved only from *within*, on the basis of:

Public Interest before Private Interest.

25. To carry out all the above we demand: the creation of a strong central authority in the Reich. Unquestioned authority by the political central Parliament over the entire Reich and over its organizations in general. The establishment of trade and professional organizations to enforce the Reich basic laws in the individual states.

The Party leadership promises to take an uncompromising stand, at the cost of their own lives if need be, on the enforcement of the above points.

Munich, February 24, 1920.

■ **DECLARATION OF THE BOYCOTT BY THE NAZI PARTY LEADERSHIP**
March 28, 1933

National Socialists! Party Comrades!

After fourteen years of inner conflict, the German *Volk*—politically overcoming its ranks, classes, professions, and confessional divisions—has elected an *Erhebung* which put a lightning end to the Marxist-Jewish nightmare.

In the weeks following January 30, a unique military revolution took place in Germany.

In spite of long years of exceedingly severe suppression and persecution, the masses of millions that support the Government of the National Revolution have, in a very calm and disciplined manner, given the new Reich leadership legal cover for the implementation of its reform of the German nation from top to bottom. On March 5 the overwhelming majority of Germans eligible to vote declared its confidence in the new regime. The completion of the national revolution, has thus become the demand of the *Volk*.

The Jewish-Marxist *Bonzen* (bigwigs) deserted their position of power with deplorable cowardice. Despite all the fuss, not a single one dared to raise any serious resistance.

For the most part, they have left the masses they had seduced in the lurch and fled abroad, taking with them their stuffed strongboxes.

The authors and beneficiaries of our misfortune owe the fact that they were spared—almost without exception—solely to the incomparable discipline and order with which this act of overthrowing was conducted.

Hardly a hair on their heads was harmed. Compare this act of self-discipline on the part of the national uprising in Germany with, for instance, the Bolshevist Revolution in Russia, which claimed the lives of over three million people, and you will begin to appreciate what a debt of gratitude the criminals guilty of the disintegration in Germany owe the powers of the national uprising. Compare the terrible battles and destruction of the Revolution of these very November Men themselves— their shooting of hostages in the years 1918 and '19, the slaughtering of defenseless opponents—and you will once again perceive how enormous the difference is between them and the national uprising.

The men presently in power solemnly proclaimed to the world that they wanted to live in international peace. In this, the German *Volk* constitutes a loyal *Gefolgschaft* [following]. Germany wants neither worldwide confusion nor international intrigues. National revolutionary Germany is firmly resolved to put an end to internal mismanagement!

Now that the domestic enemies of the nation have been eliminated by the *Volk* itself, what we have long been waiting for will now come to pass. The Communist and Marxist criminals and their Jewish intellectual instigators, who, having made off with their capital stocks across the border in the nick of time, are now unfolding an unscrupulous, treasonous campaign of agitation against the German *Volk* as a whole from abroad. Because it became impossible for them to continue lying in Germany, they have begun, in the capitals of the former Entente, to continue the same agitation against the young national uprising that they had already pursued at the outbreak of the War against the Germany of that time.

Lies and slander of positively hair-raising perversity are being launched about Germany. Horror stories of dismembered Jewish corpses, gouged-out eyes, and hacked-off hands are circulated for the purpose of defaming the German *Volk* in the world for a second time, just as they had succeeded in doing once before in 1914. The animosity of millions of innocent human beings, i.e., peoples with whom the German *Volk* wishes only to live in peace, is being stirred up by these unscrupulous criminals. They want German goods and German labor to fall victim to the international boycott. It seems they think the misery in Germany is not bad enough as it is; they have to make it worse!

They lie about Jewish females who have supposedly been killed, about Jewish girls allegedly being raped before the eyes of their parents, about cemeteries being ravaged! The whole thing is one big lie invented for the sole purpose of provoking a new world-war agitation!

Standing by and watching this lunatic crime any longer would mean being implicated.

The National Socialist Party will therefore now take defensive action against this universal crime with means that are capable of striking a blow to the guilty parties.

For the guilty ones are among us, they live in our midst and day after day misuse the right to hospitality which the German *Volk* has granted them.

At a time when millions of our people have nothing to live on and nothing to eat, while hundreds of thousands of German brain-workers degenerate on the streets, these intellectual Jewish men of letters are sitting in our midst and have no qualms about claiming the right to our hospitality.

What would America do were the Germans in America to commit a sin against America like the one these Jews have committed against Germany? The National Revolution did not harm a hair of their heads. They were allowed to go about their business as before; but, mind you, corruption will be exterminated, regardless of

who commits it. Just as belonging to a Christian confession or our own *Volk* does not constitute a license for criminals, neither does belonging to the Jewish race or the Mosaic religion.

For decades, Germany indiscriminately allowed all aliens to enter the country. There are 135 people to one square kilometer of land in this country.

In America there are less than 15. In spite of this fact, America saw it fit to set quotas for immigration and even exclude certain peoples from immigrating.

Without any regard to its own distress, Germany refrained for decades from instituting these measures. As our reward, we now have a clique of Jewish men of letters, professors, and profiteers inciting the world against us while millions of our own *Volksgenossen* are unemployed and degenerating.

This will be put to a stop now!

The Germany of the National Revolution is not the Germany of a cowardly bourgeois mentality.

We see the misery and wretchedness of our own *Volksgenossen* and feel obliged to leave nothing undone which could prevent further damage to this, our Volk.

For the parties responsible for these lies and slander are the Jews in our midst. It is they who are the source of this campaign of hate and lies against Germany. It would be in their power to call the liars in the rest of the world into line.

Because they choose not to do so, we will make sure that this crusade of hatred and lies against Germany is no longer directed against the innocent German Volk, but against the responsible agitators themselves.

This smear campaign of boycotting and atrocities must not and shall not injure the German *Volk*, but rather the Jews themselves—a thousand times more severely.

Thus the following order is issued to all party sections and party organizations:

ITEM 1: ACTION COMMITTEES FOR A BOYCOTT AGAINST THE JEWS

Action Committees are to be formed in each *Ortsgruppe* [local chapter] and organizational body of the NSDAP for conducting a practical, organized boycott of Jewish businesses, Jewish goods, Jewish doctors, and Jewish lawyers. The Action Committees shall be responsible for ensuring that the boycott does not do any harm to innocent parties but instead does all the more harm to the guilty parties.

ITEM 2: UTMOST PROTECTION FOR ALL FOREIGNERS

The Action Committees shall be responsible for providing the utmost protection for all foreigners, without regard to their religion and origins or race. The boycott is a purely defensive action that is aimed exclusively at the *Judentum* in Germany.

ITEM 3: BOYCOTT PROPAGANDA

The Action Committees shall immediately popularize the boycott by means of propaganda and enlightenment. Basic principle: no good German is still buying from a Jew or allowing the Jew or his henchmen to offer him goods. The boycott must be a universal one. It will be borne by the entire *Volk* and must hit Jewry where it is most vulnerable.

ITEM 4: THE CENTRAL MANAGEMENT: PG. STREICHER

In cases of doubt, one is to refrain from boycotting businesses until informed otherwise by the Central Committee in Munich. The Chairman of the Central Committee is Pg. Streicher.

ITEM 5: SURVEILLANCE OF NEWSPAPERS

The Action Committees shall keep the newspapers under sharp surveillance in order to ascertain the extent to which they are participating in the enlightenment crusade of the German *Volk* against the Jewish smear campaign of atrocities (*Greuelhetze*) abroad. If newspapers are not doing so or doing so only within a limited scope, it is to be seen to that they are instantly removed from every building inhabited by Germans. No German man and no German business is to continue advertising in such newspapers. These papers must become victims of public contempt, written for fellow members of the Jewish race, but not for the German *Volk*.

ITEM 6: BOYCOTT AS A MEANS OF PROTECTING GERMAN LABOR

In conjunction with the factory cell organizations of the party, the Action Committees must carry the propaganda of the enlightenment concerning the effects of the Jewish smear campaign of atrocities on German labor and thus the German worker into the factories, enlightening the workers in particular as to the necessity of a national boycott as a defensive measure for the protection of German labor.

ITEM 7: ACTION COMMITTEES DOWN TO THE LAST VILLAGE!

The Action Committees must be driven into the smallest villages in order to hit especially the Jewish traders on the flatlands.

As a basic principle, it should be stressed that the boycott is a defensive measure which was forced upon us.

ITEM 8: THE BOYCOTT IS TO COMMENCE ON APRIL 1!

The boycott shall not begin in a dissipated fashion but abruptly. For this reason all preparations are to be made instantly. The SA and SS will be given orders to set up guards to warn the population not to set foot in Jewish shops from the moment the boycott begins. The beginning of the boycott is to be publicized on posters and in the press, in handbills, etc.

The boycott shall commence abruptly at 10:00 in the morning on Saturday, April 1. It will be maintained until an order from the party leadership commands that it be discontinued.

ITEM 9: DEMAND OF THE MASSES FOR RESTRICTED ADMISSION

In tens of thousands of mass assemblies that are to reach as far as the smallest village, the Action Committees shall organize the demand for the introduction of a restriction of the number of Jews employed in all professions which should be relative to their proportion in the German population. In order to increase the impact of the action, this demand is initially to be confined to three areas:

A. admission to the German secondary school and universities;

B. the medical profession;

C. the legal profession.

ITEM 10: ENLIGHTENMENT ABROAD

Another further task of the Action Committees is to ensure that every German who upholds any connection whatsoever abroad shall make use of this to circulate in letters, telegrams, and telephone calls in an enlightening manner the truth that law and order reigns in Germany; that it is the single most ardent wish of the German Volk to be able to pursue its work in peace and live in peace with the rest of the world; and that it is fighting the battle against the Jewish smear campaign of atrocities purely as a defensive battle.

ITEM 11: CALM, DISCIPLINE, AND NO ACTS OF VIOLENCE!

The Action Committees are responsible for ensuring that this entire battle is conducted with the utmost calm and the greatest discipline. Refrain from harming a single hair of a Jew's head in the future as well! We will come to terms with this smear campaign simply by the drastic force of these measures cited.

More than ever before it is necessary that the entire party stand behind the leadership in blind obedience as one man.

National Socialists, you have wrought the miracle of sending the November State cartwheeling in a single offensive; you will accomplish this second task the same way. International *Weltjudentum* should know one thing:

The government of the National Revolution does not exist in a vacuum. It is the representation of the working German Volk. Whoever attacks it, is attacking Germany! Whoever slanders it, is slandering the nation! Whoever fights it, has declared war on 65 million people! We were able to come to terms with the Marxist agitators in Germany; they will not force us to our knees, even if they are now proceeding with their renegade crimes against the people from abroad.

National Socialists! Saturday, at the stroke of ten, *Judentum* will know upon whom it has declared war.

National Socialist German Workers' Party/Party Leadership

■ HITLER'S POLITICAL TESTAMENT, APRIL 29, 1945

More than thirty years have passed since 1914 when I made my modest contribution as a volunteer in the First World War, which was forced upon the Reich.

In these three decades love and loyalty to my people have guided all my thoughts, actions and my life. They gave me the strength to make the most difficult decisions ever to confront mortal man. In these three decades I have spent my strength and my health.

It is untrue that I or anyone else in Germany wanted war in 1939. It was wanted and provoked solely by international statesmen either of Jewish origin or working for Jewish interests. I have made too many offers for the limitation and control of armaments, which posterity will not be cowardly enough always to disregard, for responsibility for the outbreak of this war to be placed on me. Nor have I ever wished that, after the appalling First World War, there would be a second against either England or America. Centuries will go by, but from the ruins of our towns and monuments the hatred of those ultimately responsible will always grow anew against the people whom we have to thank for all this: international Jewry and its henchmen.

Only three days before the outbreak of the German-Polish war I proposed a solution of the German-Polish problem to the British ambassador in Berlin—international control as in the case of the Saar. This offer, too, cannot be lied away. It was only rejected because the ruling clique in England wanted war, partly for commercial reasons and partly because it was influenced by the propaganda put out by international Jewry.

I have left no one in doubt that if the people of Europe are once more treated as mere blocks of shares in the hands of these international money and finance conspirators, then the sole responsibility for the massacre must be borne by the true culprits: the Jews. Nor have I left anyone in doubt that this time millions of European children of Aryan descent will starve to death, millions of men will die in battle, and hundreds of thousands of women and children will be burned or bombed to death in our cities without the true culprits being held to account, albeit more humanely.

After six years of war which, despite all setbacks, will one day go down in history as the most glorious and heroic manifestation of the struggle for existence of a nation, I cannot abandon the city which is the capital of this Reich. Since our forces are too meager to withstand the enemy's attack and since our resistance is being debased by creatures who are as blind as they are lacking in character, I wish to share my fate with that which millions of others have also taken upon themselves by remaining in this city. Further, I shall not fall into the hands of the enemy who requires a new spectacle, presented by the Jews, for the diversion of the hysterical masses.

I have therefore decided to stay in Berlin and there to choose death voluntarily when I determine that the position of the Führer and the Chancellery itself can no longer be maintained. I die with a joyful heart in the knowledge of the immeasurable deeds and achievements of our peasants and workers and of a contribution unique in the history of our youth which bears my name.

That I am deeply grateful to them all is as self-evident as is my wish that they do not abandon the struggle but that, no matter where, they continue to fight the enemies of the Fatherland, faithful to the ideals of the great Clausewitz. Through the sacrifices of our soldiers and my own fellowship with them unto death, a seed has been sown in German history that will one day grow to usher in the glorious rebirth of the National Socialist movement in a truly united nation.

Many of our bravest men and women have sworn to bind their lives to mine to the end. I have begged, and finally ordered, them not do so but to play their part in the further struggle of the nation. I ask the leaders of the army, the navy and the air force to strengthen the National Socialist spirit of resistance of our soldiers by all possible means, with special emphasis on the fact that I myself, as the founder and creator of this movement, prefer death to cowardly resignation or even to capitulation.

May it become a point of honor of future German army officers, as it is already in our navy, that the surrender of a district or town is out of the question and that, above everything else, the commanders must set a shining example of faithful devotion to duty unto death.

. . . .

Before my death, I expel former Reichs Marshal Hermann Goering from the party and withdraw from him all the rights that were conferred upon him by the decree of 29 June, 1941 and by my Reichstag statement of September 1939. In his place I appoint Admiral Donitz as president of the Reich and supreme commander of the armed forces.

Before my death, I expel the former Reichsführer of the SS and the Minister of the Interior Heinrich Himmler from the party and from all his state offices. In his place I appoint Gauleiter Karl Hanke as Reichsführer of the SS and head of the German Police, and Gauleiter Paul Giesler as minister of the interior.

Apart altogether from their disloyalty to me, Goering and Himmler have brought irreparable shame on the whole nation by secretly negotiating with the enemy without my knowledge and against my will, and also by attempting illegally to seize control of the state.

In order to provide the German people with a government of honorable men who will fulfill the task of continuing the war with all the means at their disposal, I, as Führer of the nation, appoint the following members of the new cabinet:

President of the Reich: Donitz
Chancellor of the Reich: Dr. Goebbels
Party Minister: Bormann

Foreign Minister: Seyss-Inquart
Minister of the Interior: Gauleiter Giesler
Minister of War: Donitz
Supreme Commander of the Army: Schorner
Supreme Commander of the Navy: Donitz
Supreme Commander of the Air Force: Greim
Reichsführer of the SS and Head of the German Police: Gauleiter Hanke
Trade: Funk
Agriculture: Backe
Justice: Thierack
Culture: Dr. Scheel
Propaganda: Dr. Naumann
Finance: Schwerin-Crossigk
Labor: Dr. Hupfauer
Munitions: Saur
Leader of the German Labor Front and Minister Without Portfolio: Dr. Ley.

Although a number of these men, including Martin Bormann, Dr. Goebbels and others together with their wives have joined me of their own free will, not wishing to leave the capital under any circumstances and prepared to die with me, I implore them to grant my request that they place the welfare of the nation above their own feelings. By their work and loyal companionship they will remain as close to me after my death as I hope my spirit will continue to dwell among them and accompany them always. Let them be severe but never unjust and let them never, above all, allow fear to preside over their actions, placing the honor of the nation above everything that exists on earth. May they, finally, always remember that our task, the consolidation of a National Socialist state, represents the work of centuries to come, so that every individual must subordinate his own interest to the common good. I ask of all Germans, of all National Socialists, men and women and all soldiers of the Wehrmacht, that they remain faithful and obedient unto death to the new government and its president.

Above all, I enjoin the government and the people to uphold the race laws to the limit and to resist mercilessly the poisoner of all nations, international Jewry.

Berlin, 29 April, 1945, 4 a.m.

ADOLF HITLER
Witnesses:
DR. JOSEPH GOEBBELS
MARTIN BORMANN
WILHELM BURGDORF
HANS KREBS

OFFICIAL LAWS, ORDERS, AND REGULATIONS OF THE THIRD REICH

■ **LAW AGAINST THE OVERCROWDING OF GERMAN SCHOOLS AND INSTITUTIONS OF HIGHER LEARNING, APRIL 25, 1933**

The Reich government has enacted the following law, which is promulgated herewith:

1

In all schools except schools providing compulsory education, and in institutions of higher learning, the number of pupils and students is to be limited so as to ensure thorough training and to meet professional needs.

2

State governments will determine at the beginning of each school year how many pupils each school may accept and how many new students each university faculty may accept.

3

In those kinds of schools and faculties whose attendance figures are particularly out of proportion to professional needs, the number of pupils and students already admitted is to be reduced during the 1933 school year as far as this can be done without excessive rigor, in order to establish a more acceptable proportion.

4

In new admissions, care is to be taken that the number of Reich Germans who, according to the Law for the Restoration of the Professional Civil Service of April 7, 1933 (RGBI. I, p. 175), are of non-Aryan descent, out of the total attending each school and each faculty, does not exceed the proportion of non-Aryans within the Reich German population. The ratio will be determined uniformly for the entire Reich territory.

Likewise, in lowering the number of pupils and students according to section 3, a suitable proportion is to be established between the total number of persons attending and the number of non-Aryans. In doing so, a quota higher than the population ratio may be used as a base.

Paragraphs 1 and 2 do not apply to Reich Germans of non-Aryan descent whose fathers fought at the front during the World War for the German Reich or its allies, or to the offspring of marriages concluded before this law took effect, if one parent or two grandparents are of Aryan origin. These also are not to be included in calculating the population ratio and the quota.

5

Obligations incumbent upon Germany as a result of international treaties are not affected by the provisions of this law.

6

Decrees for implementation will be issued by the Reich minister of the interior.

7

The law takes effect on the date of promulgation.

■ LAW FOR THE PROTECTION OF GERMAN BLOOD AND GERMAN HONOR, SEPTEMBER 15, 1935

Imbued with the insight that the purity of German blood is prerequisite for the continued existence of the German people and inspired by the inflexible will to ensure the existence of the German nation for all times, the Reichstag has unanimously adopted the following law, which is hereby promulgated:

1

1. Marriages between Jews and subjects of German or kindred blood are forbidden. Marriages nevertheless concluded are invalid, even if concluded abroad to circumvent this law.

2. Only the state attorney may initiate the annulment suit.

2

Extramarital intercourse between Jews and subjects of German or kindred blood is forbidden.

3

Jews must not employ in their households female subjects of German or kindred blood who are under forty-five years old.

4

1. Jews are forbidden to fly the Reich national flag and to display the Reich colors.

2. They are, on the other hand, allowed to play the Jewish colors. The exercise of this right enjoys the protection of state.

5

1. Whoever violates the prohibition in paragraph 1 will be punished by penal servitude.

2. A male who violates the prohibition in paragraph 2 will be punished either by imprisonment or penal servitude.

3. Whoever violates the provisions of paragraphs 3 or 4 will be punished by imprisonment up to one year and by a fine, or by either of these penalties.

6

The Reich minister of the interior, in agreement with the deputy of the Führer and the Reich minister of justice, will issue the legal and administrative orders required to implement and supplement this law.

7

The law takes effect on the day following promulgation, except for paragraph 3, which goes into force January 1, 1936.

Nuremberg, September 15, 1935 at the Reich Party Congress of Freedom
The Führer and Reich Chancellor
ADOLF HITLER

The Reich Minister of the Interior
FRICK

The Reich Minister of Justice
The Deputy of the Führer and Reich Minister
Without Portfolio

■ **FIRST ORDINANCE TO THE REICH CITIZENSHIP LAW NOVEMBER 14, 1935)**

On the basis of article 3 of the Reich Citizenship Law of September 15, 1935 (*Reich Legal Gazette* 1, 1146) the following is ordered:

Article I

1. Until the issuance of further regulations for the award of citizenship, nationals of German or related blood who possessed the right to vote in Reichstag elections at the time when the Reich Citizenship Law entered into force or who were granted provisional citizenship by the Reich Minister of Interior acting in agreement with the Deputy of the Führer, are provisionally considered Reich citizens.

2. The Reich Minister of Interior acting in agreement with the Deputy of the Führer may revoke provisional citizenship.

Article 2

1. The regulations of Article I apply also to nationals who were part Jews (*jüdische Mischlinge*).

2. Partly Jewish is anyone who is descended from one or two grandparents who are fully Jewish (*volljüdisch*) by race, in so far as he is not to be considered as Jewish under article 5, section 2. A grandparent is to be considered as fully Jewish if he belonged to the Jewish religious community.

Article 3

Only a Reich citizen as bearer of complete political rights may exercise the right to vote in political affairs or hold public office. The Reich Minister of Interior or an agency empowered by him may make exceptions with regard to an admission to public office during the transition. The affairs of religious communities will not be affected.

Article 4

1. A Jew cannot be a Reich citizen. He is not allowed the right to vote in political affairs; he cannot hold public office.

2. Jewish civil servants will retire as of December 31, 1935. If these civil servants fought for Germany or her allies in the World War, they will receive the full pension to which they are entitled by their last position in the pay scale, until they reach retirement age; they will not, however, advance in seniority. Upon reaching retirement age their pension is to be based on pay scales which will prevail at that time.

3. The affairs of religious communities will not be affected.

4. The provisions of service for teachers in Jewish public schools will remain unaltered until new regulations are issued for the Jewish school system.

Article 5

1. Jew is he who is descended from at least three grandparents who are fully Jewish by race. Article 2, paragraph 2, sentence 2 applies.

2. Also to be considered a Jew is a partly Jewish national who is descended from two fully Jewish grandparents and

> a) who belonged to the Jewish religious community, upon adoption of the Law, or is received into the community thereafter, or
>
> b) who was married to a Jewish person upon adoption of the law, or marries one thereafter, or
>
> c) who is the offspring of a marriage concluded by a Jew (as defined in paragraph 1) after the entry into force of the Law for the Protection of German Blood and Honor of September 15, 1935 (*Reich Legal Gazette* 1, 1146), or
>
> d) who is the offspring of an extramarital relationship involving a Jew (as defined in paragraph 1) and who is born out of wedlock after July 31, 1936.

Article 6

1. Requirements for purity of blood exceeding those of article 5, which are made in Reich laws or regulations of the National Socialist German Workers' Party and its organizations, remain unaffected.

2. Any other requirements for purity of blood, exceeding those of article 4, may be made only with the consent of the Reich Minister of the Interior and the Deputy of the Führer. Insofar as requirements of this type exist already, they become void on January 1, 1936 unless they are accepted by the Reich Minister of the Interior acting with the agreement of the Deputy of the Führer. Acceptance is to be requested from the Reich Minister of the Interior.

Article 7

The Führer and Reich Chancellor may grant exemptions from the stipulations of implementory ordinances.

Berlin, November 14, 1935

The Führer and Reich Chancellor
ADOLF HITLER

The Reich Minister of the Interior
FRICK

The Deputy of the Führer
R. HESS

(Reich Minister without Portfolio)

■ **REGULATION FOR THE ELIMINATION OF THE JEWS FROM THE ECONOMIC LIFE OF GERMANY, NOVEMBER 12, 1938**

On the basis of the regulation for the implementation of the Four Year Plan of October 18, 1936 (*Reichsgesetzblatt*, I, p. 887), the following is decreed:

§ 1

1) From January 1, 1939, Jews (§ 5 of the First Regulation to the Reich Citizenship Law of November 14, 1935, *Reichsgesetzblatt*, I, p. 1333) are forbidden to operate retail stores, mail-order houses, or sales agencies, or to carry on a trade [craft] independently.

2) They are further forbidden, from the same day on, to offer for sale goods or services, to advertise these, or to accept orders at markets of all sorts, fairs or exhibitions.

3) Jewish trade enterprises (Third Regulation to the Reich Citizenship Law of June 14, 1938—*Reichsgesetzblatt*, I, p. 627) which violate this decree will be closed by police.

§ 2

1) From January 1, 1939, a Jew can no longer be the head of an enterprise within the meaning of the Law of January 20, 1934, for the Regulation of National Work (*Reichsgesetzblatt*, I, p. 45).

2) Where a Jew is employed in an executive position in a commercial enterprise he may be given notice to leave in six weeks. At the expiration of the term of the notice all claims of the employee based on his contract, especially those concerning pension and compensation rights, become invalid.

§ 3

1) A Jew cannot be a member of a cooperative.

2) The membership of Jews in cooperatives expires on December 31, 1938. No special notice is required.

§ 4

The Reich Minister of Economy, in coordination with the ministers concerned, is empowered to publish regulations for the implementation of this decree. He may permit exceptions under the Law if these are required as the result of the transfer of a Jewish enterprise to non-Jewish ownership, for the liquidation of a Jewish enterprise or, in special cases, to ensure essential supplies.

Berlin, November 12, 1938

Plenipotentiary for the Four Year Plan
GÖRING
Field Marshal General

■ ESTABLISHMENT OF JUDENRÄTE (JEWISH COUNCILS) IN THE OCCUPIED TERRITORIES, NOVEMBER 28, 1939

Regulation for the Establishment of the Judenräte, November 28, 1939

1. In each community a body representing the Jews will be formed.

2. This representation of the Jews, known as the Judenrat, will consist of 12 Jews in communities with up to 10,000 inhabitants, and in communities with more than 10,000 inhabitants, of 24 Jews, drawn from the locally resident population. The Judenrat will be elected by the Jews of the community. If a member of the Judenrat leaves, a new member is to be elected immediately.

3. The Judenrat will elect a chairman and a deputy from among its members.

4. 1) After these elections, which must he completed not later than December 31, 1939, the membership of the Judenrat is to be reported to the responsible sub-district Commander (*Kreishauptmann*), in urban districts to the City Commander (*Stadthauptmann*).

   2) The sub-district Commander (City Commander) will decide whether the Judenrat membership submitted to him should be approved. He may order changes in the membership.

5. It is the duty of the Judenrat through its chairman or his deputy to receive the orders of the German Administration. It is responsible for the conscientious carrying out of orders to their full extent. The directives it issues to carry out these German decrees must be obeyed by all Jews and Jewesses.

Cracow, November 28, 1939

The Governor General
for the Occupied Polish Territories
FRANK

■ THE MADAGASCAR PLAN, JULY 1940

The Jewish Question in the Peace Treaty

The approaching victory gives Germany the possibility, and in my view also the duty, of solving the Jewish question in Europe. The desirable solution is: all Jews out of Europe. The task of the Foreign Ministry in this is:

a) To include this demand in the Peace Treaty and to insist on it also by means of separate negotiations with the European countries not involved in the Peace Treaty;

b) to secure the territory necessary for the settlement of the Jews in the Peace Treaty, and to determine principles for the cooperation of the enemy countries in this problem;

c) to determine the position under international law of the new Jewish overseas settlement:

d) as preparatory measures:

1) clarification of the wishes and plans of the departments concerned of the Party, State and Research organizations in Germany, and the coordination of these plans with the wishes of the Reich Foreign Minister, including the following:

2) preparation of a survey of the factual data available in various places (number of Jews in the various countries), use of their financial assets through an international bank:

3) negotiations with our friend, Italy, on these matters.

With regard to beginning the preparatory work. Section D III has already approached the Reich Foreign Minister via the Department Germany [interior affairs], and has been instructed by him to start on the preparatory work without delay. There have already been discussions with the Office of the *Reichsführer* SS in the Ministry of Interior and several departments of the Party. These departments approve the following plan of Section D III:

Section D III proposes as a solution of the Jewish question: In the Peace Treaty France must make the island of Madagascar available for the solution of the Jewish question, and to resettle and compensate the approximately 25,000 French citizens living there. The island will be transferred to Germany under a mandate. Diégo Suarez Bay and the port of Antsirane, which are [sea-] strategically important, will become German naval bases (if the Navy wishes, these naval bases could he extended also to the harbors—open road-steads—Tamatave, Andevorante, Mananjara, etc.). In addition to these naval bases, suitable areas of the country will be excluded from the Jewish territory (*Judenterritorium*) for the construction of air bases. That part of the island not required for military purposes will he placed under administration of a German Police Governor, who will be under the administration of the *Reichsfürer* SS. Apart from this, the Jews will have their own administration in this territory: their own mayors, police, postal and railroad administration, etc. The Jews will be jointly liable for the value of the island. For this purpose their former European financial assets will be transferred for use to a European bank to be established for this purpose. Insofar as the assets are not sufficient to pay for the land which they will receive, and for the purchase of necessary commodities in Europe for the development of the island, the Jews will be able to receive bank credits from the same bank.

As Madagascar will only be a Mandate, the Jews living there will not acquire German citizenship. On the other hand, the Jews deported to Madagascar will lose their citizenship of European countries from the date of deportation. Instead, they will become residents of the Mandate of Madagascar.

This arrangement would prevent the possible establishment in Palestine by the Jews of a Vatican State of their own, and the opportunity for them to exploit for their own purposes symbolic importance which Jerusalem has for the Christian and Mohammedan parts of the world. Moreover, the Jews will remain in German hands as a pledge for the future good behavior of the members of their race in America.

Use can be made for propaganda purposes of the generosity shown by Germany in permitting cultural, economic, administrative legal self-administration to the Jews; it can be emphasized at the same time that our German sense of responsibility towards the world forbids us to make the gift of a sovereign state to a race

which has had no independent state for thousands of years; this would still require the test of history.

Berlin, July 3, 1940
signed RADEMACHER

SECRET NAZI DOCUMENTS

■ **REINHARD HEYDRICH'S INSTRUCTIONS FOR MEASURES AGAINST JEWS, NOVEMBER 10, 1938**

Secret

Copy of most urgent telegram from Munich
of November 10, 1938, 1:20 A.M.

To:
All headquarters and stations of the State Police
All districts and sub districts of the SD

Urgent! For immediate attention of the chief or his deputy!

RE: MEASURES AGAINST JEWS TONIGHT

Following the attempt on the life of Secretary of the Legation vom Rath in Paris, demonstrations against the Jews are to be expected in all parts of the Reich in the course of the coming night, November 9/10, 1938. The instructions below are to be applied in dealing with these events:

I. The chiefs of the State Police, or their deputies, must immediately upon receipt of this telegram contact, by telephone, the political leaders in their areas—Gauleiter or Kreisleiter—who have jurisdiction in their districts and arrange a joint meeting with the inspector or commander of the Order Police to discuss the arrangements for the demonstrations. At these discussions the political leaders will be informed that the German Police has received instructions, detailed below, from the Reichsführer SS and the chief of the German Police, with which the political leadership is requested to coordinate its own measures:

    A. Only such measures are to be taken as do not endanger German lives or property (i.e., synagogues are to be burnt down only where there is no danger of fire in neighboring buildings).

    B. Places of business and apartments belonging to Jews may be destroyed but not looted. The police are instructed to supervise the observance of this order and to arrest looters.

    C. In commercial streets particular care is to be taken that non-Jewish businesses are completely protected against damage.

    D. Foreign citizens—even if they are Jews—are not to be molested.

II .On the assumption that the guidelines detailed under paragraph I are observed, the demonstrations are not to be prevented by the police, who are only to supervise the observance of the guidelines.

III. On receipt of this telegram, police will seize all archives to be found in all synagogues and offices of the Jewish communities so as to prevent their destruction during the demonstrations. This refers only to material of historical value, not to contemporary tax records, etc. The archives are to be handed over to the locally responsible officers of the SD.

IV. The control of the measures of the Security Police concerning the demonstrations against the Jews is vested in the organs of the State Police, unless inspectors of the Security Police have given their own instructions. Officials of the Criminal Police, members of the SD, of the Reserves and the SS in general may be used to carry out the measures taken by the Security Police.

V. As soon as the course of events during the night permits the release of the officials required, as many Jews in all districts, especially the rich, as can be accommodated in existing prisons are to be arrested. For the time being only healthy male Jews, who are not too old are to be detained. After the detentions have been carried out the appropriate concentration camps are to be contacted immediately for the prompt accommodation of the Jews in the camps. Special care is to be taken that the Jews arrested in accordance with these instructions are not ill-treated.

SIGNED HEYDRICH,
SS Gruppenfürer

■ INSTRUCTIONS FOR THE DEPORTATION OF THE JEWS FROM THE PALATINATE (PFALZ), OCTOBER 1940

Secret

Notes for the Responsible Officials

1. Only full Jews will be deported. *Mischlinge*, partners in *mixed marriages* and *foreign Jews*, as long as they are not citizens of enemy nations or of areas occupied by us, will be excluded from the *Aktion*. Stateless Jews will, on principle, be detained. Every Jew is considered fit to be moved; the only exceptions are Jews who are actually bedridden.

2. In order to assemble the Jews collection points have been established. . . . The transport of those who are being held will be by buses. Every bus will be accompanied by a Crime Police official as transport leader. He will have with him, according to need, regular police, Gendarmerie or Crime Police. The transport leader is responsible for the assembly, transport and supervision of his group until the departure of the train from the collection point.

3. Every transport leader will receive a list at the concentration point, noting the bus which he has been allocated, the police officials who will work with him, and the names and addresses of the persons to be detained. Where the names of the officials to work with him have not yet been listed they will be inserted later by the transport leader.

4. The transport leader will inform the officials working with him of the names and addresses of the persons to be detained.

5. When the officials appointed for this purpose have received the personal information on the Jews, they will go to the homes of those concerned. They will then convey to them that they have been detained in order to be deported; it is to be pointed out at the same time that they must be ready to move in two hours. Possible queries are to be communicated to the head of the collection point, who will clarify the issue; no delay in the preparations is to be permitted.

6. Those who have been detained should take with them, as far as possible:

    a) A suitcase or parcel with clothing for each Jew; the weight permitted is 50 kg. for each adult, 30 kg. per child.

    b) A complete set of clothing.

    c) A woollen blanket for every Jew.

d) Food for several days.

e) Utensils for eating and drinking.

f) Up to RM 100 in cash per person.

g) Passports, identity cards or other identification papers. These are not to be packed but to be carried by each individual. . .

7. . . . .

8. A questionnaire is to be filled in for every head of a family or single Jew, in accordance with the sample provided, and is to be signed by the official in charge.

9. Attention should be paid to the following before the apartment is vacated:

a) Livestock and other live animals (dogs, cats, cage birds) are to be handed over to the local head official, chairman of the local farmers' association or other suitable person against a receipt,

b) Perishable foodstuffs are to be placed at the disposal of the NSV [Nazi welfare organization],

c) Open fires are to be extinguished,

d) Water and gas supply is to be turned off,

e) Electrical fuses are to be disconnected,

f) The keys to the apartment are to be tied together and provided with a tie-on label with the name, city, street and number of the house of the owner.

g) As far as possible the persons detained are to be searched before their departure for weapons, ammunition, explosives, poison, foreign currency, jewelry, etc.

10. After the apartment has been vacated the entrance to the apartment is to be locked by the official and sealed with the adhesive strip provided for this purpose. The key-hole must be covered by the adhesive strip.

11. After the persons detained have been taken to the bus the official will hand over to the transport leader the objects or valuables, questionnaires and keys, for delivery at the concentration point.

12. After the transport leader has handed over the detainees at the concentration point he will check the list which he received, amend it if required, and mark it as having been dealt with.

13. It is absolutely necessary that the Jews will be dealt with in a proper manner when they are detained. Excesses are in any case to be avoided absolutely.

■ **ORDER BANNING THE EMIGRATION OF JEWS FROM THE REICH, OCTOBER 1941**

Reich Security Main Office (*Reichssicherheitshauptamt*)

Berlin, October 23, 1941

IV B 4 b(Rz) 2920/41 g (984)

To. . .

The Officer appointed by the Chief of the Security Police and the SD for Belgium and France

SS *Brigadeführer Thomas*

Brussels

Secret

Re: Emigration of Jews

Reference: none

The *Reichsführer* SS and Chief of the German Police has decreed that the *emigration* of Jews is to be prevented, taking effect immediately. (Evacuation *Aktionen* will remain unaffected.)

I request that the internal German Authorities concerned in the area of service there may be informed of this order.

Permission for the emigration of individual Jews can only be approved *in single very special cases;* for instance, in the event of a genuine interest on the part of the Reich, and then only after a *prior* decision has been obtained from the Reich Security Main Office.

SIGNED MÜLLER

■ **EXTERMINATION IN GAS VANS IN THE UKRAINE, 1942**

Kiev, May 16, 1942

Reich Secret Document

To SS-*Obersturmbannführer* Rauff

Berlin

. . .I have had the vans of [*Einsatz*] *Gruppe* D disguised as house-trailers, by having a single window shutter fixed to each side of the small vans, and on the large ones, two shutters, such as one often sees on farm houses in the country. The vans had become so well known that not only the authorities but the civilian population referred to them as the "Death Vans" as soon as one appeared. In my opinion the vans cannot be kept secret for any length of time even if they are camouflaged. . . .

I also gave instructions that all personnel should stay as far away as possible from the vans when the gassing is in progress to prevent damage to their health in the event of gas leaking out. . . .

The gassing is generally not carried out correctly. In order to get the *Aktion* finished as quickly as possible the driver presses down on the accelerator as far as it will go. As a result the persons to be executed die of suffocation and do not doze off as was planned. It has proved that if my instructions are followed and the levers are properly adjusted death comes faster and the prisoners fall asleep peacefully. Distorted faces and excretions, such as were observed before, no longer occur. . . .

DR. BECKER
SS *Untersturmführer*

■ **PROPOSAL FOR THE STERILIZATION OF 2-3 MILLION JEWISH WORKERS, JUNE 23, 1942**

Reich Secret Document

Honorable Mr. *Reichsführer*!

On instructions from *Reichsleiter* Bouhler I placed a part of my men at the disposal of *Brigadeführer* Globocnik some considerable time ago for his Special Task. Following a further request from him, I have now made available more personnel. On this occasion *Brigadeführer* Globocnik pressed the view that the whole *Aktion* against the Jews should be carried out as quickly as it is in any way possible, so that

we will not some day be stuck in the middle should any kind of difficulty make it necessary to stop the *Aktion*. You yourself, Mr. *Reichsführer*, expressed the view to me at an earlier time that one must work as fast as possible, if only for reasons of concealment. Both views are more than justified according to my own experience, and basically they produce the same results. Nevertheless I beg to be permitted to present the following consideration of my own in this connection:

According to my impression there are at least 2-3 million men and women well fit for work among the approx. 10 million European Jews. In consideration of the exceptional difficulties posed for us by the question of labor, I am of the opinion that these 2-3 million should in any case be taken out and kept alive. Of course this can only be done if they are at the same time rendered incapable of reproduction. I reported to you about a year ago that persons under my instruction have completed the necessary experiments for this purpose. I wish to bring up these facts again. The type of sterilization which is normally carried out on persons with genetic disease is out of the question in this case, as it takes too much time and is expensive. Castration by means of X-rays, however, is not only relatively cheap, but can be carried out on many thousands in a very short time. I believe that it has become unimportant at the present time whether those affected will then in the course of a few weeks or months realize by the effects that they are castrated.

In the event, Mr. *Reichsführer*, that you decide to choose these means in the interest of maintaining labor-material, *Reichsleiter* Bouhler will be ready to provide the doctors and other personnel needed to carry out this work. He also instructed me to inform you that I should then order the required equipment as quickly as possible.

VIKTOR BRACK
SS *Oberführer*

NAZI CORRESPONDENCE

■ GÖRING ORDERS HEYDRICH TO PREPARE A PLAN FOR THE "FINAL SOLUTION OF THE JEWISH PROBLEM," JULY 31, 1941

To the Chief of the Security Police and the SD,

SS *Gruppenführer* Heydrich

Berlin

In completion of the task which was entrusted to you in the Edict dated January 24, 1939, of solving the Jewish question by means of emigration or evacuation in the most convenient way possible, given the present conditions, I herewith charge you with making all necessary preparations with regard to organizational, practical and financial aspects for an overall solution (*Gesamtlösung*) of the Jewish question in the German sphere of influence in Europe.

Insofar as the competencies of other central organizations are affected, these are to be involved.

I further charge you with submitting to me promptly an overall plan of the preliminary organizational, practical and financial measures for the execution of the intended final solution (*Endlösung*) of the Jewish question.

GÖRING

■ DANNECKER LETTER REQUESTING PERMISSION TO DEPORT CHILDREN FROM PARIS, JULY 10, 1942

[Commanding Officer, Security Police and Security Service in France] IV J, Paris to Reich Security Main Officer IV B 4,

Berlin
July 10, 1942
Urgent, to be submitted immediately!
Subject: Removing Jews from France

Previous: Discussion between SS-Lieutenant Colonel Eichmann and SS-Captain Dannecker on July 1, 1942 in Paris, my dispatch of July 6, 1942, IV J SA 225a.

French police will carry out the arrest of stateless Jews in Paris during July 16–18, 1942. It is to be expected that after the arrests about 4000 Jew-children will remain behind. For the moment French public welfare will care for these children. Inasmuch, however, as any lengthy togetherness of these Jew-children and non-Jewish children is undesirable, and since the "Union of the Jews in France" is not capable of accommodating in its own children's homes more than 400 children, I request an urgent decision by letter as to whether the children of the stateless Jews about to be deported may be removed also, starting with the 10th transport or so.

At the same time I request once more an urgent decision in the matter I raised in my dispatch of July 6, 1942.

By instruction
DANNECKER

■ HITLER BANS PUBLIC REFERENCE TO THE "FINAL SOLUTION OF THE JEWISH QUESTION," JULY 11, 1943

National Socialist German Workers' Party
Party Sectretariat
Head of the Party Secretariat
Führer Headquarters, July 11, 1943

Circular No. 33143 g.

Re: Treatment of the Jewish Question

On instructions from the Führer I make known the following:

Where the Jewish Question is brought up in public, there may be no discussion of a future overall solution (*Gesamtlosüng*).

It may, however, be mentioned that the Jews are taken in groups for appropriate labor purposes.

signed
M. BORMANN

Distribution:
Reichsleiter
Gauleiter
Group leaders

■ LETTER FROM ARTHUR SEYSS-INQUART TO MARTIN BORMANN REGARDING THE "JEWISH QUESTION" IN THE NETHERLANDS

Reich Commissar for the Occupied Netherlands Territories
The Hague
to Party Chancellery Chief Bormann

copies to General Commissars in Netherlands and
Plenipotentiary Dr. Schröder

February 28, 1944

Dear Party Comrade Bormann:

We have cleaned up the Jewish question in the Netherlands insofar as now we only have to carry out decisions that have already been formulated. The Jews have been eliminated from the body of the Dutch people and, insofar as they have not been transported to the East for labor, they are enclosed in a camp. We are dealing here first of all with some 1500 persons who have not been transported to the East for special reasons such as interventions by churches or by personalities who are close to us. In the main I have warded off the interference of the churches in the whole Jewish question in that I held back the Christian Jews in a closed camp where they can be visited weekly by clergy. About 8–9000 Jews have avoided transport by submerging [going into hiding]. By and by they are being seized and sent to the East; at the moment, the rate of seizures is 5–600 a week. The Jewish property has been confiscated and is undergoing liquidation. With the exception of a few enterprises which have not yet been Aryanized, but which have been placed under trusteeship, the liquidation is finished and the property converted into financial papers of the Reich. I count on a yield of ca. 500 million Guilders [more than $250,000,000]. At some appropriate time the future utilization of this money is to be decided on in concert with the Reich Finance Minister; however, the Reich Finance Minister agrees in principle to the use of these funds for purposes in the Netherlands.

The question of Jews in mixed marriages is still open. Here we went further than the Reich and obliged also these Jews to wear the star. I had also ordered that the Jewish partner in a childless mixed marriage should likewise be brought to the East for labor. Our Security Police processed a few hundred such cases, but then received instructions from Berlin not to go on, so that a few thousand of these Jews have remained in the country. Finally, Berlin expressed the wish that the Jews in mixed marriages be concentrated in the Jewish camp Westerbork, to be employed here in labor for the moment. Herewith we raise the problem of mixed marriages. Since this matter is basic I turn to you. The following is to be considered with respect to marriages in which there are children: if one parent is brought to a concentration camp and then probably to labor in the East, the children will always be under the impression that we took the parent away from them. As a matter of fact, the offspring of mixed marriages are more troublesome than full Jews. In political trials, for example, we can determine that it is precisely these offspring who start or carry out most of the assassination attempts or sabotage. If we now introduced a measure that is sure to release the hatred of these people, then we will have a group in our midst with which we will hardly be able to deal in any way save reparation. If, in short, there is a plan which is aimed at the removal of Jewish partners from mixed marriages with children, then the children of these marriages will sooner or later have to travel the same road. Hence I believe that it may be more appropriate not to start on this course, but to decide in each instance whether to remove the whole family or—with due regard to security police precautions—to permit the Jewish member to remain in the family. In the first case, the couple, complete with children, will have to be segregated, possibly like the Jews in Theresienstadt. But in that case one must remember that the offspring will get together to have more children, so that practically the Jewish problem will not be solved lest we take some opportunity to remove this whole society from the Reich's sphere of interest. We are trying the other way in that we free the Jewish partner who is no longer able to have children, or who allows himself to be sterilized, from wearing the star and permit him

to stay with his family. These Jews—at the moment there must be 4–5000 in the Netherlands—remain under a certain amount of security police control with respect to residence and employability. For example, they are not permitted to direct an enterprise which has employees or occupy a leading position in such an enterprise. There are quite a few volunteers for sterilization. I believe also that we have nothing to fear any more from these people, since their decision indicates a willingness to accept conditions as they are. The situation with the Jewish women is not so simple, since the surgical procedure is known to be difficult. All the same I believe in time this way will yield results, provided one does not decide on the radical method of removing the whole family. For the Netherlands then, I would consider the following for a conclusion of the Jewish problem:

1. The male Jewish partner in a mixed marriage—so far as he has not been freed from the star for reasons mentioned above—is taken for enclosed labor to Westerbork. This measure would signify no permanent separation, but action of a security police nature for the duration of exceptional conditions. These Jews will be employed accordingly and will also receive appropriate wages with which they can support their families who will remain behind. They will also receive a few days' leave about once in three months. One can proceed with childless female partners in mixed marriages in the same way. We have here in the Netherlands 834 male Jews in childless mixed marriages, 2775 Jews in mixed marriages with children, and 574 Jewesses in childless mixed marriages. Under certain circumstances these Jews can return to their families, for example, if they submit to sterilization, or if the reasons for separation become less weighty in some other way, or if other precautions are taken or conditions develop which make separation no longer seem necessary.

The Jewish women in mixed marriages with children— the number involved is 1448—should be freed from the star. The following considerations apply here: it is impossible to take these Jewish women from their families—the Reich Security Main Office agrees—if there are children under 14. On the other hand the women with children over 14 would in most cases have reached an age which would entitle them to request freedom from the star because it is hardly likely that they will have more children.

3. I am now going to carry out the Law for the Protection of Blood in the Netherlands, and

4. make possible divorce in mixed marriages by reason of race difference.

These four measures together will constitute a final cleanup of the Jewish question in the Netherlands. Since this regulation could in a certain sense produce a precedent for the Reich, even while in the long run the regulation of mixed marriages in the Reich will also apply in the Netherlands, I am informing you, Mr. Party Director, of my intentions in the hope that I may have your reactions. I wrote in the same vein to the *Reichsführer-SS*.

With best regards

Heil Hitler!
Your
Seyss-Inquart

JEWISH RESISTANCE

■ **A SUMMONS TO RESISTANCE IN THE VILNA GHETTO, JANUARY 1942**

Let us not be led like sheep to the slaughter!

Jewish youth! In a time of unparalleled national misfortune we appeal to you! We do not yet have the words to express the whole tragic struggle which transpires before our eyes. Our language has no words to probe the depths to which our life has fallen nor to vociferate the anguish which strangles us.

It is still too hard to find the proper definition for the state in which we find ourselves, for the extraordinary cruelty with which the annihilation of the local Jewish population has been carried out.

The community of Jerusalem of Lithuania [Vilna was called "the Jerusalem of Lithuania"] numbered 75,000. On entering the ghetto, 25,000 were already missing, and today only 12,000 remain. All the others have been killed! Death strolls in our streets; in our tents—powerlessness. But the anguish at this huge misfortune is much greater in the light of the ignoble conduct of the Jews at the present time. Never in its long history of martyrdom has the Jewish people shown such abjectness, such a lack of human dignity, national pride, and unity, such communal inertia and submissiveness to the murderers.

The heart aches even more at the conduct of Jewish youth, reared for twenty years in the ideals of upbuilding and halutz defense, which now is apathetic, lost, and does not respond to the tragic struggle.

There are, however, occasions in the life of a people, of a collective, as in the life of an individual, which seize you by the hair of your head, shake you up, and force you to gird up all your strength to keep alive. We are now experiencing such an occasion.

With what can we defend ourselves? We are helpless, we have no possibilities of organizing any defense of our existence. Even if we are deprived of the possibility of an armed defense in this unequal contest of strength, we nevertheless can still defend ourselves. Defend ourselves with all means—and moral defense above all—is the command of the hour.

Jewish youth!

On none but you rests the national duty to be the pillar of the communal defense of the Jewish collective which stands on the brink of annihilation!

I *Let us defend ourselves during a deportation!*

For several months now, day and night, thousands and tens of thousands have been torn away from our midst, men, the aged, women, and children, led away like cattle—and we, the remainder, are numbed. The illusion still lives within us that they are still alive somewhere, in an undisclosed concentration camp, in a ghetto.

You believe and hope to see your mother, your father, your brother who was seized and has disappeared.

In the face of the next day which arrives with the horror of deportation and murder, the hour has struck to dispel the illusion: There is no way out of the ghetto, except the way to death!

No illusion greater than that our dear ones are alive.

No illusion more harmful than that. It deadens our feelings, shatters our national unity in the moments before death.

Before our eyes they led away our mother, our father, our sisters—enough!

We will not go!

Comrades! Uphold this awareness and impart to your families, to the remnants of the Jerusalem of Lithuania.

—Do not surrender into the hands of the kidnappers!

—Do not hand over any other Jews!

—If you are caught, you have nothing to lose!

—Let us defend ourselves, and not go!

Better to fall with honor in the ghetto than to be led like sheep to Ponary!

II *On guard over national honor and dignity*

We work for Germans and Lithuanians. Everyday we come face to face with our employers, the murderers of our brothers. Great the shame and pain, observing the conduct of Jews, stripped of the awareness of human dignity.

Comrades!

—Don't give the foe the chance to ridicule you!

—When a German ridicules a Jew—don't help him laugh!

—Don't play up to your murderers!

—Denounce the bootlickers at work!

—Denounce the girls who flirt with Gestapo men!

—Work slowly, don't speed!

—Show solidarity! If misfortune befalls one of you—don't be vile egotists—all of ou help him. Be united in work and misfortunes!

—Jewish agents of the Gestapo and informers of all sorts walk the streets. If you get hold of one such, sentence him—to be beaten until death!

III *In the presence of the German soldier*

Instead of submissiveness and repulsive bootlicking, you are given the possibility in daily encounters with German soldiers to perform an important national deed. Not every German soldier is a sworn enemy of the Jews, not every German soldier is a sworn Hitlerite. But many have false ideas about Jews. We, the youth, by our conduct, in word and deed, can create in the mind of the German soldier another image of a Jew, a productive one, a Jew who has national and human dignity.

Comrades, show the Jews with whom you work and live together that this is the approach to the German soldier.

IV *To the Jewish police*

Most tragic is the role of the Jewish police—to be a blind tool in the hands of our murderers. But you, Jewish policemen, have at least a chance to demonstrate your personal integrity and national responsibility!

—Any act which threatens Jewish life should not be performed!

—No actions of mass deportation should be carried out!

—Refuse to carry out the orders which bring death to Jews and their families!. . .

—Do not let service in the police be turned into national disgrace for you!

—Jewish policeman, sooner risk your own life than dozens of Jewish lives!

Comrades!

Convey your hatred of the foe in every place and at every moment!

Never lose the awareness that you are working for your murderers!

Better to fall in the fight for human dignity that to live at the mercy of the murderer!

Let us defend ourselves! Defend ourselves until the last minute!

■ **THE LAST LETTER FROM MORDECAI ANIELEWICZ, WARSAW GHETTO REVOLT COMMANDER, APRIL 23, 1943**

It is impossible to put into words what we have been through. One thing is clear, what happened exceeded our boldest dreams. The Germans ran twice from the ghetto. One of our companies held out for 40 minutes and another—for more than 6 hours. The mine set in the "brushmakers" area exploded. Several of our companies attacked the dispersing Germans. Our losses in manpower are minimal. That is also an achievement. Y [Yechiel] fell. He fell a hero, at the machine-gun. *I feel that great things are happening and what we dared do is of great, enormous importance. . . .*

Beginning from today we shall shift over to the partisan tactic. Three battle companies will move out tonight, with two tasks: reconnaissance and obtaining arms. Do you remember, short-range weapons are of no use to us. We use such weapons only rarely. What we need urgently: grenades, rifles, machine-guns and explosives.

It is impossible to describe the conditions under which the Jews of the ghetto are now living. Only a few will be able to hold out. The remainder will die sooner or later. Their fate is decided. In almost all the hiding places in which thousands are concealing themselves it is not possible to light a candle for lack of air.

With the aid of our transmitter we heard a marvelous report on our fighting by the "Shavit" radio station. The fact that we are remembered beyond the ghetto walls encourages us in our struggle. Peace go with you, my friend! Perhaps we may still meet again! *The dream of my life has risen to become fact. Self-defense in the ghetto will have been a reality. Jewish armed resistance and revenge are facts. I have been a witness to the magnificent, heroic fighting of Jewish men of battle.*

M. Anielewicz
Ghetto, April 23, 1943

■ **LIFE OF JEWISH PARTISANS AND JEWISH FAMILY CAMPS IN THE FOREST, FROM A DIARY BY A JEWISH PARTISAN, 1942–1943**

August 12, 1942

. . . The idea of the forest returned and came to life. After the second mass-murder all of us were certain that the Germans made no difference between one Jew and another. . . They deceived the Judenrat and the Jewish Police when they promised them that they would stay alive if they helped to carry out the slaughter, and in the end they killed them too. Once more we began to search or ways of escape outside the ghetto. . . .

The first to escape were Jews from the neighborhood Naliboki Forest. They disappeared and nothing more was heard of them. The people from Zhetl also went, to Lipiczanka Forest, and they were joined by some from Nowogrodek, who returned after a while to take with them their relatives and friends. From them we heard details of life in the forest. They have arms, they carry out attacks on Germans traveling on the roads; the peasants are afraid of them and supply them with

food. There are Russian partisans in the forest who live on good terms with the Jews and carry out joint attacks on the Germans with them.

Young boys of 15 to 17 snatch arms from the Germans and fix stocks to pistols and rifles. . . .

[1943]

As a result of our many attacks on the Germans in the area of our camp, a German assault was to be expected any day. Information reached us that the Germans knew where we were. The Staff decided to dissolve the separate groups and to re-establish the Brigade.

At the beginning of April all the groups were ordered to leave their valleys and move within 24 hours to Brozova Forest, in Stara-Huta.

We packed our belongings, filled our knapsacks, and fastened our blankets on top of them. The cooking gear and other things were loaded on carts and we moved out. The night was cloudy and the sky full of rain. The damp penetrated into the very marrow of our bones. The dry, bare branches of the young trees waved and bent hither and thither. Our thoughts were black too. Many of us had been lost in our wanderings from forest to forest, from base camp to base camp. They had fallen, and who knew what awaited us at the next base?

By day the snow began to melt. Long pools of water stretched along the sandy paths. We had many kilometers to go. Our feet sink in the mud as though it were soft dough. You want to rest and there is no place to sit. Everything is wet and damp. Now we have found a kind of hillock from which the water has run off. The people sit down, rest, eat their fill and then continue on their way. . . .

In the course of a few days all the groups gathered in one place. We began to live according to the plan that had applied before the winter. Every evening the whole unit assembled. One platoon was selected for guard duty for the next 24 hours; several groups were sent out to get food; the people were divided up according to kitchens, each group doing its own cooking. The groups received their supplies from a central store, in accordance with the number of its members. . . .

LIFE IN THE GHETTOS

■ ORDER BY LUDWIG FISCHER ON THE ESTABLISHMENT OF A GHETTO IN WARSAW, OCTOBER 2, 1940

1. On the basis of the Regulation for Restrictions on Residence in the Government-General of September 13, 1940 (V.Bl.G.G.I., p. 288), a Jewish quarter is to be formed in the city of Warsaw, in which the Jews living in the city of Warsaw, or still to move there, must take up residence. The [Jewish] quarter will be set off from the rest of the city by the following streets: [here follows a list of streets and sections of streets]. . . .

2. Poles residing in the Jewish quarter must move their domicile into the other part of the city by October 31, 1940. Apartments will be provided by the Housing Office of the Polish City Hall.

Poles who have not given up their apartments in the Jewish quarter by the above date will be forcibly moved. In the event of forcible removal they will be permitted to take only refugee style luggage (*Flüchtlingsgepäck*), bed-linen, and articles of sentimental value.

Poles are not permitted to move into the German quarter.

3. Jews living outside the Jewish quarter must move into the Jewish area of residence by October 31, 1940. They may take only refugee luggage and bed-linen. Apartments will be allocated by the Jewish Elder (*Judenältester*).

4. The Appointed Mayor of the Polish City Hall and the Jewish Elder are responsible for the orderly move of the Jews to the Jewish quarter, and the punctual move of the Poles away from the Jewish quarter, in accordance with a plan yet to be worked out, which will provide for the evacuation by stages of the individual Police districts.

5. The Representative of the District Governor of the city of Warsaw will give the necessary detailed instructions to the Jewish Elder for the establishing and permanent closure of the Jewish quarter.

6. The Representative of the District Governor of the city of Warsaw will issue regulations for the execution of the Decree.

7. Any person contravening this Decree, or the Regulations for its execution, will be punished in accordance with the existing laws on punishment.

Head of the Warsaw District
DR. FISCHER
Governor

■ **EXTRACT FROM THE DIARY OF CHAIM A. KAPLAN ON THE WARSAW JUDENRAT, 1941**

April 23, 1941

The Community Council—the Judenrat, in the language of the Occupying Power—is an abomination in the eyes of the Warsaw community. . . . If it were not for fear of the Authorities there would be bloodshed. . . . It was not elected by the Community, but reached its position of power through appointment and with the support of the Nazi Authorities, and as a result of the general situation. . . . Starzynski appointed Czerniakow, whom nobody had known prior to this appointment. There were thousands like him. . . . According to rumor, the President is a decent man. But the people around him are the dregs of humanity. . . . I shall not list their names because they are not worthy of having their names recorded officially in the history of the Jewish Community of Warsaw. They are known as scoundrels and corrupt persons, who did not avoid ugly dealings even in the period before the war. The community has become for them . . . an unending opportunity to take bribes, to rob the poor and crush the oppressed. Everything is done in the name of the President. But in truth, everything is done without his knowledge and even without his consent, and perhaps also against his decisions and wishes. . . .

■ **FROM THE DIARY OF ADAM CZERNIAKOW ON THE EVE OF THE DEPORTATION FROM THE WARSAW GHETTO, 1942**

July 20, 1942

At the Gestapo at 7:30 in the morning. I asked Mende how much truth there was in the rumors. He answered that he had heard nothing about it. After this I asked Brandt; he answered that he knew of nothing of the kind. . . . I went to his superior officer, Commissar Böhm. He said that it was not his department. . . . I observed that according to the rumors the deportation was due to start at 19:30 today. He answered that he would certainly know something if it were so. . . .

Finally I asked [Scherer] whether I could inform the population that there was no reason for fear. He said I could, that all the reports were nonsense and rubbish. . . .

July 22, 1940 [1942]

At the Community at 7:30 in the morning. The borders of the small ghetto are guarded by a special unit in addition to the usual one. . . .

At 10 o'clock *Sturmbannführer* Höfle appeared with his people. . . .

It was announced to us that the Jews, without regard to sex or age, apart from certain exceptions, would be deported to the East. Six thousand souls had to be supplied by 4 o'clock today. And this (at least) is how it will be every day. . . .

Sturmbannführer Höfle . . . called me into the office and informed me that my wife was free at the moment, but if the deportation failed she would be the first to be shot as a hostage.

■ FROM THE DIARY OF A JEWISH YOUTH ON EDUCATION AND CULTURE IN THE VILNA GHETTO, 1942

Sunday the 13th [December 1942]. . .

Today the ghetto celebrated the circulation of the 100,000th book in the ghetto library. The festival was held in the auditorium of the theater. We came from our lessons. Various speeches were made and there was also an artistic program. The speakers analyzed the ghetto reader. Hundreds of people read in the ghetto. The reading of books in the ghetto is the greatest pleasure for me. The book unites us with the future, the book unites us with the world. The circulation of the 100,000th book is a great achievement for the ghetto, and the ghetto has the right to be proud of it.

TESTIMONY

■ TESTIMONY OF VICTOR BRACK REGARDING TERMINATION OF THE MENTALLY DISABLED IN GERMANY

Q: Witness, when adult persons were selected for euthanasia and sent by transport to euthanasia stations for that purpose, by what methods were the mercy deaths given?

A: The patients went to a euthanasia institution after the written formalities were concluded—I need not repeat these formalities here, they were physical examinations, comparison of the files, etc. The patients were led to a gas chamber and were there killed by the doctors with carbon monoxide gas (CO).

Q: Where was that carbon monoxide obtained, by what process?

A: It was in a compressed gas container, like a steel oxygen container, such as is used for welding—a hollow steel container.

Q: And these people were placed in this chamber in groups, I suppose, and then the carbon monoxide was turned into the chambers?

A: Perhaps I had better explain this in some detail. Bouhler's basic requirement was that the killing should not only be painless, but also imperceptible. For this reason, the photographing of the patients, which was only done for scientific reasons, took place before they entered the chambers, and the patients were completely diverted thereby. Then they were led into the gas chamber which they were told was a shower room. They were in groups of perhaps 20 or 30. They were gassed by the doctor in charge.

. . . .

Q: What was done with the bodies of these people after mercy deaths were given?

A: When the room had been cleared of gas again, stretchers were brought in and the bodies were carried into an adjoining room. There the doctor examined them to determine whether they were dead.

Q: Then what happened to the bodies?

A: After the doctor had determined death, he freed the bodies for cremation and they were cremated.

Q: After he had freed the bodies, had determined that they were dead, they were then cremated? Is that correct?

A: Yes.

Q: There was a crematory built for every one of these institutions?

A: Yes. Crematoriums were built in the institutions.

. . . .

Q: And these people thought that they were going in to take a shower bath?

A: If any of them had any power of reasoning, they had no doubt thought that.

Q: Well now, were they taken into the shower rooms with their clothes on or were they nude?

A: No. They were nude.

Q: In every case?

A: Whenever I saw them, yes.

Resources for Further Study

OVERVIEW OF THE HOLOCAUST

Aly, Gotz. *"Final Solution": Nazi Population Policy and the Murder of the European Jews*. London: Arnold, 1999.

Bachrach, Susan D. *Tell Them We Remember: The Story of the Holocaust*. New York: Little, Brown, 1994.

Bauer, Yehuda, and Nili Keren. *A History of the Holocaust*. New York: Franklin Watts, 1982.

Berenbaum, Michael. *The World Must Know: The History of the Holocaust as Told in the United States Holocaust Memorial Museum*. New York: Little, Brown, 1993.

Broszat, Martin. *The Hitler State: The Foundation and Development of the Third Reich*. New York: Longman, 1981.

Dawidowicz, Lucy S. *The War Against the Jews 1933–1945*. New York: Holt, Rinehart and Winston, 1985.

Dippel, John V. H. *Bound Upon a Wheel of Fire*. New York: Basic Books, 1996.

Edelheit, Abraham J., and Hershel Edelheit. *History of the Holocaust: A Handbook and Dictionary*. Boulder: Westview Press, 1994.

Edelheit, Abraham J., and Hershel Edelheit. *A World in Turmoil: An Integrated Chronology of the Holocaust and World War II*. Westport: Greenwood Press, 1991.

Gilbert, Martin. *The Holocaust: A History of the Jews in Europe during the Second World War*. New York: Holt, Rinehart, Winston, 1986.

Hilberg, Raul. *The Destruction of the European Jews*. Chicago: Quadrangle Books, 1961. Reprint, revised and definitive edition, New York: Holmes and Meier, 1985.

Holocaust. Eight-volume library series. Woodbridge, CT: Blackbirch Press, 1998.

Kershaw, Ian. *Hitler: 1889–1936*. New York: Norton, 1998.

Kershaw, Ian. *Hitler: 1937–1945*. New York: Norton, 2000.

Roth, John. *The Holocaust Chronicles: A History in Words and Pictures*. New York: Publications International, 2000.

Yahil, Leni. *The Holocaust: The Fate of European Jews*. Oxford: Oxford University Press, 1991.

MULTIMEDIA

Historical Atlas of the Holocaust [CD-ROM]. U.S. Holocaust Memorial Council, 1996.

Kitty: Return to Auschwitz [Videorecording]. Home Vision Cinema, 1986.

Majdanek 1944 [Videorecording]. National Center for Jewish Film, 1986.

Shoah [Videorecording]. New Yorker Video, 1985.

LIFE UNDER THE NAZIS

Auerbacher, Inge. *I Am a Star: Child of the Holocaust.* New York: Puffin Books, 1993.

Bankier, David. *The Germans and the Final Solution: Public Opinion under Nazism.* Bloomington: Indiana University Press, 1999.

Barnett, Victoria J. *Bystanders: Conscience and Complicity During the Holocaust.* Westport: Greenwood Press, 1999.

Beck, Gad, et al., eds. *An Underground Life: Memoirs of a Gay Jew in Nazi Berlin (Living Out).* New York: Henry Holt, 1999.

Berenbaum, Michael. *A Mosaic of Victims: Non-Jews Persecuted and Murdered by the Nazis.* New York: New York University Press, 1990.

Bitton-Jackson, Livia. *I Have Lived a Thousand Years: Growing Up in the Holocaust.* New York: Scholastic, 1997.

Boehm, E. H. *We Survived: Fourteen Histories of the Hidden and Hunted of Nazi Germany.* Santa Barbara: ABC-Clio, 1985.

Browder, George. *Hitler's Enforcers.* New York: Oxford University Press, 1996.

Browning, Christopher. *Ordinary Men: Reserve Police Battalion 101 and the Final Solution in Poland.* New York: HarperCollins, 1992.

Browning, Christopher. *The Path to Genocide: Essays on the Launching of the Final Solution.* Cambridge: Cambridge University Press, 1992.

Czerniakow, Adam. *The Warsaw Diary of Adam Czerniakow: Prelude to Doom, and the Reexamined.* Edited by Raul Hilberg. Chicago: Ivan R. Dee, 1999.

Dippel, John V. H. *Bound Upon a Wheel of Fire: Why So Many German Jews Made the Tragic Decision to Remain in Nazi Germany.* New York: Basic Books, 1996.

Dobroszycki, Lucjan, ed. *The Chronicle of the Lodz Ghetto.* New Haven: Yale University Press, 1984.

Drucker, Olga. *Kindertransport.* New York: Henry Holt, 1995.

Dwork, Deborah. *Children with a Star: Jewish Youth in Nazi Europe.* New Haven: Yale University Press, 1991.

Feig, Konnilyn. *Hitler's Death Camps.* New York: Holmes and Meier, 1981.

Fogelman, Eva. *Conscience and Courage: Rescuers of Jews during the Holocaust.* New York: Anchor Books/Doubleday, 1994.

Frank, Anne. *The Diary of a Young Girl.* Definitive edition. New York: Anchor Books/Doubleday, 1996.

Friedlander, Henry. *The Origins of Nazi Genocide: From Euthanasia to the Final Solution.* Chapel Hill: North Carolina University Press, 1995.

Friedlander, Saul. *Nazi Germany and the Jews: The Years of Persecution, 1933–1939.* New York: HarperCollins, 1997.

Gallagher, Hugh Gregory. *By Trust Betrayed: Patients, Physicians, and the License to Kill in the Third Reich.* New York: Henry Holt, 1990.

Hilberg, Raul. *Perpetrators, Victims, Bystanders: The Jewish Catastrophe, 1933–1945.* New York: Aaron Asher Books, 1992.

Greenfeld, Howard. *The Hidden Children.* New York: Ticknor & Fields, 1993.

Horwitz, Gordon. *In the Shadow of Death: Living Outside the Gates of Mauthausen.* New York: Free Press, 1990.

Kaplan, Marion. *Between Dignity and Despair: Jewish Life in Nazi Germany.* New York: Oxford University Press, 1998.

Klein, Gerda Weissmann. *All But My Life.* Revised edition. New York: Hill and Wang, 1995.

Klemperer, Victor. *I Will Bear Witness: A Diary of the Nazi Years, Vol. I, 1933–1941.* New York: Random House, 1998.

Klemperer, Victor. *I Will Bear Witness: A Diary of the Nazi Years, Vol. II, 1941–1945.* New York: Random House, 2000.

Lacqueur, Walter. *The Terrible Secret: Suppression of the Truth about Hitler's Final Solution.* Boston: Little, Brown, 1980.

Levi, Primo. *Survival in Auschwitz: The Nazi Assault on Humanity.* New York: Collier Books, 1986.

Massaquoi, Hans J. *Destined to Witness: Growing Up Black in Nazi Germany.* New York: William Morrow, 1999.

Plant, Richard. *The Pink Triangle: The Nazi War Against Homosexuals.* New York: Henry Holt, 1986.

Smelser, Ronald, and Rainier Zitelmann, eds. *The Nazi Elite.* London: Macmillan, 1993.

Tec, Nechama. *Dry Tears: The Story of a Lost Childhood.* New York: Oxford University Press, 1984.

Tec, Nechama. *When Light Pierced the Darkness: Christian Rescue of Jews in Nazi-Occupied Poland.* New York: Oxford University Press, 1986.

Wiesel, Elie. *All Rivers Run to the Sea: Memoirs.* New York: Knopf, 1995.

Wiesel, Elie. *And the Sea Is Never Full: Memoirs 1969.* New York: Knopf, 1999.

Wiesel, Elie. *Night.* New York: Bantam Books, 1982.

Zar, Rose. *In the Mouth of the Wolf.* Philadelphia: Jewish Publication Society, 1983.

Ziemian, Joseph. *The Cigarette Sellers of Three Crosses Square.* Minneapolis: Lerner, 1975.

MULTIMEDIA

Children in the Holocaust [Videorecording]. Phoenix/Coronet/BFA Films and Video, 1983.

A Day in the Warsaw Ghetto—A Birthday Trip in Hell [Videorecording]. Filmakers Library, 1993.

Genocide [Videorecording]. Simon Wiesenthal Center, 1981.

Genocide [Videorecording]. World at War series. HBO Home Video, 1975.

Kovno Ghetto: A Buried History [Videorecording]. The History Channel, 1997.

The Nazis—Witness to Genocide [Videorecording]. MPI Home Video, 1990.

Survivors: Testimonies of the Holocaust [CD-ROM]. Simon & Schuster Interactive, 1999.

Theresienstadt: Gateway to Auschwitz [Videorecording]. Ergo Media, 1987.

Weapons of the Spirit [Videorecording]. First Run/Icarus Films, 1988.

Witness to the Holocaust [Videorecording.] National Jewish Resource Center.

PERSPECTIVES ON THE HOLOCAUST

Ayer, Eleanor, with Helen Waterford and Alfons Heck. *Parallel Journeys.* New York: Aladdin Paperbacks, 1995.

Berenbaum, Michael, and Abraham J. Peck, eds. *The Holocaust and History: The Unknown, the Disputed, and the Reexamined.* Bloomington: Indiana University Press, 1998.

Breitman, Richard. *Official Secrets: What the Nazis Planned, What the British and Americans Knew.* New York: Hill and Wang, 1998.

Bridgman, Jon. *The End of the Holocaust: The Liberation of the Camps.* Portland: Areopagitica Press, 1990.

Bukey, Evan Burr. *Hitler's Austria: Popular Sentiment in the Nazi Era, 1938–1945.* Chapel Hill: University of North Carolina Press, 2000.

Eliach, Yaffa. *There Once Was a World.* New York: Little, Brown, 1998.

Fein, Helen. *Accounting for Genocide.* New Brunswick: Free Press, 1979

Feingold, Henry L. *The Politics of Rescue: The Roosevelt Administration and the Holocaust, 1938–1944.* New Brunswick: Rutgers University Press, 1970.

Feliciano, Hector. *The Lost Museum: The Nazi Conspiracy to Steal the World's Greatest Works of Art.* New York: Basic Books, 1997.

Gilbert, Martin. *The Boys: The Story of 732 Young Concentration Camp Survivors.* New York: Henry Holt, 1997.

Gutman, Israel, Michael Berenbaum, and Raul Hilberg, eds. *Anatomy of the Auschwitz Death Camp.* Indianapolis: Indiana University Press, 1998.

Hassler, Alfred A. *The Lifeboat Is Full: Switzerland and the Refugees, 1933–1945.* New York: Funk & Wagnells, 1969.

Herbert, Ulrich. *Hitler's Foreign Workers: Enforced Foreign Labor in Germany Under the Third Reich.* Cambridge: Cambridge University Press, 1997.

Klee, Ernst, Willi Dreesen, and Volker Riess, eds. *"The Good Old Days": The Holocaust as Seen by Its Perpetrators and Bystanders.* New York: Free Press, 1991.

Lipstadt, Deborah E. *Beyond Belief: The American Press and the Coming of the Holocaust, 1933–1945.* New York: Free Press, 1988.

Marks, Jane. *The Hidden Children: The Secret Survivors of the Holocaust.* New York: Fawcett Columbine, 1993.

Meredith, James H. *Understanding the Literature of World War II: A Student Casebook to Issues, Sources, and Historical Documents.* Westport, CT: Greenwood Press, 1999.

Rittner, Carol, and Sondra Myers, eds. *The Courage to Care: Rescuers of Jews during the Holocaust.* New York: New York University Press, 1986.

Rochman, Hazel, and Darlene Z. McCampbell. *Bearing Witness.* New York: Orchard Books, 1995.

Spiegelman, Art. *Maus: A Survivor's Tale.* Volumes I and II. New York: Pantheon, 1986, 1991.

Volovkova, Hana, ed. *I Never Saw Another Butterfly: Children's Drawings and Poems from Terezin Concentration Camp, 1942–1944.* New York: Schocken, 1994.

Weiner, Miriam. *Jewish Roots in Poland.* Secaucus/New York: Routes to Routes Foundation/YIVO, 1997.

Weiner, Miriam. *Jewish Roots in Ukraine and Moldova.* Secaucus/New York: Routes to Routes Foundation/YIVO, 1999.

Young, James E. *The Texture of Memory: Holocaust Memorials and Meanings.* New Haven: Yale University Press, 1993.

Ziegler, Jean. *The Swiss, the Gold and the Dead: How Swiss Bankers Helped Finance the Nazi War Machine.* New York: Penguin, 1998.

Zuckerman, Abraham. *A Voice in the Chorus: Life as a Teenager in the Holocaust.* Hoboken: Ktav, 1991.

Zuroff, Efraim. *Occupation: Nazi Hunter; The Continuing Search for Perpetrators of the Holocaust.* Los Angeles: Simon Wiesenthal Center, 1994.

MULTIMEDIA

America and the Holocaust [Videorecording]. Shanachie Entertainment, 1994.

Breaking the Silence [Videorecording]. National Center for Jewish Film, 1984.

Kristallnacht: The Journey from 1938 to 1988 [Videorecording]. PBS Video, 1988.

Lessons the Holocaust Can Teach Us Today [Videorecording]. Snell Media Video.

The Long Way Home [Videorecording]. BWE Video, 1997.

The Quarrel [Videorecording]. BMG, 1993.

Return to Life: The Story of Holocaust Survivors [CD-ROM]. Sponsored by Yad Vashem.

Photo Credits

Photographs appearing in *Learning About the Holocaust* were reproduced with permission from the following sources:

VOLUME 1

p. 12, USHMM Photo Archives; p. 22, Leah Hammerstein Silverstein/ USHMM Photo Archives; p. 32, Gift of Sol Scharfstein, Museum of Jewish Heritage, New York; p. 36, USHMM Photo Archives; p. 38, Yad Vashem Photo Archives; p. 42, USHMM Photo Archives; p. 45, USHMM Photo Archives; p. 49, Yad Vashem Photo Archives; p. 50, © Martin Gilbert; p. 53, National Archives/USHMM Photo Archives; p. 59, Gift of Claire Glazer, Museum of Jewish Heritage, New York; p. 60, Gift of Rosette Bakish, Museum of Jewish Heritage, New York; p. 61, Hulton-Getty/The Gamma Liaison Network; p. 62, Yad Vashem Photo Archives; p. 64, © Martin Gilbert; p.78, Yad Vashem Photo Archives; p. 80, USHMM Photo Archives; p. 83, Hadassah Rosenaft Collection/USHMM Photo Archives; p. 85, National Archives/USHMM Photo Archives; p. 90, Yad Vashem Photo Archives; p. 92, Archives of the YIVO Institute for Jewish Research; p. 93, Yad Vashem Photo Archives; p. 94, USHMM Photo Archives; p. 98, © Martin Gilbert; p. 100, Archive Photos, Inc.; p. 102, USHMM Photo Archives; p. 105, USHMM Photo Archives; p. 106, USHMM Photo Archives; p. 108, Yad Vashem Photo Archives; p. 113, Private Collection, courtesy of Hélène Potter; p. 115, Sidney Harcsztark Collection/USHMM Photo Archives; p. 120, Eve Nisencwajg Bergstein/USHMM Photos Archives; p. 124, Yad Vashem Photo Archives; p. 127, Main Commission for the Investigation of Nazi War Crimes/USHMM Photo Archives; p. 133, Central State Archive of Film, Photo and Phonographic Documents/USHMM Photo Archives; p. 135, USHMM Photos Archives; p. 138, © Martin Gilbert; p. 141, Yad Vashem Photo Archives; p. 145, USHMM Photos Archives; p. 146, USHMM Photos Archives; p. 150, USHMM Photos Archives; p. 152, USHMM Photos Archives; p. 159, Frihedsmuseet/ USHMM Photo Archives; p. 164, National Museum of American Jewish History/USHMM Photo Archives; p. 169, Collection of Ben Kaplan. Museum of Jewish Heritage, New York; p. 171, Yad Vashem Photo Archives; p. 173, Yad Vashem Photo Archives; p. 177, Archives of the YIVO Institute of Jewish Research; p. 178, Library of Congress; p. 180, Hulton-Getty/Tony Stone Images; p. 182, Yad Vashem Photo Archives; p. 184, Yad Vashem Photo Archives; p. 187, Stadtarchiv Nuerenberg/USHMM Photo

Archives; p. 191, National Archives/USHMM Photos Archives; p. 193, © Polish Scientific Publishers PWN.

VOLUME 2

p. 3, Archive Photos, Inc.; p. 5, Yad Vashem Photo Archives; p. 14, National Archives/USHMM Photo Archives; p. 16, USHMM Photo Archives; p. 20, Snark/Art Resource; p. 21, Archive Photos, Inc.; p. 27, AP/Wide World Photos; p. 29, UPI/Bettmann Archive. Corbis Corporation; p. 32, Bildarchiv Preussischer Kulturdesitz; p. 33, Lena Fagen/USHMM Photo Archives; p. 34, Rijksinstituut Voor Oorlogsdocumentatie/USHMM Photo Archives; p. 38, National Museum in Majdanek/USHMM Photo Archives; p. 40, © Martin Gilbert; p. 46, Yad Vashem Photo Archives; p. 48, © Martin Gilbert; p. 53, Landesbildstelle Baden/USHMM Photo Archives; p. 55, National Archives/USHMM Photo Archives; p. 56, © Martin Gilbert; p. 57, © Martin Gilbert; p. 60, Popperfoto/Archive Photos, Inc.; p. 64, Archives of the YIVO Institute for Jewish Research; p. 65, Yad Vashem Photo Archives; p. 66, AP/Wide World Photos; p. 72, Yad Vashem Photo Archives; p. 75, Archives of the YIVO Institute for Jewish Research; p. 79, Yad Vashem Photo Archives; p. 80, USHMM Photo Archives; p. 82, Jerzy Ficowski/USHMM Photo Archives; p. 85, USHMM Photo Archives; p. 88, AP/Wide World Photos; p. 89, Archive Photos, Inc.; p. 93, © Corbis Corporation; p. 98, The Beate Klarsfeld Foundation. Museum of Jewish Heritage, New York; p. 106, Library of Congress; p. 107, Archive Photos, Inc.; p. 109, Yad Vashem Photo Archives; p. 112, Yad Vashem Photo Archives; p. 117, National Archives/USHMM Photo Archives; p. 118, © Bettmann Archives/Corbis Corporation; p. 122, USHMM Photo Archives; p. 119, © Martin Gilbert; p. 125, Yad Vashem Photo Archives; p. 126, Yad Vashem Photo Archives; p. 133, Yad Vashem Photo Archives; p. 139, American Jewish Joint Distribution Committee/USHMM Photo Archives; p. 141, National Museum of American Jewish History/USHMM Photo Archives; p. 145, Yad Vashem Photo Archives; p. 146, Archives of the YIVO Institute for Jewish Research; p. 147, Jewish Community Center of New Orleans; p. 152, Pafal Imbro Collection/USHMM Photo Archives; p. 154, Yad Vashem Photo Archives; p. 156, © Corbis Corporation; p. 157, AP/Wide World Photos; p. 160, Ghetto Fighters House/USHMM Photo Archives; p. 168, Main Commission for the Investigation of Nazi War Crimes/USHMM Photo Archives; p. 169, National Archives in Krakow/USHMM Photo Archives; p. 171, Imperial War Museum/USHMM Photo Archives; p. 172, Anthony Potter Collection/Archive Photos, Inc.; p. 174, Archives of the YIVO Institute for Jewish Research.

VOLUME 3

p. 2, © Martin Gilbert; p. 5, Archive Photos, Inc./Popperfoto; p. 6, Library of Congress; p. 8, Yad Vashem Photo Archives; p. 9, Yad Vashem Photo Archives; p. 18, Yad Vashem Photo Archives; p. 20, USHMM Photo Archives; p. 25, Archives of the YIVO Institute for Jewish Research; p. 31, Yad Vashem Photo Archives; p. 35, Yad Vashem Photo Archives; p. 38, Yad Vashem Photo Archives; p. 45, USHMM Photo Archives; p. 49, Mauthausen Museum Archives/USHMM Photo Archives; p. 50, USHMM Photo Archives; p. 55, Yad Vashem Photo Archives; p. 61, Hulton Getty Collection/Archive Photos, Inc.; p. 63, Archive Photos, Inc.; p. 65, Archives of the YIVO Institute for Jewish Research; p. 71, USHMM Photo Archives; p. 75, Max Reed/USHMM Photo Archives; p. 77, Susan D. Rock; p. 81, © Corbis Corporation; p. 85, © Martin Gilbert; p. 87, Yad Vashem Photo Archives; p. 89, Yad Vashem Photo Archives; p. 93, © Martin Gilbert; p. 95, Yad Vashem Photo Archives; p. 101,

AP/Wide World Photos; p.105, USHMM Photo Archives; p. 109, Yad Vashem Photo Archives; p. 116, USHMM Photo Archives; p. 113, Archives of the YIVO Institute for Jewish Research; p. 121, USHMM Photo Archives; p. 125, © Polish National Publishing House; p. 129, Archives of the YIVO Institute for Jewish Research; p. 132, © Martin Gilbert; p. 142, Yad Vashem Photo Archives; p. 143, John Menszer/Shep Zitler; p. 147, Yad Vashem Photo Archives; p. 150, Library of Congress; 155, USHMM Photo Archives; p. 159, Archives of the YIVO Institute for Jewish Research; p. 161, Bildarchiv Preussischer Kulturbursitz; p. 167, Hulton Getty Collection/Archive Photos, Inc.; p. 170, Government Press Office, Jerusalem/USHMM Photo Archives; p. 175, Yad Vashem Photo Archives; p. 178, Yad Vashem Photo Archives; p. 180, Yad Vashem Photo Archives; p. 183, Yad Vashem Photo Archives; p. 183, Gallagher Collection/USHMM Photo Archives; p. 185, Instytut Pamieci Narodowej/Institute of National Memory/USHMM Photo Archives.

Volume 4

p. 2, USHMM Photos Archives; p.3, USHMM Photos Archives; p. 5, Instytut Pamieci Narodowej/Institute of National Memory/USHMM Photo Archives; p. 6 Yad Vashem Photo Archives; p. 8, Yad Vashem Photo Archives; p. 11, © Martin Gilbert; p. 13, Yad Vashem Photo Archives; p. 16, Yad Vashem Photo Archives; p. 20, Yad Vashem Photo Archives; p. 29, Yad Vashem Photo Archives; p. 34, AP/Wide World Photos; p. 38, © Corbis; p. 39, © Hulton-Deutsch Collection/ Corbis; p. 40, Snark/Art Resource; p. 45, Yad Vashem Photo Archives; p. 52, Beit Hannah Senesh/USHMM Photos Archives; p. 54, Yad Vashem Photo Archives; p. 57, Gift of Erna Levi, Museum of Jewish Heritage, New York; p. 58, YIVO Institute for Jewish Research; p. 67, Yad Vashem Photo Archives; p. 70, AP/Wide World Photos; p. 73, AP/Wide World Photos; p. 89, Yad Vashem Photo Archives; p. 99, National Archives/USHMM Photos Archives; p. 103, Yad Vashem Photo Archives; p. 109, Gift of Katalin Szeekely, Museum of Jewish Heritage, New York; p. 110, UPI/Corbis-Bettmann; p. 120, Bildarchiv Preussischer Kulturbesitz; p. 127, USHMM Photos Archives; p. 130, Bildarchiv Preussischer Kulturbesitz; p. 133, National Archives/USHMM Photos Archives; p. 136 USHMM Photos Archives; p. 137, AP/Wide World Photos; p. 139, Corbis Corporation; p. 141, National Archives/USHMM Photos Archives; p. 146, USHMM Photos Archives; p. 156, USHMM Photos Archives.

Text Credits

The editors wish to thank the copyright holders of the excerpted criticism included in this volume and the permissions managers of many book and magazine publishing companies for assisting us in securing reproduction rights. We are also grateful to the staffs of the Detroit Public Library, the Library of Congress, the University of Detroit Mercy Library, Wayne State University Purdy/Kresge Library Complex, and the University of Michigan Libraries for making their resources available to us. Following is a list of the copyright holders who have granted us permission to reproduce material in *Learning About the Holocaust*. Every effort has been made to trace copyright, but if omissions have been made, please let us know.

COPYRIGHTED EXCERPTS IN *Learning About the Holocaust* **WERE REPRODUCED FROM THE FOLLOWING PERIODICALS:**

Congressional Record, v. 14, October, 1968.

COPYRIGHTED EXCERPTS IN *Learning About the Holocaust* **WERE REPRODUCED FROM THE FOLLOWING BOOKS:**

Anielewicz, Mordecai. From a letter in *Documents on the Holocaust.* **Yitzhak Arad, Israel Gutman, and Abraham Margaliot, eds. Ktav Publishers House, 1982, in association with Yad Vashem. Reproduced by permission of Yad Vashem.—Becker, Dr. From a letter in** Documents on the Holocaust. Yitzhak Arad, Israel Gutman, and Abraham Margaliot, eds. Ktav Publishers House, 1982, in association with Yad Vashem. Reproduced by permission of Yad Vashem.—Bormann, M. From "Hitler Bans Public Reference to the 'Final Solution of the Jewish Question,' July 11, 1943," in **Documents on the Holocaust. Yitzhak Arad, Israel Gutman, and Abraham Margaliot, eds. Ktav Publishers House, 1982, in association with Yad Vashem. Reproduced by permission of Yad Vashem.—Brack, Viktor. From "Proposal for the Sterilization of 2-3 Million Jewish Workers, June 23, 1942," in** Documents on the Holocaust. Yitzhak Arad, Israel Gutman, and Abraham Margaliot, eds. Ktav Publishers House, 1982, in association with Yad Vashem. Reproduced by permission of Yad Vashem.—Central Construction Office. From a letter in **Documents of Destruction: Germany and Jewry, 1933-1945. Edited by Raul Hilberg. Quadrangle Books, 1971. Copyright © 1971 by Raul Hilberg. All rights reserved.—Cohen, Judy (Weissennberg). From Auschwitz-Birkenau. May 4, 1997. Women and Holocaust, http://interlog. com/~mighty/poetry/poetry5.html. Reproduced by permission. (May 24, 2000). Reproduced by permission from the author.—Czerniakow, Adam. From a diary entry in** Documents on the Holocaust. Yitzhak Arad, Israel Gutman,

Index

A

Abegg, Elisabeth, **3:** 179
Adamowicz, Irena, **2:** 165, **3:** 179-180
AFSC. *See* American Friends Service
    Committee (Quakers)
AGFA Camera Company, **2:** *14*
Aid to Jews
    by Allies after the War, **1:** 167
    by Belorussians, **1:** 91
    by Catholic church in Belgium, **1:** 66
    donations of foreign currency for
        travel, **1:** 51
    by Poles, **1:** 1-3, 91**4:** 128
    by Ukrainians, **1:** 55
    See also Non-Jews who aided Jews
    See also Rescue of European Jews
Akiva, **4:** 148
    in Kraków, **2:** 170
Aktion, **4:** 28
Aktion, Intelligenz, **2:** 169
Aktion "Erntefest." *See* Erntefest ("Harvest
    Festival")
Aktion 1005, **1:** 4-6
    at Babi Yar, **1:** 55
    map of, **1:** *5*
Aktion M ("Operation Furniture"), **3:** 88
Aktion Reinhard, **1:** 6-9
    See also Erntefest ("Harvest Festival")
Aktion T4. *See* Euthanasia Program
Algeria, **3:** 171
Aliya Bet, **1:** 9-13
Allied Control Council Law No. 10, **4:** 75
Allies
    definition of, **1:** 64
    effect on Jews of Allies' German policy,
        2: 69
    efforts to aid displaced persons, **1:** 167,
        4: 90
    liberation of Jews in southern Italy, **2:**
        120
    postwar disunity among, **1:** 155-156
    refusal to bomb Auschwitz, **1:** 47
    responses to Jewish refugees, 1942-
        1945, **4:** 95

American Friends Service Committee
    (Quakers), **1:** 13-14, **3:** 167
American Jewish Committee, **1:** 15, 17
American Jewish Conference, **1:** 16
American Jewish Congress, **1:** 14, 17, **4:** 143
American Jewish Distribution Committee.
    See Joint Distribution Committee
American Jewish literature about the
    Holocaust, **3:** 11-12
American Jewish organizations, **1:** 14-16, 17
    founded by Stephen Samuel Wise, **4:**
        140-*141*
        Rescue Committee of United States
            Orthodox Rabbis, **3:** 164-166
        for rescue of Jewish children, **3:** 166
        See also Joint Distribution Committee
            (JDC)
American Jews
    advisors to Franklin D. Roosevelt, **1:**
        17-18, **3:** 69-*71*
    and the Holocaust, **1:** 16-19
    and the Joint Distribution Committee
        (JDC), **2:** 138-139
    Orthodox Rabbis, **3:** 165
    and the Rescue Committee of the
        United States
American press and the Holocaust, **1:** 20-21
American Quakers' reaction to Nazism, **1:**
    13
American zone
    denazification, **1:** 154
    displaced persons' camps, **1:** 168
    United States Army role, **4:** 90-92
Amsterdam, **3:** 85, 86-87
    deportations from, **3:** 89
    Anne Frank's life in, **2:** 26-33
Anielewicz, Mordecai, **1:** 21-24, *22*, **4:** 155,
    196
Anne Frank Foundation, **2:** 32
Anne Frank house, **2:** 31-*32*
Annex, The (Anne Frank), **2:** 30
Anschluss, **1:** 50-51
    historical context of, **2:** 54
Anti-Defamation League (ADL), **1:** 15
Antifascist Bloc, **2:** 130

Antifascist Struggle Organization, **2:** 165
Anti-Gypsy legislation, **2:** 81, 82-84
Anti-Jewish boycotts, **1:** *102*-104
Anti-Jewish legislation
    Croatia, **1:** 139
    France, **2:** 135-136
    Germany, **1:** 24-27, **2:** 51, 52, 54
    Hungary, **2:** 108
    Italy, **2:** 120
    "Jewish Code" in Slovakia, **4:** 12
    Lösener, Bernard, **3:** 28
    Nazi marriage laws, **1:** 25, **2:** 90, **3:** 66,
        96, **4:** 180-181
    by Ustaša in Croatia, **1:** 139
    See also Nuremberg Laws
Anti-Jewish measures
    Austria, **1:** 50, *52-53*, **2:** 171-174
    Belgium, **1:** 64-65
    Berlin, **1:** 84-86
    Bohemia and Moravia, **1:** 97-98
    Budapest, **1:** 109
    Croatia, **1:** 139
    Dvinsk, **1:** 174
    France, **2:** 22-23
    by French police, **2:** 35-36
    Generalgouvernement, **2:** 40
    German-occupied countries, **2:** 56
    Germany, **2:** 50-55, 56-57, 171-174
    Hungary, **2:** 109-110, 113, 114
    Kovno, **2:** 164
    Łódź, **3:** 20
    Lublin, **3:** 30
    Lvov, **3:** 37
    Netherlands, **3:** 87-88
    Order Banning the Emigration of Jews
        from the Reich **4:** 188-189
    Paris, **3:** 111-112
    Poland, **3:** 131-132
    Prague, **1:** 99
    Riga, **1:** 176
    Slovakia, **4:** 12
    by Soviets, **1:** 72, **4:** 22
    Tarnów, **4:** 52-53
    Ternopol, **4:** 55-56
    Ukraine, **2:** 109-110